1 (*overleaf*) WOOLMEN'S PERPENDICULAR
Cirencester, Gloucestershire: the nave,
early sixteenth century

English Historic Architecture

English Historic Architecture

Bryan Little

B. T. BATSFORD LTD

London

Made and Printed in Great Britain by
William Clowes and Sons Ltd, London and Beccles
for the publishers
B. T. BATSFORD LTD
4 Fitzhardinge Street, Portman Square, London W.1

PREFACE

This book's title, and its inevitably modest length, at once pose two questions: 'What is Architecture?' and 'What does one mean by Historic?' The second is the easier to answer. 'Historic' architecture, as I see it, is that whose constructional nature and decorative style are clearly and finally of the past. That does not mean that there have not been many neo-Gothic or neo-Renaissance buildings put up, since 1914, on virgin sites where no respect had to be paid to genuinely Gothic or Georgian buildings nearby. But such buildings, though sometimes seemly or impressive, are of little architectural or intellectual significance; they were the swan-songs of traditions whose message, by the 1920s and still more by the 1960s, was essentially complete. Significant architecture, since 1914, has used building techniques and styles which were foreshadowed in the nineteenth century but by no means fully worked out. Their story, moreover, is still far from fully told. I therefore end this 'historic' survey with the beginning of the First World War. I am well aware of the growing importance of what this country has seen built in the last fifty years. But such architecture, along with what follows till the end of this century, will be the fitting material for another, very different volume in some four decades' time.

Far more delicate and difficult is a sane definition of 'architecture'. A trained architect can now be employed to design the most humble, utilitarian buildings as well as those of more obvious pretension and dignity. Yet there have been periods when this has not been so, and when 'mason-builders' or 'surveyors' were far more common than 'architects' in the modern sense of the term; the rise of the architectural profession is a topic which must find a place even in so short a book as this. But for many reasons such a brief study must concentrate on buildings of the more important and monumental type, or on those which display a reasonable degree of conscious design and artistry of style. Barns, industrial buildings, and a wide range of domestic architecture need not be excluded, but cottages, hovels, and

7

sheds inevitably tend to fall outside my scope. Yet neither they, nor buildings which seem more akin to civil engineering than what is normally accepted as 'architecture', should be left wholly out of account. The latter, in particular, will be seen as the early industrial forerunners of what are now the architect's common medium.

One last point concerns both scale and grandeur (where these have been achieved in England), and succeeding phases of aesthetics and artistry. Architecture, of whatever kind, can only be fully understood as one visible sign of a long human story. England's building achievement is closely bound up with her varied periods of power, poverty, and wealth. Her architectural styles, in their turn, reflect England's acceptance, or rejection, of the main artistic trends, whether Romanesque, Gothic, Renaissance, or imitationally eclectic, on the Continent and elsewhere. Insularity and internationalism have alike been apparent, at different times, in the story of our historic architecture.

Clifton, Bristol   B.D.G.L.
Christmas, 1963

CONTENTS

THE ILLUSTRATIONS

ACKNOWLEDGMENT

The Author and Publishers wish to thank the following for permission to reproduce the illustrations included in this book:

Aerofilms and Aero Pictorial Ltd for figs. 20 and 37; Stewart Bale Ltd for figs. 78, 81 and 83; British Railways (Western Region) for fig. 69; J. Allan Cash, F.R.P.S. for fig. 64; the late Brian Clayton for figs. 12 and 19; Corporation of Cheltenham for fig. 60; Corporation of the City of Leeds for fig. 74; The Council of Industrial Design for fig. 68; Eric de Maré for figs. 67 and 80; Herbert Felton, F.R.P.S. for fig. 25; Leonard and Marjorie Gayton for figs. 8, 10, 22, 63 and 65; A. F. Kersting, F.R.P.S. for figs. 1, 2, 5–7, 9, 11, 14, 15, 17, 18, 21, 27, 28, 30, 32, 33, 35, 40–54, 56–59, 61, 70, 76, 79 and 82; Ministry of Public Buildings and Works for fig. 36; National Buildings Record for figs. 62, 73 and 77; L. Shaw for fig. 75; Edwin Smith for figs. 4, 24, 26, 39, 71 and 72; J. W. Whitelaw for fig. 3; Reece Winstone, A.R.P.S. for figs. 31 and 66.

NOTE

To avoid interrupting the flow of the narrative, all references to illustrations have been placed at the end of paragraphs. The numerals, in bold type and square brackets, refer to the figure-numbers of the illustrations. The caption of the illustration will, in each case, make it apparent exactly which part of the text is being illustrated.

CHAPTER ONE

Saxon Beginnings

Until 1066

The principles of ordered design, and style as an expression of structural method, are both of them basic elements in succeeding periods of architecture. So our story might fairly start with such pre-historic works of architectural geometry as Avebury and Stonehenge. Fischer von Erlach, that leading exponent of Imperial Austrian Baroque, clearly saw the point when in 1721 he put Stonehenge among the illustrations of his *Historische Architektur*. Beehive huts and the burial chambers in long or round barrows were also not without their constructional meaning. But as architecture is also a matter of conscious artistry we may safely pass on from these relics of prehistory. For sophisticated architecture, provincial in scale yet clearly sharing in the great classic traditions of Mediterranean Europe, we wait till Britain was an outlying province of the Roman Empire. Yet here again a real difficulty arises. For Colchester, Bath, Cirencester, and the rest were not the beginnings of an unbroken story. Modern historians can reasonably claim that habitation continued, more vigorously than was once thought likely, amid the blight and slow ruination of some Romano-British towns. But *architectural* continuity was none the less severed. England's historic architecture restarted fairly soon in those long centuries between Hengist and Harold. Only from the earliest Anglo-Saxon buildings do we enter on an unbroken tradition.

Dark-Age Britain's waves of immigrants from the thickly wooded regions of Germany were carpenters, not masons, by instinct and experience. Timber was thus their main building material. Not one of their early structures has survived above ground. But from the digging

out of post-holes and foundations, and from what we can still see in
Germany of later barns and houses in the same 'Saxon' tradition, we
can tell that the halls and homesteads of Anglo-Saxon England were of
more structural interest than artistic note. The main building materials
were round logs or squared beams of timber, wattle and daub, and reed
thatch. Stylistic points of distinction, such as those which in Roman
times had clearly separated Doric, Ionic, or Corinthian buildings, were
unknown. When craftsmanship and deliberate artistry first appeared
among these unlettered settlers, and when they came to know more of
the arts still flourishing in cultured southern Europe or the Near East,
the decorative arts, and the sculpture of simple buildings and upstand-
ing mission crosses, were the spheres in which new fashions were
found.

The first Anglo-Saxon houses which could reasonably qualify as
'architecture' were the palaces of the heptarchic kings and the halls
or larger homesteads of their thegns and lesser gentry. Fortresses, at
this stage, were not the great masonry piles of the post-Conquest age,
but were simple 'burhs', with timber buildings enclosed by earthen
ramparts capped by timber palisades. In the palaces and early 'manors'
large, rectangular buildings had high-pitched roofs whose beams and
rafters, on their supports of great vertical baulks, were no mean feats
of carpentry. They covered large spaces and they must, in some ways,
have been like the great timber-framed barns of the late Middle Ages.
Many of them, like the earlier, pre-Conquest hall in the Saxon palace
at Cheddar, would have been simple rectangles inside. The wider,
more ambitious buildings had rows of upright piers to help support
the timbers of their roofs. The post-holes of such piers have been excavated in the site of the seventh-century palace at Yeavering in Northumberland. The roofs of these buildings descended low towards the
ground, but at each end a high-gabled wall displayed a larger timbered
expanse. The walls of these spacious 'mead halls' would be timber-
framed, with the spaces between the timbers filled in with wattle and
clay, or else of logs, split down the middle and then laid crossways or
upright. The technique of this second kind of walling was really the
same as that used for their log cabins by early settlers in Colonial
America; primeval Virginia and Massachusetts had much in common
with the deeply wooded England that was slowly cleared and settled by
her Germanic colonists.

These Saxon halls were communal buildings—the living, eating, and sleeping places of the leading families, and of their servants and dependants who would gather for warmth round a central hearth. The smoke from that hearth would escape, past blackened beams, through a hole in the roof. In farmsteads of this type the animals would be quartered at one end. At the other end, partitions screened off an area for the more private convenience of the owners. These early houses, with no windows and with light coming in through doorways in their narrow ends, were places of smoke and dark shadow. The design was basically that which long outlasted the Saxons as that of the unfortified manor house of post-Conquest times. Its methods of construction, particularly in the timber-framed buildings, were those which in stoneless districts lingered on till the time of Charles II. The 'log-cabin' technique of continuous wooden walling demanded more timber and has left fewer traces. But near Ongar in Essex the nave of Greenstead church has amazingly survived from early in the eleventh century, with a much later chancel and with modern brickwork to keep its vertical split logs from the rising damp. It well shows us how many Saxon buildings were fashioned, by axe and chisel and with no finesse of decorative style.

Greenstead church is the only above-ground survival of pre-Conquest timber construction. All the other Anglo-Saxon buildings are of rubble (sometimes liberally mixed with Roman brick) or dressed stone. Every one of them was built for religious uses, and nearly all have been greatly altered since they were new. Here in these churches (in some cases from early in the period of Anglo-Saxon architecture) we see a definite architectural style. Our Saxon churches, particularly the early cathedrals and other important buildings of which the merest traces remain, formed a remote, outlying element in the wider artistic movement known as early Romanesque. Rome, with the round-arched architecture of its imperial period, was the basic model. But the basilican churches of early Christian Rome, not the temples and public buildings of paganism, were those whose influence was strongest. So when in England the time came to imitate Roman models the Anglo-Saxon church builders and their clerical patrons turned more to what they knew of Italian churches than to the crumbling Roman remains in Britain itself. The Roman buildings of England were probably less ruined and more evident than they are today, so that surviving round arches and classical columns may have had some slight influence on

Saxon builders, and still more on the carvers and decorative artists who gave our early churches a measure of barbaric splendour. Where the Saxons certainly used Roman buildings was as a source of ready-made materials. Bricks at Dover, and worked stonework in the churches at Hexham and Corbridge still prove how useful they found the wreckage of Roman Britain.

The disappearance, above ground level, of most Anglo-Saxon buildings has much hampered the study of that period of our story. But excavation has added considerably to our knowledge, particularly the very recent diggings at places like Winchester and Much Wenlock which suggest that churches of some elaboration, and of fine workmanship, were not uncommon in pre-Conquest England. Saxon churches, including those of the early period whose square east ends and carved decoration looked rather to Celtic inspiration, were first built soon after A.D. 600.* They continued at least till 1066. So the Saxon period in our English architecture, with a great interruption caused by the Danish invasions and ravages of the ninth century, was longer that that of any other English style.

The smaller churches, both early and late in the Saxon period, were of the simple design which lasted, in the poorer, less populous parishes, throughout the Middle Ages. A plain rectangular nave led, through a chancel arch which was often low and narrow, to a smaller chancel. This contained the altar, and its eastern end was round-apsed or sometimes square. Such, in unpretending simplicity, was Rochester's first cathedral. At Escomb in County Durham there is a long, very narrow early church of the same 'two-compartment' design; Irish influence may have affected the plan of such simple churches in the North. Smaller and later churches, such as those at Corhampton and Boarhunt in Hampshire, have a similar plan.

More elaborate churches had more subdivisions. They were, however, unambitious as architecture. Their primitive planning may partly have been due to the inexperience and modest skill of the builders then available in England. What happened was that separate compartments, misleadingly called *porticus* but really a series of secluded chapels for burials or for private prayer, were built along the sides, and sometimes

---

* The small oratory of St Piran, near Perranzabuloe in Cornwall, was of course a church of wholly Celtic character, contemporary with the first Saxon churches but standing outside their tradition.

also round the west end, of the central nave. Similar projections are
also found in some early Italian churches. These chapels would sometimes be added to earlier, simple designs. Elsewhere, the churches had
them from the start. They were usually entered by narrow doorways
piercing the solid masonry of their walls. One such chapel, probably
of the tenth century, survives intact as part of the Saxon church at
Bradford-on-Avon. With its plain masonry and narrow arch it speaks
clearly of the unaspiring simplicity of its designers. The earlier church
at Bradwell-on-Sea in Essex also had these projecting chapels in its
original plan. [5]

More impressive architectural effects could best be provided by
building pillars and arches in the Roman manner. A screenlike arcade
of three round arches sometimes spanned the entrance to the chancel;
such an arcade survived till 1805 in the important seventh-century
church of Reculver in Kent. Round-arched arcades, of the type much
more common in the later Romanesque periods, were also built. We
can best see them at Brixworth in Northamptonshire, where the
seventh-century 'minster' church of missionary priests had full-sized
arches, made of Roman brick from nearby ruins, which led from the
nave to its set of flanking chapels.* At Wing, near Aylesbury, an aisled
church once thought to be late Saxon now seems to be of about the
same period as Brixworth, while in the eighth century, in the time of
the Mercian King Offa who was a figure of international note, Continental influences seem to have been at work. But in general, for reasons
not surprising in the primitive setting of early Saxon society, England's
first Christian architecture was plain and unimpressive. It was in the
carving of friezes and mission crosses, in metalwork and in superb
illuminated manuscripts like the Lindisfarne gospels, that real splendour was achieved. [3]

The architectural story was taken up again after the great interruption caused by the chaos and destruction of the great Danish attacks.
Most of our Saxon churches are of this later period, the majority being
on or near the 'limestone belt' of fine building stone which stretches
across from East Yorkshire to Dorset. Some churches still had *porticus*,
with few attempts at adventurous construction or style. Others, in two
or three unaisled sections, were simply rectangular. Some, though unaisled, were cruciform (as at Worth, near Crawley, in Sussex) with

* These arches were later blocked, so that the nave is now aisleless.

unaisled transepts and sometimes, as one sees at Breamore in western Hampshire, with a central tower. A few, however, were clearly basilican in the Continental manner, with transepts as in North Elmham Cathedral in Norfolk, short apsidal sanctuaries, and round-arched arcades. Such arcades existed at Sherborne and Canterbury Cathedrals and impressively survive, with simply clustered columns and 'cushion' capitals, at Great Paxton in Huntingdonshire. A few of these basilican churches had western towers, like those which adorn some German Romanesque basilicas, as well as those over the eastern crossing. The larger buildings, cathedrals for instance or some of the Benedictine abbeys reformed and restored under St Dunstan's inspiration, must have been truly if modestly imposing, with painted decoration and vigorous figure sculpture to reinforce their architectural effect. Altogether more ambitious, and foreshadowing the great octagon at Ely between that cathedral's eastern and western limbs, was the octagonal structure, built about 1050 at St Augustine's Abbey, Canterbury, to form a striking link between two simpler, and once separate churches. It seems likely that this 'rotunda' was inspired by a similar feature in St Bénigne at Dijon; important ecclesiastics like Abbot Wulfric of St Augustine's would have known of this church from their Continental contacts or from visits on the way to Rome. [6]

Western towers in Saxon England were by no means confined to the churches of cathedrals and monasteries. They were fairly common in parish churches; they sometimes served both for defence and as living quarters for the priest. In East Anglia, where good stone for the ashlar dressings of squared corners is lacking, these towers were often round. Most of them, however, were square in plan. That at St Benet's, Cambridge, has a specially fine rounded entrance arch of about 1015, with vigorously sculptured lions above the rolled and moulded capitals on each side. Here, and in the somewhat later West tower of St Michael's by the North Gate at Oxford the windows are grouped in pairs, with moulded stone balusters between them. St Alban's Cathedral has some Saxon stone balusters, of a more advanced type, which may have come from similar arches. They are well turned, as if from a lathe, and were reused in the triforium of the great Norman church which replaced the Saxon abbey.

The best known late Saxon tower is that of Earls Barton in Northamptonshire. Its topmost stage has groups of five small windows which are

2   *Earls Barton, Northamptonshire: the Saxon tower, early eleventh century*

parted from each other by rude balusters, and the tower's whole surface is adorned with thin strips of stone, a few of them imitating the
rounded heads of Romanesque arches but mostly diagonal or upright.
These 'applied' or 'pilaster' strips were derived from examples in
Carolingian Germany and were commonly used by England's Saxon
builders on towers and on the side walls of churches. It seems likely
that they were meant to imitate the effect of the timber framing and
plaster infilling seen in most houses, and in many churches not built
of stone. Another decorative effect now rendered in stone was 'long
and short' work—long, narrow strips of horizontally laid stone alternating with similar strips running upwards. This is often seen on the
corners of towers (as at Earls Barton) or of the body of a church. [2]

Windows, doorways, and archways were mostly round-headed in
this long period of Saxon Romanesque. A few, however, had triangular tops, perhaps because untried masons found it easier to lean
straight pieces of stone or timber together at an angle than to frame and
build an arch. The round arch, however, was normally used under the
influence of Continental Romanesque. Direct though unskilful copying
from Roman work, and perhaps from examples still standing in
England, occurred when the masons and carvers carried out rough
fluting on piers or pilasters, or carved their primitive imitations of
Corinthian capitals. Masonry of the 'zigzag' or 'herringbone' type is
likewise found in Saxon churches, but also occurs in buildings, like
some walls at Corfe Castle, put up soon after the Conquest. [4]

Yet although some aspects of our late Saxon architecture were still
but faltering imitations of Continental models, and though ornamental
detail was often rude and unsophisticated, the masons of that time
were not without a fair measure of skill. Though their churches, and
particularly the naves, were often lofty in relation to their width, the
builders were able to erect them with walls much thinner than those
thought necessary by their post-Conquest successors. The windows,
though small and unglazed and sometimes cut through a single stone
slab, were often set in the middle of the wall's thickness, so that they
were 'double-splayed', with the masonry widening out on both sides
and not merely towards the church's interior. Towers like those at
Earls Barton and Barnack, the arcades and clerestory windows at
Great Paxton, and arches like those at Coln Rogers in the Cotswolds
and at Britford near Salisbury, all prove that the Anglo-Saxon builders

A SAXON SELECTION

3 Brixworth, Northamptonshire: *basilican, seventh century*
4 Deerhurst, Gloucestershire: *round and triangular headed openings*
5 Bradford-on-Avon, Wiltshire: *side chapel, tenth century*
6 Worth, Sussex: *rounded apse, tenth or eleventh century*

had come far along the architectural road by the time of the Norman Conquest. [2]

Yet the range of architecture was still extremely small. Timbered halls and churches of various types seem to have made up its sum total. Public buildings, of the kind that were occasionally built in the later Middle Ages, seem not to have existed in Saxon times. Nor were the fortifications of those days very worthy to be classed as military architecture. Such bridges as existed were of timber piles, and domestic building, below the more notable houses, was not at an 'architectural' level.

Another striking feature of late Saxon architecture in England was its marked isolation. Despite all the Continental influences, from pagan or early Christian Rome, from Carolingian Germany or Romanesque France, that had gone to their making, the buildings of England, as they stood in the first decades of the eleventh century, were far behind what was now being achieved in the neighbouring countries of Europe. Early Saxon England, with such men as Bede and Alcuin as its leading personalities, had been in the cultural vanguard. When Edward the Confessor became king it had sadly fallen back. Politically and socially it had achieved much, particularly in its unified monarchy. But in many ways it seemed, as indeed it was geographically, on Europe's outer fringe. England's church life, despite the vigour of its Benedictine monasteries as rejuvenated by St Dunstan and his colleagues, was out of touch with Continental movements and stood much in need of reform. The whole story of English architecture has been, and is, one of alternating phases when English builders have worked in isolation or under influences from abroad. The late Saxon period was one of the insular times. Despite such buildings as the basilican cathedrals and Abbot Wulfric's Rotunda at Canterbury, English builders seemed little aware of important new movements, and dynamic forces, at work across the Channel. But before Duke William of Normandy arrived in Sussex with his army the country had seen the first stirrings of new things.

The Norman Conquest was in many respects a great act of Europeanisation. The pattern of English life was bound closer to Continental practice, particularly that of northern France. The process neither started nor ended in 1066; some aspects of it had got well under way in Edward the Confessor's reign. The king, with his pro-Norman and other Continental leanings, had actively promoted a policy whereby ideas and personalities flowed in from abroad. Estates in southern England were given to such Norman churches as Rouen Cathedral and the abbey of Fécamp. Important posts, particularly the bishoprics of Old Sarum, Hereford, and Wells, were held by churchmen from Normandy or the 'Lotharingian' territories of the Rhineland and eastern France. So too, in architecture, the king and his family showed favour to the Norman Romanesque style, more spacious and grandiose than anything in England, now seen in the great new abbeys of Normandy. The new nunnery church at Wilton, rebuilt of stone by Edward the Confessor's wife Queen Edith and consecrated in 1065 by the 'Lotharingian' bishop Herman of Old Sarum, may well have been one such 'Norman' church. The Confessor's own abbey at Westminster, erected at exactly the same period and with its eastern half finished just in time for the Confessor's funeral and the Conqueror's Coronation, was certainly another. It came as an architectural advance guard of the great outburst of Anglo-Norman Romanesque which soon transformed all England's more important churches, and which again accustomed Britain to major works of military architecture.

CHAPTER TWO

The Anglo-Normans

1066–c. 1180

The year 1066 was more of a political landmark than the decisive
marking of artistic change. Westminster, and perhaps Wilton also, had
already introduced England to 'Norman' Romanesque. Had the Confessor lived longer the new style might also have been seen in some
secular buildings. The new rulers of England soon gave a tremendous
impetus to the rebuilding of its more notable churches, and military
architecture of a new type was not long in appearing. But there was
little chance, for the first few years, of any great novelty in the design
and building of the smaller churches which served the laity in the
parishes. The people themselves, and the masons and builders in small
towns and villages, were still of Anglo-Saxon or Danish stock. So in
many churches built between 1060 and about 1100 it is bafflingly hard
to tell whether they were built just before or soon after the Conquest;
features like 'herringbone' masonry occur each side of the political
watershed of 1066. Nor are any documents available to help us date
them. One cannot put an exact term to the overlap between 'Saxon'
and 'Norman' Romanesque. Both belonged to the same broad art
movement, and they prove that essentially political titles are seldom
wholly apt for phases in art and culture. We may also assume that
'non-stylistic' construction in timber continued after the Conquest; a
new wooden hall or a palisade would look much the same in 1080 as in
1060.

As a military operation the Norman Conquest was effectively over
within six years of Hastings. The founding of Battle Abbey on the
site of William's victory, the rebuilding of the gutted Cathedral at

Canterbury, and other works had already set in train a vast process of architectural expansion, a 'building boom' with few parallels in England's history. In a country whose population may not have exceeded two million a fantastic amount was done. Dynamic new figures appeared on the scene. The king and the new aristocracy made haste to strengthen their hold by a great network of strategically placed castles. New parish churches often replaced older, more primitive structures on those same magnates' estates. Above all, the Normans or Lotharingians who gradually replaced the Saxon holders of abbacies and bishoprics soon felt themselves bound to destroy the churches they found standing, and to replace them with new, much larger buildings. New foundations like those at Battle, Chester, Shrewsbury, and Reading joined those of the Benedictines already in existence. New priories of modest size were founded, as the dependencies of abbeys in France, on estates presented to the mother houses by followers of the Conqueror. These were, above all, the monastic centuries; not only were pre-Conquest monasteries enlarged to receive greater floods of inmates, but new orders of monks, nuns, and canons arose to join the Benedictines. The new buildings were larger and more splendid than the old, and throughout the land new building became the fashion. Even St Wulstan, the bishop of Worcester and the last of the pre-Conquest bishops to remain in office, was obliged in the end to make a start, and a splendid start, on the replacement of his Saxon cathedral. So much was undertaken, and largely carried out, by the middle of the twelfth century that great strains were thrown on the available supplies of building manpower. A shortage of skilled builders, and the large-scale use of unskilled Saxon labourers in the lower grade, may account for much of the poor and slipshod work which went into many seemingly massive Anglo-Norman churches. [9]

Most of England's larger churches built in the Norman period or just after it were monastic; the same applies to the bulk of those, like Norwich and Gloucester Cathedrals or the nuns' church of Romsey Abbey, whose fabric is still mainly Norman Romanesque. A few, however, were churches of secular canons. Among these were St John's at Chester (for a short time a cathedral), the cathedrals at Chichester and Hereford which are still mainly Norman, Old St Paul's in London where the great Romanesque nave stood till 1666, the extremely important cathedral of Old Sarum, and Exeter Cathedral whose pair of

Romanesque towers are still its most striking feature. Many of the monastic churches, with the varied alterations made by the time of Henry VIII, have wholly or mainly disappeared. Of the numerous survivors not one has come down to us exactly as its eleventh or twelfth century builders left it; the castle chapels of St John in the Tower of London and at Dover give a better impression of how a Norman place of worship looked when architecturally unaltered. At Durham the seemingly unchanged windows are the result of Victorian 're-Normanisation' by Sir Gilbert Scott.

THE GREATER NORMAN CHURCHES

The 'greater' churches of the Norman period were cruciform, with their naves far longer than their eastern limbs. Some naves, as at Norwich and Winchester, were of a quite disproportionate length. The cloisters and other monastic buildings lay along these naves for most of their length, while the bays next to the central crossing were filled by the stalls and transverse screen of the monks' choir. Even so, their vast length is sometimes hard to explain. Some, before the building of numerous parish churches outside the monastic precincts, may have been used by the laity, and there is also a feeling that some monastic communities 'kept up with the Joneses' by building naves larger than those of their neighbours. But the nave was anyhow the least essential part of a monastic or collegiate church. It would be the portion built last, so that its western end, as at Romsey and Selby, is sometimes in a later style than that of the arches nearest the tower. Such changes, within the same part of a single building, did not always seem incongruous to mediaeval builders. They would, however, have been out of the question for a sensitive ancient Greek architect, for by classical standards it was unthinkable for a design to be carried out except as a unified whole. The bottom end of a great Romanesque nave in England would sometimes broaden out into a great western structure, or *westwerk*, of a type probably inspired by Germanic rather than Norman French examples. The great western transepts at Ely and Bury St Edmund's were structures of this type; the same idea was less impressively carried out when Bishop Alexander enlarged Lincoln Cathedral's western end about 1140. In other cases, a pair of towers provided a western termination.

7 *Durham Cathedral: the Norman nave, 1099–1133*

The most interesting part of a great Norman Romanesque church was its eastern half. Over the crossing a central tower, like those at Romsey Abbey and Winchester Cathedral, would be comparatively low; loftier, richly arcaded towers like those at Tewkesbury and Wimborne were a later improvement. In two cathedrals, the small one built at Old Sarum under the 'Lotharingian' Bishop Herman, and at Exeter which was probably inspired by Old Sarum, two flanking towers in the Rhenish manner took the place of one over the crossing.

The eastern limb of these Norman Romanesque abbeys and cathedrals would normally end in a rounded apse. Variety came in the relationship of the central section (containing the High Altar) to the aisles and lesser chapels. In some churches, and fairly commonly in those started before 1100, there was a set of parallel apses, divided from each other by solid walls and with the central presbytery projecting beyond the other elements in the design. No eastern limb of this type survives to-day, but this plan existed in the Confessor's church at Westminster, at Canterbury and Lincoln, and most notably in the new abbey church at St Alban's which may well have derived from the Abbaye aux Dames at Caen.

In most of the remaining large-scale churches of the Norman period, and certainly in most of those built just before and soon after 1100, an aisle or ambulatory was carried all the way round the eastern end. An arcade had thus to be built to divide it from the central space, and this arcade would continue behind the High Altar. The effect, as one still sees at Norwich Cathedral, was most impressive, the more so as the design included an upper row of 'triforium' arches, and then the top windows of the clerestory. A series of small chapels sometimes led out of the aisle of such an eastern limb. Where, as at Gloucester, the presbytery had below it a lower church or crypt, there were corresponding chapels at a lower level.

The third possible shape for a church's eastern limb was that of the square east end. This had been a popular feature in Saxon parish churches, and in the twelfth century we find some major churches returning to this older tradition. This was the shape of the original presbytery at Southwell Minster, and of the outside of the splendidly enlarged choir at Old Sarum. We still see it at Romsey Abbey. It occurs also in many parish churches and in the fine late Romanesque hospital

8 *Southwell Cathedral, Nottinghamshire: the Norman nave, 1108–50*
9 *Worcester Cathedral: the early Norman crypt, 1084–92*

church of St Cross at Winchester. We shall see how this type of east end later became more prevalent.

From the ground plan we go on to the exterior and inner 'elevations' of the great Anglo-Norman churches. Basic principles of design were now laid down, and these were followed in later centuries. The building of arches, walls, and windows was closely linked to the great structural problems presented by the support of ceilings and roofs spanning wide and lofty spaces. Constructional methods and stylistic expression became ever more linked.

The greater church of the Norman period was aisled, with windows whose inner faces were splayed so that more light could reach the interior from the actual openings. Below the roof an upper row of clerestory windows gave extra light to what would otherwise have been a gloomy interior. Even so, the windows were of modest size. This was partly because of their smallness, and partly because the scarcity of glass at this time made it necessary to fill windows with oiled and transparent textiles, or sometimes with wooden shutters which let in no light when closed. Later on, when glass and tracery were normal, these single-light, round-headed windows were provided, as at Ely, Gloucester, and Winchester, with mullions and tracery inserted into their frames. These Norman windows used up comparatively little of the available wall space, and the designers aimed at structural strength through large expanses of massive masonry walls, the buttresses of this period being shallow and unable to exert much counter-thrust. The piers which supported their round-arched nave and choir arcades were thick in proportion to their height, though as the masonry which one sees is only a veneer over a rubble core they are much less sturdy than they seem. The arcades of rounded arches spring from pillars which are sometimes square in plan, like those of many parish churches and the piers in St Alban's Cathedral made up of Roman bricks from the nearby ruins of Verulamium. More often they are cylindrical, particularly in the West Midlands where round pillars of great diameter survive at Great Malvern Priory, at St Chad's at Stafford, at Tewkesbury Abbey, and in Gloucester Cathedral. The most elaborate are those built on a 'clustered' or composite plan, with separate shafts to support the successive 'orders' of the arches above. Pillars on this plan in some cases alternate with others which are round, the more elaborate piers being specially well seen at Norwich, and at Ely and Durham in conjunction with the circular variety. [7]

Above the main arcades a second storey or triforium consisted of an upper row of arches, in many cases leading through to a broad gallery above the aisle below it. At Southwell Minster, in Norwich Cathedral, and in the eastern limb at Gloucester these upper arches were nearly as large as those of the main arcade below them, while at Gloucester the upper aisle of the presbytery had a third storey of projecting chapels exactly corresponding to those below them at ground level and in the crypt. Elsewhere, however, and most notably in the naves of Tewkesbury and Gloucester, these triforium arches were made very small, and this second storey in the overall design seems to have served no liturgical purpose; we shall see how as time went on it was often eliminated. But where a spacious triforium gallery existed it sometimes served a structural purpose by containing, and hiding from outer view, a series of transverse supports to help carry the weight and support the downward thrust exerted by the topmost element in the church's design. [8]

The highest storey in the wall design was the clerestory. As the wall itself, at this height, was still of considerable thickness an upper passageway was frequently built between its outer and inner surfaces. On the outer side the window consisted, as elsewhere in the church, of a single opening. The inner side often has an arcade of small, attractively grouped arches, the central one being higher than the other two.

Finally, the principal roof of a great Norman church was nearly always of timber; its main beams corresponded to the pillars and wall spaces which divided the bays below, and in some cases rested on shafts running all the way up from the church's floor. Nearly all these timber Norman roofs were later replaced by Gothic stone vaults. But in Peterborough Cathedral the Norman timber ceiling survives, and that over the nave at Rochester, though of the early Tudor period, convincingly keeps up the impression conveyed by these long, timberroofed churches of the eleventh and twelfth centuries. The aisles, being narrow and presenting fairly simple constructional problems, were fairly often covered by simple groined vaults. But the stone vaulting of the main central spaces was a more daunting proposition. It may have been intended in the nave at Norwich (whose actual vaults are of the late fifteenth century), but the pioneering building where this form of ceiling was first achieved was the superb Norman Romanesque cathedral at Durham. This was started in 1093, though building work went on for nearly forty years. It was designed, from the start, to have a ribbed vault, and some of its cylindrical pillars are notable for the incised decoration which also occurred in other churches such as those at Orford and Waltham Abbey. The vaults are of the simple, quadri-partite type, with the four ribs intersecting in the middle of each rect-angular compartment. The section of the nave vault at Durham is slightly pointed, it being found that this gave greater strength than a semicircular shape; this important new feature is best seen in the great cross arches which define each double bay from its neighbour. [7]

The most notable outside views of the great Norman churches are of their central towers, of the end elevations of their transepts, and of their western composition. The eastern ends must also have been important, but even where these were not wholly rebuilt in later cen-turies they have been drastically altered by the putting in of new win-dows, vaults, and other features. The frontages of naves and transepts are composed of wall spaces, windows which often have exterior side shafts, carved capitals, and other decoration outside as well as within. Corner towers and turrets also appear; at Southwell Minster the tri-angular gable was filled with an interesting pattern of incised decor-ation. Rows of miniature arcading were a much favoured way of decorating the wall surfaces of towers or western façades. The little arches were often grouped in an attractive interlacing pattern; this same technique was used to adorn indoor wall surfaces in church aisles and on the walls of monastic chapter houses like those at Much Wen-lock Priory and Bristol Cathedral. West fronts, like other parts of these Norman Romanesque churches, have been much altered; large win-dows, in particular, changed much of their previous appearance at Rochester, Castle Acre, Hereford, Malmesbury, and elsewhere.

ANGLO-NORMAN DECORATION

We now come to the important subject of the decoration of the archi-tectural features of Anglo-Norman churches. The same decorative touches were also applied to secular buildings, and the amount of decoration increased greatly as the Norman period continued.

Archways, and particularly the important, readily visible transverse arches which separated naves from chancels, were specially chosen for

carved and chiselled adornment. So too were doorways, in particular
the main entrance of a church. Corbel tables, that is to say the rows of
carved stone blocks between the eaves of a building and its side walling,
were usually given decorative treatment, and we have seen how panelling and wall arcading was used to decorate expanses of wall which
would have seemed dull had they been left plain.

Chancel arches and doorways are really the most important places
for displays of Anglo-Norman decorative art. Parish churches are often
the buildings where this art is best studied. For as they are smaller and
more intimate than the great cathedral and monastic churches their
decoration can be seen and studied at closer range. The earliest doorways, with or without side shafts and semicircular tympana above the
actual door, are usually simple and not always easy to distinguish from
late Saxon work. But as time goes on the degree of decoration greatly
increases, and the severe austerity one associates with some of the
greater Norman churches is wholly absent from such profusely ornate
small churches as those of Barfreston in Kent, Compton Martin and
Lullington in Somerset, Kilpeck in Herefordshire, and Elkstone in the
Gloucestershire Cotswolds. [10, 12]

Chancel arches inevitably have no tympana, but present a fully arched
opening from one part of a church to the other. So their decoration is
mainly found on their concentric 'orders', and on the side shafts and
capitals which support them. Doorways, on the other hand, can be of
two types. Some display the 'concentric' treatment, continuously all
round the archway (as in the superb south porch of Malmesbury Abbey)
or else with side shafts and capitals. Others have their archway blocked
in by a semicircular tympanum. This itself provides a space for carved
decoration in low relief; some have symbolic subjects such as the Tree
of Life, others have religious scenes like Christ in Glory or St Michael
defeating Satan. Fonts of the Norman period, mostly of stone but sometimes of lead, gave more opportunities for sculpture, often arranged in
an 'architectural' setting of continuous arcading. These carved fonts
are often the only Norman feature remaining in a church which
has otherwise been wholly rebuilt. This is particularly true in such
fifteenth-century Cornish churches as Altarnun and Bodmin. [31]

The subject of carved decoration in Anglo-Norman Romanesque
buildings is too large for detailed treatment here. Capitals, an important structural link between the piers and the arches above them, are of

various types. Some are simply moulded. Some are squared at the top, but cut away at the sides to form what is known as the 'cushion' capital; Professor Geoffrey Webb has suggested that these are of Germanic origin and yet another example of 'Lotharingian' influence. Many of twelfth-century date are attractively carved with 'scalloped' decoration, while some, as in the crypt of Gloucester Cathedral which was started soon before 1100, are rendered with foliate carving in a crude imitation of classical Corinthian columns. [9]

The best-known decoration of Norman arches, whether in the arcades of some cathedrals and parish churches or round chancel arches and doorways, is the chevron, or zig-zag, moulding. Many other motifs, in comparatively shallow relief and rendered with the chisel, are also found; billet, lozenge, and cable are among the other mouldings used. More three-dimensional in their nature, and producing a great effect of barbaric splendour and profusion, are the figure sculpture and foliate carving of some capitals, side shafts, fonts, and other features. A specially important local school of this type was at work in the south-west Midlands and Welsh border counties, at Kilpeck, Rock, Shobdon, Brinsop, and elsewhere. Celtic and Scandinavian influences, as well as those from Romanesque France and the Germanic countries, seem clearly to have been at work with the carvers of twelfth-century England, while the strongly barbaric 'beakheads', whose grotesque probosces avidly grip the plainer mouldings of archways, are more local to this country. [7]

PARISH CHURCHES

I have pointed out that many aspects of Norman Romanesque decorative art can be studied as well in parish churches as in cathedrals and abbeys. Nor should the numerous parish churches of the Anglo-Norman period be disregarded as architecture. Their construction and design are less challenging and ambitious than in the 'greater' churches, but they are none the less of great importance, though only a few remain in anything like their original form; early windows, in particular, have made way for larger, traceried openings letting in more light. The majority were built on a simple unaisled plan, with a nave and a sanctuary and sometimes with a third compartment between these two. Sanctuaries end in rounded apses or have a square termination. Most of them seem to have had no towers. But towers in a central position were fairly numerous. Some, as at Stewkley in Buckinghamshire and Coln St Dennis in the Cotswolds, were built over the rectangular spaces allowed between sanctuaries and naves. Others crowned the crossings of cruciform churches; excellent, and relatively ornate examples of Norman Romanesque central towers survive at Castor in Northamptonshire and East Meon in Hampshire.

Narrow aisles were also built on to many of the naves of Norman parish churches. The arcades required for this particular plan are often crude and simple, the arches being cut through older masonry, leaving chunks of the walls standing as heavy, square piers. More often, the arcades have proper pillars of cylindrical or other shapes; the two types of pier are found together at Shrewton in Wiltshire. The pillars and arches often have the decorative techniques and designs which I have mentioned. Far less frequent, in Norman parish churches, are clerestory ranges of upper windows. Steyning in Sussex, Melbourne in Derbyshire, Compton Martin in Somerset, and St Margaret's at Cliffe near the South Foreland are in this respect great rarities.

Hardly anything is known of the master masons who worked on the great Romanesque churches of the Anglo-Norman period. Stylistic evidence makes it clear that Gloucester, Tewkesbury, and Pershore were built under the same inspiration, and strong affinities are clear between such buildings in the eastern counties as the naves at Ely and Peterborough. The personalities and preferences of abbots and bishops could also lead to the employment of the same masons in different places. The great likenesses between the late eleventh-century work at Winchester and Ely no doubt derive from the move of Simeon from the post of cathedral prior at Winchester to the abbacy of Ely, while the imperious Bishop Roger of Old Sarum may well have employed the same masons alike on his cathedral choir and on the great new castles with which he strengthened his political position. But in the absence of documents the architectural authorship of Norman Romanesque buildings must remain less well charted than that of major churches in the Gothic styles. What remains past question is the vast importance in our architectural story of the period between about 1070 and 1150. Parish churches apart, cathedrals, monastic churches, and collegiate churches were built all over the country, and even where their eastern halves have been refashioned or wholly replaced there are many large or moderate-sized churches whose naves were far less altered and have wholly or

partly survived. Selby and Blyth, Binham and Wymondham, Shrewsbury and Great Malvern, Dunstable and Elstow, St James's at Bristol,
Leominster and Leonard Stanley, Malmesbury and Christchurch,
Wimborne and St German's all show important Norman work in
churches which have never attained cathedral status. Elsewhere, as
at Lindisfarne, Castle Acre, and even in the sad wreck of the vast
westwerk of Bury St Edmund's, there are substantial ruins which
bear witness to Anglo-Norman achievements in design and decoration.

Of less merit, despite its first impression of massive solidity, was the
Norman Romanesque achievement in terms of construction. Much of
the work done was unscientific. Vast churches like that at Winchester
were built on sites where the ground was too soft to take them. Foundations were sometimes inadequate for the weight they were expected
to bear. Central towers, like that at Winchester a few years after it had
been built, and like that at Ely in 1323, would collapse entirely.
Arcades would in time lean sharply to one side, particularly in many
parish churches and smaller monastic ones such as St James's at Bristol.
Piers which seemed strong and massive, like those at Gloucester,
Tewkesbury, and Reading, had no more than a thin skin of ashlar
masonry cast round a loosely bound core of rubble. Not much thought,
apparently, was given to the problems of stress or to the balancing support of thrust; all round massiveness was preferred to the intelligent
checking of pressures at sensitive points. The Anglo-Norman designers
did not as a rule realise that the round arch is not the strongest type of
arch, and their massive piers, comparatively small 'single-light' windows, and the general absence of wide stone vaults were as much the
result of limited technique as of artistic preference. At Durham, however, the slightly pointed section of the vaults and the well conceived
transverse arches in the triforium gallery point clearly to greater finesse
in the coming century. Windows, moreover, are often more ambitious
in twelfth-century work. For paired openings, well grouped beneath
single containing arches, would take the place of single lights, particularly in the upper stages of towers and in some domestic buildings.
Larger openings in the walls were thus required, and one thus gets a
feeling of greater confidence by designers and masons in their building
technique.

A great problem, no less acute for the Anglo-Norman Romanesque

10 *Barfreston, Kent: the south doorway, late Norman*

designers than for their Gothic successors, was that of building materials. Timber, in a densely wooded country, was no problem, and the churches of poor village communities had perforce to make do with what stone, whether rubble, flint, limestone, or sandstone, lay close to hand. For the greater churches in stoneless districts the problem was that of transporting large tonnages of high grade stone of a type that fitted the prestige and importance of the communities concerned. The answer lay largely in freightage by water. Rivers, and even a few artificial 'lodes' or channels ending in a cul de sac, were much used, so that the richer churches like Ely and Norwich could have stone, via the numerous Fenland waterways, from the oolitic limestone quarries of Rutland and Northamptonshire. In some stoneless districts of the southern counties it was even found best to ship stone across the Channel from Caen in Normandy, and so up estuaries and navigable rivers to such places as Christchurch or Winchester.

By the middle decades of the twelfth century Anglo-Norman Romanesque had reached its fullest structural development and elaboration. The achievement since 1066 had been stupendous. But round-arched architecture, whether under inspiration from Normandy, Lotharingia, or elsewhere, had little more to say. Though the revolutionary new ideas of the fully Gothic designers were hardly foreseen, the limits of what could be done with the round arch had apparently been reached. The pointed arch, a constructional device needing no tips or inspiration from returning Crusaders,* had been used in the great Durham design made soon before 1100. It appears again, as a constructional necessity, on the north and south sides of the central crossing of St John's church at Devizes which was probably built not long after 1140. In a few more years the splendid nave at Malmesbury Abbey, a pioneering and most sophisticated masterpiece of late Romanesque, has slightly pointed arches all along the length of each arcade, while the vault section in the aisles, and the cross arches which divide each bay of an aisle from its neighbour, are noticeably acute. No traces of Gothic or 'Transitional' decoration appear in this noble nave, while the arches of its triforium, of its wall arcading, of its remaining Romanesque windows, and of its southern doorway, are conventionally Norman. But from such a work it is clear that Romanesque, as it had long

* The attractive artistic effect of interlaced arcading may, however, have contributed to it.

11   *Late Norman manor : Boothby Pagnell, Lincolnshire, c. 1180*
12   *Late Norman church : Elkstone, Gloucestershire*

been known, would not long outlast the coming of the Plantagenet dynasty.

HOUSES AND CASTLES

Churches of various types and sizes by no means made up the full achievement of the Anglo-Norman builders. A few of their stone houses, and many of their castles, remind us forcibly that secular architecture was a serious competitor of churches in its call on the available supply of carpenters, labourers, and skilled masons.

The more important private houses, the ceremonial halls, and the few public buildings of the Norman period were architecturally akin to the naves, whether aisled or otherwise, of parish churches. Their main structure was rectangular, not cruciform, and as such apartments as kitchens seem often to have been fitted out in separate buildings their ground plan was apt to be less complicated than that of many manor houses and town residences in the later Middle Ages. Some were built of wood, and houses of this material must have differed comparatively little from the barnlike 'hall houses' of Saxon times. Shallow buttresses, large spaces of wall, and fairly small window openings were all features of those built of rubble or dressed stone.

The basic elements in the more important Anglo-Norman dwelling house were the great hall, some private apartments, and provision for storage space. For defensive and other reasons these main elements of the house were compact, and were contained within the area of a simple rectangle. So at least in the stone-built houses the storage space was in cellars, directly below the hall and dimly lit by narrow rectangular slits. The ceiling of these cellars was often stone-vaulted, with transverse ribs and wall shafts like those in the late twelfth-century cellar of a merchant's house which survives beneath the Fleece Inn at Gloucester. Others, however, had their ceilings framed with massive timber baulks. But in the timber-built houses, which we may assume to have been the type more often built in the early Norman period, this ground-level cellar space seems not to have been provided. The storage of goods was then arranged in separate buildings. The same single-storey design seems to have been followed where stone halls were large and spacious enough to be built with pillars and aisles, and the cellars or undercrofts of private houses and halls are in this respect less

ambitious than the crypts of great churches where the piers of the
presbytery are carried down to foundation level in the crypt.

The main apartment of the house was the hall, as a rule unaisled like
a small parish church's nave, and often with a hearth in the middle of
its floor; the smoke from the fire would rise towards a hole in the timber roof. It was there drawn out by a louvre, or chimney, of stone or
pottery, pitched carefully above the hearth on the peak of the roof.
But the important late Norman houses whose remains survive at Christchurch and Southampton show that in some 'manorial' dwellings, as in
the great tower keeps of contemporary castles, the fireplaces were
apt to be recessed in the side walls. This, of course, is how most
fireplaces have been ever since, diminishing the amount of smoke
allowed to circulate in the rooms and the amount of warmth thrown
out into their living space. The smoke of the fires in these built-in
fireplaces was drawn up by means of stone hoods, projecting on brackets some distance beyond the side walls of the rooms.

The rectangular hall was the main living apartment of such a house.
It lay at first-floor level, and an outside staircase led up from outdoors.
The indoor activities of the household were here pursued, and at night
the servants gathered to sleep round the central hearth, or in a semi-
circle before the fireplace if this was in one of the side walls. But the
owner of the house and his family claimed greater privacy. So this was
contrived by partitioning off one end of the rectangular hall by a wood-
en screen. Behind this the 'solar', or private parlour, gave a measure
of seclusion; in some cases, as at Christchurch, an upper room or loft
provided yet more private accommodation above the main parlour.

Such were the better-class dwelling houses of the Norman and early
Plantagenet periods. A fair number of such houses survive, in ruins or
in a much altered state. All were built in the second half of the twelfth
century. That at Christchurch was designed as a dwelling house, pre-
sumably for the castellan in times of peace, within the confines of a
castle, so much so that one of its walls is incorporated into the outer
wall of the castle itself. Some, as at Lincoln, Bury St Edmund's, and
Southampton, were the town houses of merchants and traders; those
at Lincoln and Bury St Edmund's are said to have belonged to wealthy
Jews. Others, like the manor house at Saltford between Bristol and
Bath, the Norman portion of Horton Court in Gloucestershire, and
the manor at Boothby Pagnell near Grantham in Lincolnshire, were

unfortified country manor houses. So too, when new, was the 'Stone House' at Cambridge later known as the School of Pythagoras; this building is late enough for the inner apertures of its windows to be Transitional Gothic in character. [11]

A few of the larger manors, and several palaces and castles, had halls which were aisled, and which were some of them built of wood. Recent excavation has shown that the Saxon royal palace at Cheddar was much enlarged in the early Norman period by the building of a spacious aisled hall whose pillars were of timber. In the Bishop's Palace at Hereford some piers and arches of the Great Hall still stand among many later floors and partitions; they show bell-shaped scalloped capitals and billet moulding—features one normally associates with Norman Romanesque architectural adornment in stone. The great rectangular building of Westminster Hall, started by William II and perhaps finished by 1100, was certainly split up into a central nave and two flanking aisles. Its windows, and the arcading between them, were of an ambitious design, and the two rows of pillars may possibly have been of massive timber work.

MONASTIC BUILDINGS

The earliest Guildhalls, like that built at Exeter about 1160, may also have been rectangular buildings like the halls of manors or castles. But public buildings, as we know them now, were still in their infancy under the Norman Kings. The living quarters of the monasteries are more important for those who would study early mediaeval architecture. Though built as part of religious establishments, and closely linked to the great churches which existed for the corporate worship of the monks, they stand somewhat apart from architecture of the strictly ecclesiastical type.

The buildings of the important monasteries, as gradually enlarged and rebuilt in the century after the Norman Conquest, were most carefully planned for the purposes they were meant to serve. With the churches I have dealt already. The domestic buildings, for working, sleeping, eating, and recreation, would follow the church. They included a chapter-house for the business meetings of the convent, an infirmary for the lodging of sick and decrepit monks, and other buildings required by a mainly self-supporting community. They might, at first, be temporarily built of wood while the church was being got ready for worship, but the monks' eventual aim was to have their living quarters constructed of stone. The chapter-house, sometimes vaulted and approached from the cloister by a central doorway, flanking windows, and at Bristol and elsewhere by a beautiful vestibule, was nearer in its architecture to a church than to a purely domestic building. At Worcester Cathedral, before the end of the Norman period, a splendid chapter-house, with a central pillar and a circular interior, foreshadowed the beautiful polygonal buildings which later became a special glory of English Gothic architecture. But the other buildings, in reality a series of simple rectangular halls, come more within the domestic heading. We must, however, bear in mind that they and the manorial halls are not, in their construction and roofing, very different from the naves of parish churches. The main point in which their design diverged from the pattern normal in parish churches was that many of these domestic blocks were built in two storeys.

The chief domestic buildings of mediaeval monks were the refectories, the dormitories, the carefully contrived latrine blocks built close to the dormitories, and the western ranges of the cloister quadrangles which contained storage and administrative space and sometimes a separate dwelling for the head of the convent.* All these would be grouped round the quadrangle of the cloister garth. To the east of the cloister buildings the infirmary would usually resemble an aisled parish church, its 'nave' being the hall containing the beds for the sick and the 'chancel' being the infirmary chapel.

Many monastic buildings which are still used or survive in ruins were started or rebuilt in the periods when the Gothic styles had succeeded Romanesque. But the main principles of their arrangement were laid down in the Norman period, and in some places important parts of surviving monastic buildings are in the Norman style. The undercrofts, or crypts, below monks' dormitories and refectories were apt to be more ambitious than those below manor house halls; this is clear at Westminster and Durham, and at Chester in the undercroft which served for storage in the western range. [16]

The manor houses, castle halls, and monastic buildings of the Norman Romanesque period had their share of carved decoration and

---

* In Cistercian Abbeys, being built by the end of the Norman period, these western ranges originally housed the lay brothers.

chiselled adornment. This ornament, and the motifs which composed
it, differed little from much of what was also found in the churches.
Chevron and billet mouldings, cushion and scalloped capitals, figure
and foliate carving of a somewhat crude yet vigorous type, all these
would appear on arches, doorways, and window frames. Doorways like
those at Horton and in the Jew's House at Lincoln, and 'two-light'
windows as at Christchurch, Saltford, and Southampton, are much the
same as one might find them in an ecclesiastical setting. Now and
throughout the Middle Ages there were functional differences, but no
chasms of style, between sacred and secular architecture. What is true
of the rectangular halls, in their varied uses as living rooms, refectories,
or places for the well ordered communal sleeping of monks, is also true
of the ornamental portions of the Anglo-Norman castles.

CASTLES

Military and civil engineering are architecture's kindred arts, and no
short account of the Anglo-Norman building record could be complete without its note on castles. Those built in England, and in the
border zone of Wales, can be grouped in two types—the motte and
bailey castle which came first, and the more imposing, more sophisticated tower and bailey fortress which continued as the standard pattern
for over a hundred years.

The common factor to both was the bailey, or large fortified enclosure. As this bailey was placed, in the manner of an Iron Age camp
or a Saxon *burh*, on the top of some hill or commanding eminence it
would normally be irregular in shape, with its fortified outline con-
forming to the sinuous contours of its hill. Only castles built on flat
ground, like the Tower of London or Portchester whose Roman fortress walls made a rectangular framework for an inner enclosure, were
laid out on neatly geometrical lines. In the early Norman period the
defences of the bailey were not of stone, but consisted of earthen
ramparts crowned by a sturdy timber palisade. They were thus no
architectural advance on the Saxon *burhs*, or for that matter on the
ramparts, palisades, and ditches of the Iron Age.* Where the earliest
Norman castles improved on their predecessors was in their provision

* At Old Sarum and Thetford, Iron Age ramparts were actually used as the outer
fortifications of Norman castles.

of a single strongpoint, harder to take than the rest of the castle and so offering a last centre of refuge for hard-pressed defenders.

This dominant strongpoint of a Norman castle was first provided by

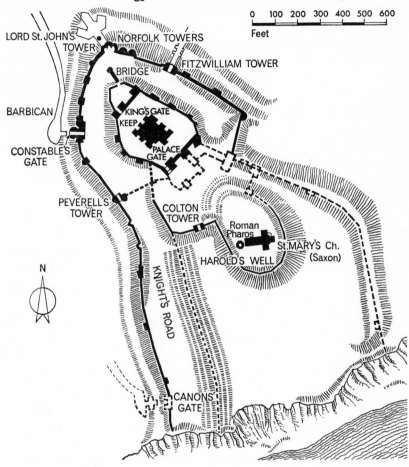

13 *Dover Castle, Kent, c. 1179–97: a great keep-and-bailey castle developed late in the twelfth century and enlarged under Henry III. (The outer curtain wall is of the thirteenth century and foreshadows the 'concentric' planning of Edwardian castles)*

the piling up of a tall, conical mound of earth. This was known as the *motte*, and around it the engineers provided an inner ditch. On the top of this mound, or encircling its upper portion, a circular tower, or shell keep, provided a final rallying point and some cramped living

quarters for the owner himself, his family, and the leading elements in
the garrison. These 'pillbox' towers were built at first, like the palisades on the ramparts, of timber baulks. But where castles were allowed
to survive the turbulent middle decades of the twelfth century the
towers on the mottes were replaced (not always in the Norman period,
as one sees at Christchurch and York) by circular towers, or 'shell
keeps' of stone. Lincoln, Totnes, Tonbridge, and Warwick were all
good examples of this treatment. In some castles, and most notably at
Berkeley, the shell keep encircled not the upper portion but the base
of the mound; in such a case, as also in the roomy circular keeps at
Restormel and Windsor, the circular tower allowed reasonable space
for living quarters within.

But the circular shell keep was by no means the final masterpiece of
the Anglo-Norman military engineers. Before the eleventh century had
ended, and all through the next hundred years, the country saw the rise,
above many a stone-girt fortified enclosure, of what were, in effect,
the ancestors of the tower blocks or point blocks which some people
now find a disconcerting intrusion into our urban townscape. No less
menacing, to those who counted themselves a subject people, were
the great tower keeps which still plentifully exist to prove the skill
and calculation of their builders.

The tower keeps of the late eleventh and twelfth centuries are
among England's finest memorials of the Norman régime. In their own
way they are no less impressive than the greatest churches. In the
strength of their construction, moreover, they surpassed the abbeys
and cathedrals. Not only was the portentously thick masonry of their
walls a strong insurance against collapse, but those walls, revetted or
splayed outwards near their base to ensure a firmer hold on the ground
below, descended straight to massive foundations built on solid chalk
or rock. A tower keep, on such supports, had better chances of standing upright than an abbey's central tower on its rubble-packed piers
and sometimes inadequate foundations.

Many of these tower keeps survive, though some of great splendour,
as at Bristol, Devizes, and Bridgwater, have disappeared above ground.
They were square, or nearly so, in plan. The lowermost rooms, ill lit
and only just above the foundations, were used, as were the lower
compartments of manor houses, for storage. A well, within those
cellars or sometimes, as in the excavated foundations at Bristol, in the

actual thickness of the walls, was vital for the needs of a garrison cut off in this ultimate citadel. Above the cellars several storeys were built, while higher still the topmost parapet, and sometimes four corner turrets, dominated the inner and outer baileys and gave views of the country around. Shallow buttresses, as in churches, would slightly diversify the wall expanses. Windows, of one or two lights, lit the various apartments within. The entrance doorway, as in the manor houses whose halls were entered by means of outside stairways, was usually some distance above the ground, at first or perhaps second floor level. The stairway approaching it was often masked, as one still sees in the great keep at Rochester, by a 'forebuilding' projecting from the main bulk of the keep.

The living rooms, on their succeeding floors, were the lord of the castle's living quarters. In some castles, which had halls and parlours out in the bailey, these rooms in the keep were only used in times of stress. Elsewhere, and especially in such spacious keeps as at London, Colchester, Rochester, Norwich, and Hedingham, they were large and comfortable enough for more permanent use. Halls, parlours, and bedrooms could all be provided in the main expanse of a tower keep's interior, while smaller rooms and latrines could be fashioned in the thickness of the walls. A chapel, as in the Tower of London and at Dover where they are of some size and architectural pretension, was also provided. The larger keeps, as we can still well see at Rochester and Hedingham, had their living space divided along one axis by an arcade or a great transverse arch. The embellishment of those arches, and of the round-arched fireplaces built into the great thickness of the walls, employed the same motifs—chevron, cable, billet, and the rest—that were chiselled at the same time on the ornamental parts of the churches. The keep, or White Tower, of the Tower of London, with the round columns, unornamented arches, and plain capitals of its chapel arcades, very clearly displays its building period as being the last years of the eleventh century. Dover, Sherborne, Richmond, Hedingham, and others have keeps which are just as obviously of dates well into the twelfth. We have indeed, to remember that many of these supposedly 'Norman' keeps and outer fortifications were part of the political and military policy of Henry II, the first Plantagenet King; neither here nor in churches is the political adjective very apt to designate an architectural or artistic phase. [14]

Before 1200 some new structural ideas were being worked out in the design and building of certain tower keeps. A weak point in those built on a quadrangular plan was the existence of squared corners which were comparatively easy for attackers to loosen with picks and other demolition devices. So at Orford in Suffolk, at Conisborough in York-shire, and elsewhere the main structure of the late twelfth-century tower keeps was made polygonal, with the corners obtuse-angled instead of the right-angled, more exposed corners of the square or rectangular towers. Projecting turrets were included in the fabric, making it easier for defenders to cast missiles on mining and burrowing attackers below. In military architecture, as in that of the great churches, new methods were being tried to meet problems which were always likely to recur.

CHAPTER THREE

Early Gothic

c. 1180–1250

As the last square tower keeps were rising above their baileys the earliest truly Gothic churches of England were also being built. The 1170s, in this connection, were a revealing decade. The new castle at Orford was finished in 1173, a year when the King's eldest son and some of his barons were in open rebellion, and when Scotland had joined the malcontents in their open struggle against Henry II. Next year, only two months after Henry had undergone his penitential scourging at Becket's tomb, the great late Norman choir at Canterbury, built in the manner of Cluny with an eastern pair of transepts, was reduced by fire to a blackened shell. Within its outer walls, and above its surviving crypt, a new choir was duly built whose style and structure marked it out as a pioneering English essay in what was now, in northern France, the accepted architectural manner. The new tendencies had, indeed, been foreshadowed in some Cistercian abbey churches in the North. But here in the primate's church, now popular as never before as a centre of national pilgrimage, the slow transition from Romanesque to Gothic achieved its most influential display.

Within the range of buildings to which architectural treatment was applied some important departures had, indeed, been made already from the solidity of Anglo-Norman building practice, and from the largely Continental influences which had come in with the new generation of barons and churchmen from Normandy or Lotharingia. The squared east end had become overwhelmingly predominant in the later twelfth century. The Galilee chapel at the west end of Durham Cathedral, contemporary with the new Gothic choir at Canterbury yet

Norman Romanesque in the roundness of its arches and in its rich zig-zag mouldings, had columns, with moulded bases, of a clustered slenderness which belonged to the coming architectural fashion.* The aisled castle hall at Oakham, a brilliant example of 'Transitional' work in the manner of a church nave, has paired windows and rounded arches in the Romanesque manner; but its foliate capitals, dogtooth moulding, and its general feeling of a greater lightness and delicacy, look forward to an age of more slender and more scientific construction. In some of the greater churches experiments were made to vary the horizontal 'three-tier' design of arcade, triforium, and clerestory. For the two lower stages would be combined into one on the inner side, the lower arch of the arcade and a 'blind' triforium stage both being contained within a single arch of 'giant' proportions. Experiments of this kind had been made in the presbytery at Tewkesbury, in the nave at Romsey, and perhaps elsewhere. The new fashion now appeared again, with round arches but with moulding and decoration of a more novel type, in the eastern limb of St Frideswide's Priory (now the Cathedral) at Oxford. In the last years of the century this same design, a bold innovation but somewhat awkward in appearance, was used in the more completely Gothic choir built at Glastonbury to replace the great Norman church burnt out in 1184. The logic of these experiments was the total cutting out of the second, or triforium, stage. Parish churches, some small Benedictine priories and several of the new Cistercian abbeys had already done without it; the time duly came when it wholly disappeared.

Two main things stand out about England's buildings of this half-century which saw the transition from Romanesque to Gothic. Structure, especially that of the more important churches, was planned on new, more scientific lines. Decoration, as in the carved and chiselled work round arches and on capitals, sometimes expressed new motifs. Carefully wrought mouldings and round arches were more in evidence, while foliage was carved with greater freedom than before.

What mattered most, in the earliest churches which can truly be called Gothic, was a new structural emphasis less on strength by mere masses of masonry than on the channelling of weights and stresses to points where they could be met by the counterthrust of fairly slender

* Very similar columns, with pointed arches, are in the York church of St Michael, Spurriergate.

14 *Castle Hedingham, Essex: the keep, c.1140*

masses of masonry run up to take them. Stone vaults in particular, with their structure expressed and emphasised by ribs running diagonally across each rectangular section, were supported by more delicate stonework fabrics than those thought needful for Norman vaults or timber roofs. Windows would still for the most part pierce the walls in single units, but the arcade pillars of such a structure could be much more slender and delicate than their forerunners in Norman Romanesque. These are the main elements of early Gothic as worked out in northern France. With some limitations, and some decorative features carried over from the Norman period, they are well seen in the eastern limb of Canterbury as this was reconstructed after the fire of 1174. The original designer of the new work was William of Sens, a master mason from the very part of France where the Gothic manner of building was first evolved. The inward narrowing of the sanctuary towards the High Altar was forced upon this designer from abroad by his orders to build within the surviving shell of the older, apsidal choir. But other features, among them the eastern apse, the great use of dark polished marble, paired columns (as in the cathedral at Sens itself), and the strongly classical character of the capitals of his slender pillars, were brought in by William from what he knew in France. So the general feeling of the eastern limb of the cathedral at Canterbury is strongly French Gothic, drawing back towards Continental practice the building work of a country that was tending, as in late Saxon times, to go its own way. [15]

The arches and window heads of Canterbury Cathedral's eastern limb are most of them pointed; round the eastern apse they are sharply so. The same shape of arches appears in several other buildings of this Transitional or early Gothic period. From now onwards the pointed arch, found stronger and more graceful by the scientific builders of this time, becomes much more common. Yet it was not wholly essential to their new constructional style. Round arches, as in the new retrochoir at Chichester Cathedral, still appeared in buildings of the new type, while at Furness Abbey, Haughmond Abbey and elsewhere entrance arches with mouldings and carvings of the new pattern could still be semicircular. At the same time arcades and doorways of an essentially Norman type were often built in many parish churches, at Durham Castle, and in the naves of Buildwas Abbey in Shropshire and the Cornish priory of St German's; these arches none the less displayed a

15 EARLY GOTHIC *Canterbury Cathedral: the eastern apse, 1179–84*

pointed outline. The rounded arch was not essential to the last expression of the Romanesque tradition, nor were pointed arches, as yet, an
essential of advancing Gothic.

The new choir at Canterbury, with the Frenchman William of Sens
as its pioneer designer, was soon followed by other buildings which
well showed some of the newly introduced artistic tendencies. We
have seen how the new retrochoir at Chichester still clung to rounded
arches in its main arcades. But the clustered columns and stiffly foliate
capitals of those arches, and the paired arches of the triforium stage,
were wholly in the new fashion. The south-eastern counties, being
close to the Continent, were early in their French stylistic borrowing.
So in the Sussex port of New Shoreham the fine vaulted choir of the
parish church is early Gothic in character, though with strong Romanesque survivals. In London the round nave of the Temple church well
blended an early Gothic main arcade with a triforium stage whose
interlaced arcade was residually Romanesque.

The leading patrons of architecture in the late twelfth century included the first builders of many monastic establishments. Some of the
numerous houses of Canons Regular were founded at this time. Most
of their buildings, however, have been destroyed, but churches such as
that of Keynsham Abbey, founded soon after 1167 by the wealthy and
prominent Earl of Gloucester, may well have been notable works in
the Transitional manner. More important, for students of architecture
whose main interest must lie in what still stands above ground, were
the churches and domestic buildings of the twelfth-century Cistercians.
Unlike many older monasteries, which had been the result of slow
growth on long-occupied sites, these abbeys were new foundations on
virgin soil. The churches, and most of the many domestic buildings,
were usually built in one operation. Their plan and arrangement were
carefully and unsentimentally calculated for the particular life led within the precincts. They were controlled by the precise instructions of a
centrally directed Rule which all abbeys of the Order were bound to
observe; excessive decoration, central towers, and coloured glass were
all banned. So standardised was the Cistercian plan, in England, Ireland, Italy, France, Denmark, or elsewhere, that the study of early
Cistercian abbeys is dull and unvaried compared to that of the other
religious orders. But once the third dimension is reached the churches
are often of great importance for the way in which early Gothic and

late Romanesque tendencies are seen side by side. So at Buildwas in Shropshire, not far from the famous eighteenth-century Iron Bridge over the Severn, slightly pointed arches are held up on pillars and scalloped capitals of a Romanesque type. But in Yorkshire, in the naves at Kirkstall and Fountains, the arcades with their pointed arches are far more Gothic in character, the triforium stage (as also in the smaller church at Buildwas) is left out; and in general one finds the influence of Burgundian Gothic, as modified by the English masons who must have worked for these Cistercian monks.

I have said that the Gothic style, as a rule with its arches and windows pointed, had mainly been shown constructionally, in the meeting of stress and thrust with a new economy of masonry and mass. As such, it had started in France. Certain changes of emphasis marked it as it first developed in England. Two modern writers have well observed that English Gothic was apt to consist less in structural essentials than in the architectural treatment, by what amounted to applied ornament, of long wall surfaces.* This is clear in the elaborate treatment of the windows and wall arcading (at window level) which survives in the unaisled nave of the Yorkshire nunnery church of Nun Monkton: the same idea was also fully exploited in the originally unaisled nave of Ripon Cathedral. Elsewhere, on outside walls, early Gothic arcading, like that of the Norman Romanesque designs, is used more as an applied, non-structural, decoration than as an essential element in a building's composition. In this respect it foreshadows the veneer of Gothic decoration applied by the late Georgians to buildings whose design was symmetrically conceived on classical lines.

Meanwhile, much building work was done in parish churches which showed late Romanesque and early Gothic detail side by side. Pointed arches thus rise from plain round pillars with scalloped capitals. A new and daring freedom, and a greater sculptural effect, are found in the treatment of chevron moulding. The little pyramids of 'dogtooth' moulding, and foliate capitals of the new, more classically motivated type, begin to appear. Soham in the Isle of Ely, Margate in Kent, Downton and Tisbury in Wiltshire, St Oswald's and St Margaret's at Durham, and Faringdon in Berkshire are among the many churches where one can study this fertile process of architectural evolution and

* Peter Kidson and Peter Murray, *A History of English Architecture*, 1962.

rebirth. This half-century between 1150 and 1200 was formative and exciting as were few other periods in England's architectural story. For one great artistic tradition was making way for another; the same excitement, more or less in reverse, occurred when the Renaissance slowly ousted Gothic.

At Canterbury and elsewhere mediaeval England had been shown its first sample of French Gothic. Some people might have felt that this, perhaps with some modification, might become a tradition. But native insularity, and a political severance, soon steered things the other way. England's Gothic was destined to be a Gothic apart.

Some great churches in the western counties, started shortly before 1200, more typically foreshadow the splendid architectural idiom which held sway in thirteenth-century England. The new choir and transepts of the cathedral at Wells were started soon after 1180. Above their richly carved capitals, they have squared abaci of a Romanesque type. But in the main the style and detail of the new work was Gothic, and the sculpture of the capitals blends figures and foliage more flowing and natural in character than in the more rigidly classic capitals of the same time in Kent or Sussex. The clustered columns at Wells (with no dark marble to diversify their colour-scheme) are sturdier than those at Canterbury, and though neither Wells nor the Canterbury choir have the loftiness of Continental Gothic the horizontal emphasis is greater at Wells; length, not height, was what came to distinguish the Gothic of England. The new abbey church at Glastonbury had much of Wells's character, though the combining, under single giant arches, of arcade and triforium must have lessened its long-drawn impression. These Westcountry churches, along with Canterbury's choir and eastern transepts, may have had their influence on St Hugh when in 1186 he moved from his Somerset Carthusian priory to the see of Lincoln, there starting the unattractive, unsymmetrically vaulted choir which still bears his name. [17]

From soon after 1200, with a brief interruption caused by the Papal Interdict in King John's reign, England settled down to its own version of Gothic. With very few exceptions the buildings erected were in the style not ineptly known as 'Early English'. England's master masons, now clearly emerging as the main fashioners of architecture, had already begun to go their own way. Political severance aided their natural isolationism. For by the end of 1204, when the last of Normandy was

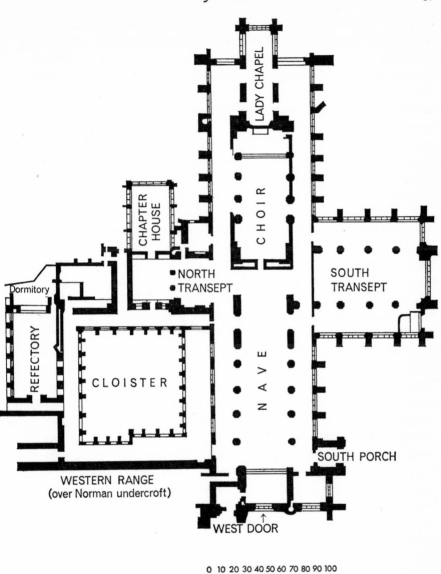

16 *Chester Monastery and Cathedral, 1093 onwards: ground plan*

lost, large areas of northern and western France had passed from the
sway of the English Crown; the whole atmosphere was less favourable
to fruitful contacts with the central forcing ground and homeland of
the French Gothic tradition. So England's existing preference for such
things as fairly low vaults and square east ends was reinforced. Square
east ends, in particular, became almost universal in the churches; the
apsidal presbytery at Beaulieu Abbey, a Cistercian house directly colon-
ised from Citeaux and thus displaying strong influences from eastern
France, was a rare exception in the first decade of the thirteenth century. As England was cut off from the architectural idioms of the
Continent, so too her own influence on other countries was small.
Scotland and Ireland for a time were parts of the Early English architectural province. Norway, and the outer Scandinavian territories of Ice-
land, the Faroes, and even Greenland were well within the English
sphere; alone of the countries which shared in the great Gothic tradition they consistently preferred the square east end.

The Early English, or 'lancet' style, as matured and widely used
between 1200 and about 1250, is the simplest, most readily understood subsection of English Gothic. We may, in this matter of purist
simplicity, compare it to the Doric of the Greek world in the fifth
century before Christ; in such a context one may think of Salisbury
Cathedral as England's Parthenon. Nowadays, one senses a certain
chaste coldness in Greek Doric and Early English alike. We must,
however, recall that their restrained simplicity of outline and style was
at first set off by rich colour effects of painted stone, and in the mediaeval Gothic buildings of glass as well. These are absent now after
long years of alteration, vandalism, and outright ruin.

In the more important church buildings the Early English of the
first decades of the thirteenth century displays the methods of construction which had now firmly replaced the more elementary building
technique of Norman Romanesque. The stresses unavoidable in arched
vaults of stone are concentrated on the curved stone ribs, and are so
transmitted to the key points where bays, or compartments, of vaulting
are separated from one another, and where external buttresses rise to
take the downward thrust. The vaults themselves are still simply
planned; before 1250 they were usually quadripartite, with no more
than the four compartments in each rectangle which are produced by
plain diagonal ribs. Along the centre lines of the vaults the intersection

points of the ribs are marked, as in the choir at Hereford where a
thirteenth-century vault crowns an older structure, by deeply carved
bosses. These act alike as the keystones of the structure, and as the
most striking adornments of the vaulted ceilings. Buttresses, as at
Salisbury, Worcester, Wells, and elsewhere, are still of a modest
projection, and some are charmingly gabled. The lancet, tall and narrow and curved to a point at the top, was the standard window opening
of the time. Many appear singly, but many are also in groups of two,
three, or sometimes more. But as thirteenth-century lancets were of
modest width the spaces of wall between windows were still wider
than they were in the later Gothic period. A few windows, in the
gable ends of large churches and in parish church clerestories where
these occurred, were circular.

The Early English period saw important new ways of adorning interior surfaces and so redeeming them from dull severity. Wall arcading
was still much in favour. The arches, like the heads of some lancets,
were fairly often designed in a trefoil pattern. In Beverley Minster, and
the eastern transepts at Lincoln, this wall arcading is 'two-tiered', a
set of trefoiled arches being placed in advance of a row of the normal
two-centred type; the effect so produced is rich and elaborate. The
heads of lancets are often richly moulded on the inner side, while
dignified shafts of stone or dark marble part the lancets from each other.
Niches and piscina recesses (for the washing during Mass of the sacred
vessels) show the same tricks of design as windows and wall arcades. A
new grace and freedom appeared in the design and fitting out of many
churches, or of the chancels and chapels added to older naves.

The basic design of the 'greater' churches in the thirteenth century
showed many changes from what had been normal before Gothic became the accepted style. The precedent of a long eastern limb, already
set at Canterbury and followed at Lincoln, was eagerly accepted;
eastern transepts, in particular, became fairly common. The extensions at Rochester, the new eastern limb at Worcester, the superb
church at Beverley and the new choir at Carlisle, the new presbytery
at Rievaulx, the enlargements at Southwell and elsewhere, all emphasised England's obvious preference for length at the expense of loftiness.
At Hereford, Southwark, Salisbury, and later on in other great churches
retrochoirs and Lady Chapels continued, at lower levels, the main
eastward elongations. Crypts, however, were far fewer than in Norman

times. Hereford and Wimborne have small ones of the thirteenth century below the extreme eastern end of their buildings, while Rochester's splendid crypt under all of its new eastern arm, and that built as the first stage of the new chapter-house at Wells, were brilliant exceptions to the normal trend. But the undercrofts of monastic buildings, simply vaulted ground-floor rooms in those same buildings, and some cellars in castles, manors, and town houses better proved the skill of the thirteenth-century masons on construction of this type.

The architectural composition of the greater churches was much as before, with the sequence of a main arcade, a triforium stage, and an upper row of clerestory windows. Here and there, as in the exquisitely beautiful new presbytery built at Pershore Abbey, the triforium and clerestory stages were neatly combined into one; the 'vertical' effect so given was important as the harbinger of much yet to come in English Gothic. Where a great church had to be built anew, or where new work replaced an older structure, the building process was slow, so that a complete uniformity of design was not maintained. Differences in such points as columns, capitals, carved detail, and vaulting ribs, occur between the earlier part of a church and that which was finished later. This is most noticeable when one carefully studies the presbytery and transepts at Hexham Priory. Even at Salisbury, the great example of a 'pattern book' thirteenth-century cathedral, started on a virgin site and most of it continuously built from 1220 to about 1270, there are certain differences, particularly in the amount of carved detail allowed as an embellishment, between the eastern and western halves of the church.

Apart from lancet windows, there are certain well known features by which the Early English of the thirteenth century can be distinguished. Columns, as at Wells, Abbeydore, and Pershore, are sometimes beautifully clustered and built all of stone. At Salisbury, in the choir at Worcester, and in some other churches stone columns are girt round with dark marble shafts. Some capitals, most notably at Salisbury and in Cistercian churches, are simply moulded. Others are splendidly sculptured with foliate carving so deeply cut that a hand can be buried between the stiffly curving leaves. Arches in the greater churches, and the hoods of lancets as one sees them on the choir of Jesus College Chapel (originally a nunnery church) at Cambridge, tend to be richly moulded. But in parish churches and the simpler monastic buildings the plainer device of the backward-sloping chamfer is used to relieve

17   *Wells Cathedral: the nave, 1192–c.1230*

the sharpness of their outline. Outside, the 'corbel table', or row of simply carved blocks just below the eaves, was still used; it had, however, less sculptural daring than in such Norman churches as Barfreston and Kilpeck. Not many central towers of the Early English period now survive. But that at Christ Church, Oxford, with its short spire and corner pinnacles, is a most important piece of building. Spired towers, however, are far more typical of parish churches, and the thirteenth-century builders were responsible for some of the stone spires which gracefully rise above the East Midland landscape. **[17]**

Parish churches of various sizes also made their contribution to the sum total of Early English, or lancet Gothic. Many friary churches and their attendant buildings were also of this period, but very few of these show surviving buildings of much note. In the parish churches clustered columns are sometimes found, but less often than those of simpler round or polygonal plans. Many columns, as at Berkeley and Slymbridge in Gloucestershire, West Walton in Norfolk, and Eaton Bray in Bedfordshire, have beautiful foliate capitals. Chancels of the period are apt to be long and dignified, with rows of side lancets and eastern groups (almost always in odd numbers) which often number five and at Blakeney in Norfolk and Ockham in Surrey run up to seven, producing thereby the effect of a single window right across the chancel wall. Some chancels, like those at St Mary de Lode, Gloucester, Almondsbury in Gloucestershire, St Mary's, Guildford, and the splendid one at Hythe in Kent, are vaulted, while the side lancets are sometimes crowned and connected by beautiful internal arches with shafts between them; Cherryhinton near Cambridge has a specially beautiful example of this treatment. Some notable parish churches are wholly or mainly in the lancet style. Chipstead in Surrey, Haltwhistle in Northumberland, and the noble church of Bishop's Cannings near Devizes, all prove that the greater churches were not alone in their display of this technique. Doorways as well as windows, chancel arches, and arcades show such Early English features as moulded archways, shafts, and dogtooth ornament; a few have heads which are shallow and segmental, not pointed, in outline.

DOMESTIC WORK AND CASTLES

In the stone-built houses of an increasing middle class, the builders of early thirteenth-century England also produced fair amounts of

18 *Salisbury Cathedral: the chapter-house, c.1280*

domestic architecture. Rude peasant homesteads of wood and wattle, like that whose stone lower courses were lately excavated near North Tawton in Devon, we may well pass over. But other dwellings were of a more genuine architectural note.

The manor houses of the early thirteenth century were basically like those built in the late Norman period. Some had the hall and solar floor raised up above ground level on stone-roofed cellars whose vaults were some of them ribbed. Others had their halls, and their lowermost private apartments, at ground floor level. The windows in the upper rooms of these rectangular houses were like those in parish churches. In the cellars, however, they were simpler and more utilitarian in design. Some were rectangular slits, with slanting splays to allow more light to reach the dim storage space within. Others had windows whose narrow, square-headed tops were supported by curved 'shoulders'; the same design was used for many of the fireplace openings, with their hoods projecting into the room the better to draw up the smoke, now found (as one well sees in the Prioress's room at Polslo Priory, Exeter) in a room's side walls.

Castle design developed considerably between 1200 and about 1250. We have seen how at Orford and Conisborough the problem of vulnerable right-angled corners had been met by building polygonal, obtuse-angled tower keeps. In the thirteenth century the military engineers devised tower keeps and bastions which were rounded in shape, presenting no angles to the sappers' picks. Subsidiary towers would project more boldly, so the defenders could better enfilade the burrowers along the wall. Round keeps of this period are well preserved at Longtown in the Black Mountain country of Herefordshire and at Skenfrith lower down the Monnow valley. The new fashion was even better displayed in Rochester's great keep. For when in 1215 one of its square corner towers was ruined in a siege, the replacement was made rounded in plan. Semi-circular bastions of the new type, scientifically built out with arrow slits to command the walls between them, are numerous at the White Castle in Monmouthshire. They also project from town fortifications of the time; one sees them, for example, at Caernarvon and in the garden of New College at Oxford.

Meanwhile, the courtyards of royal and baronial castles were being partly filled with more domestic buildings, designed for use in the long spells when the castles were not under siege. Great halls with their parlours and kitchens were a particular feature; what really happened was that manorial dwellings arose within fortified enclosures. Chapels, as in the earliest part of St George's at Windsor, were also built away from the keeps. Most notable of all these buildings is the fine pillared hall built by Henry III in Winchester Castle. Its basic design is that of the open, spacious nave of a friary or large parish church. Its thin marble pillars and lofty aisles recall those of the contemporary choir of the Temple Church in London. Its general impression, as in Salisbury's Lady Chapel with its unattractively spindly pillars, is that of the 'hall church' already built in Anjou and Poitou. The general design of such a building, and the early tracery of the windows inserted in place of the original lancets, looked forward to the type of Gothic which soon displaced the lancet idiom.

Gothic Florescence

1250–1350

The French Gothic designers were earlier than those of England in abandoning lancets, and in the use of stone tracery. The mullioned and traceried filling of a window opening was something one could attain by two methods. A master mason could accept, at a single jump, the full logic of Gothic construction. By this the effectiveness of his vault ribs or main timbers, and the counterthrusting strength of his buttresses, made it needless for the intervening wall spaces to contain more than the minimum of two-dimensional stonework. He could, on the other hand, proceed by a more evolutionary process, slowly whittling down his expanses of stone infilling until he could fill his windows and triforium openings with nothing more than spindly bars of stone to hold in place the iron, lead, and glass of the windows. It was not, perhaps, surprising that the more logical approach, and the swifter intellectual leap, were first found in the fully traceried windows of early thirteenth-century France, while in England a similar, and in the end a more ambitious, result was reached by the more pedestrian methods of trial and error.

From the middle decades of the thirteenth century to the equivalent years of the sixteenth, window tracery was the clearest distinguishing mark of English Gothic work. More than anything else it is the tracery of windows that serves to distinguish periods and delineate styles. Geometrical, Decorated, and Perpendicular—the titles whereby the subsections of our Gothic period are usually known—all mainly relate to successive changes in tracery design. A traceried window is one where the lower part is subdivided into 'lights' by mullions, or narrow strips of vertical stone, and where the arched or upper portion is split up, by thinner stone partitions, into the varied patterns of the actual tracery.* So thin are the mullions and the stonework of the tracery that plane surfaces of masonry are kept out. The third dimension cannot, of course, be wholly avoided, and the total square footage of stonework in a traceried window is bound to be considerable. But the whole essence of the design lies in its linear quality. A traceried window is often beautiful and interesting. What the original designers, like those of pinnacles and gargoyles, seem not to have realised, and what modern clergy and architects have found a terrible burden, is how much such a window must suffer from the ceaseless attacks of wind, rain, and rust.

Before we look further at the evolution and design of the earliest English tracery we must remember that large, traceried windows were made possible by the design and construction of the buildings they lit, and that the basic nature of Gothic construction long remained the same. The ribbed vault of finely moulded stonework, with the spaces between its ribs filled by simpler masonry, and with its thrust taken at critical points by external buttresses, was the key element in most large churches. In parish churches, where the roof structures were mostly of timber, the weight and thrust of the largest beams would still be met from outside by buttresses whose depth grew greater, and whose 'stepping' became more pronounced. What also happened, in the late thirteenth century and after 1300, was the coming of richer and more varied design in the vaults themselves; in this respect late English Gothic (like that of Germany and Spain) was more interesting than that of countries working in the northern French tradition.

So we find, in the nave at Lincoln, in the new presbytery and retro-choir built at Ely, and in the Lady Chapel at Exeter which was the first step in a systematic rebuilding of the older cathedral, that the ribs would increase in number beyond those needed for the earlier quadripartite vaults. Bosses at their points of intersection would be larger and more richly carved. The 'branching' effect of these many-ribbed vaults of the mid-thirteenth century was specially splendid in the magnificent polygonal chapter-houses built by many abbeys and collegiate

---

* Windows *wholly* filled with tracery, without vertical mullions, are very rare except for 'rose' or 'wheel' windows and those built on a convex triangular plan. They occur, however, at Dorchester Abbey in Oxfordshire, at Barsham in Suffolk, and in the private chapel at Clevedon Court in Somerset.

churches. Lichfield, Westminster, and Salisbury soon followed the examples of Margam, Dore, and Lincoln; at Westminster and Salisbury the windows were of a traceried, geometrical type. The chapter-houses of this many-sided type became a special glory of English Gothic. [18]

Our earliest properly traceried windows may well have resulted from direct borrowing from abroad by the masons (often foreigners) employed by the Crown. This was certainly true when geometrical tracery in the fully French manner appeared in the triforium and upper windows of Henry III's new abbey church at Westminster. But for the most part the lancets of England's earliest Gothic only slowly made way for windows of the new type.

We have seen how the placing, side by side, of as many as five or seven lancets gave the impression of a single large window. That impression was reinforced, particularly on the inner walls of parish-church naves, where pairs or trios of adjacent lancets were gathered under a 'rear' or 'retaining' arch. The same effect was given when in a triforium arcade each arch was not left wholly separate, as in Wells and Southwark cathedrals, but when pairs of arches were put together, as in the choir at Worcester built soon after 1224, under one larger arch. This had already been done in the Transitional retrochoir at Chichester. The flat space which naturally occurred above the two small arches of each pair had been filled, in each case, by the carved figure of an angel.

The next stage was when the flat space above two lancets, or over two small arches in an inside triforium gallery, was pierced by some geometrically shaped opening. A trefoil, or the four-lobed piercing known as a quatrefoil, was often so used. An opening shaped as a vesica (or two curves meeting at the top and bottom in points) was sometimes employed. Some churches, as one sees in every other quartet of triforium arches in the choir at Salisbury, had their 'plate tracery' contrived in more fanciful forms, and as the edges of these geometrical shapes would be delicately moulded the area of flat masonry was cut down to a minimum. The triforium arches at Salisbury are most important for the early use of plate tracery, for here we see it in a great church whose window groupings still adhered to the lancet form. But as the thirteenth century progressed plate tracery became more common alike in parish churches and those of greater pretension. Hexham Priory shows it at an early stage and so does St Hugh's choir at Lincoln. The new eastern limb at Rievaulx Abbey, the nave at Lincoln, and the brilliantly ornate easternmost portion of Ely all show, in their triforium stages if not in their windows, how English masons of the top class were working towards the fully traceried filling of arched openings in their structural walls.

Between the early plate tracery of the Hexham and Salisbury master masons and the completely geometrical 'bar' tracery of the last decades before 1300, the new abbey church at Westminster was started soon after 1245; the chief patron was King Henry III. Like the newly fashioned choir at Canterbury some 70 years before, it brought England face to face with very different architecture imported from northern France. For Westminster Abbey, with some detailed modifications and with its nave not finished till soon before the Reformation, is in essence a lofty, apsidal church of the French Gothic school. Henry de Reynes its chief designer seems likely to have hailed from Rheims. Not all Englishmen, and fewer foreign visitors to Westminster Abbey, quite realise how exotic, in a country by now accustomed to low vaults and square east ends, was this great Coronation church which duly became the country's national shrine. Of the great mediaeval churches now surviving in England's capital it is Southwark Cathedral, not Westminster Abbey or Wren's St Paul's, which most fully expresses a specially English talent in building design. The windows and triforium arches at Westminster were filled by the King's masons with wiry, geometrically designed bar tracery in the French manner, while in the end wall of the north transept a traceried rose window of the French type* was placed above rows of windows of a more English kind. The tracery and decorative details of this church, if not its ground plan and basic design, were important and influential, for the next few decades, in the minds of England's masons and carvers. Yet it seems to have been impossible to shake English clerics and master masons from their liking for square east ends. The Cistercian abbey of Hayles in Gloucestershire, founded about the time of Westminster's rebuilding, and inspired perhaps by its mother house of Beaulieu, was rare in its own time in having a fine apsidal eastern limb; the same feature occurred, in the next century, at Croxden and Vale Royal.

English Gothic thus continued along new lines. It took certain main features from the Continent but in other respects it adhered to its

---

* Wheel or rose windows were not, however, unknown in England before 1245. A few had been put up in the Transitional period, and in Lincoln Cathedral's north transept the 'Dean's Eye' dates from about 1220.

somewhat insular character. Clustered pillars, deeply moulded arches, foliate capitals of boldly cut stone, and dogtooth ornament remained for some time. But window design broke away from the grouping of lancets and the piercing with circles and quatrefoils of flat stone surfaces. In some parish churches the new patterns were very simple. A large pointed window of this time can contain what are, in effect, some odd-numbered lancets, the central one being the tallest. But thin stone mullions, not narrow strips of walling, divided them one from another, while the upper spaces are left for their filling with glass. In other windows, as at Bere Ferrers in Devon and other churches where economy compelled simplicity, the mullions curved gracefully towards the top of the window and would then intersect in a simple basket pattern. Elsewhere, however, geometrical tracery was far more elaborate, though always rigidly, and somewhat stiffly, based on plain circles or their segments. French patterns were often surpassed where large expanses of walling, and the square east ends of England, allowed vast spaces for stonework tracery and coloured glass. Binham Priory in Norfolk and Lincoln's Angel Choir of about 1260, the chapter-house windows at Westminster and Salisbury, the chapel of the Palace at Wells and the northern window of the Nine Altars Chapel at Durham, the nave at Lichfield and the great east window at Ripon, all these demonstrated the great skill of the tracery designers working between 1250 and about 1300. Parish churches also boldly displayed the new, wiry and sometimes unattractive geometrical windows. This was very much so in the eastern Midlands, at Grantham, Raunds, Melton Mowbray, and other churches in a region which early gained great prosperity from the export trade in wool. Northamptonshire churches became particularly splendid, and are still famous for their middle-Gothic architecture and slender spires. This region, unhappily when we think of the swarm of banal Victorian imitations which it inspired, became the happy hunting ground for those nineteenth-century admirers of Gothic who specially venerated the achievements of the hundred years or so which followed 1250. Nor were windows of the ordinary shape the only ones created at this time. Triangular windows, with convex sides and filled with geometrical tracery in a pattern of circles, were seen at Westminster, in the splendid north transept at Hereford, in the nave clerestory at Lichfield, and even in the gables of the beautiful new barn built close to the abbey at Glastonbury. [18, 19, 20]

19   *Lichfield Cathedral: inside the nave, c.1270*

BARNS AND HOUSES

Large barns on monastic and other estates now became worthy of their place among England's architecture. They were long, rectangular buildings, with their low side walls pierced by narrow slits, and with massive timber roofs whose main beams had their thrust met, as in timber-roofed churches or halls, by buttresses of suitable size. One, or perhaps more than one transeptal section would project from the roof, the higher walls of each transept allowing for doorways large enough to admit carts loaded with corn or wool. These great barns, like that at Glastonbury and the much larger building whose imposing ruins survive at St Leonard's Grange near Beaulieu, were not merely for storing tithes in kind, or the produce of single manors. They were the fore-runners of the great warehouses of the early industrial age, storehouses for the saleable produce of large estates. With such notions of bulk storage in our minds, we need not be surprised that the Hereford *Mappa Mundi* of about 1290 shows Joseph's granaries in Egypt as a vast, triply-transepted barn. [20]

Houses of the better type were still, in these last decades of the thirteenth century, planned on lines similar to those already laid down. But some of the survivors have more projecting rooms, and slightly more complex plans, than the earlier, severely rectangular, stone houses. 'Licences to crenellate', or to strengthen one's home against casual robbers and raiders, were now issued to some owners, so that fortified elements could be given to previously defenceless houses. The massive, multiangular tower at Stokesay, with its paired windows and narrow lancets contrasting with the far larger windows of its older hall, was built about 1291 near one end of the rectangular domestic block. More interesting still is the sturdy, four-square Suffolk manor house of Little Wenham Hall. Its plan, rectangular with a projecting wing, is less notable than its materials. For here, from about 1280, is a house mainly built of brick, specially made and not robbed from Roman ruins. Brick building was now well established in such Continental regions as the Low Countries and northern Germany. It came thence to England, the more easily as the nearest English districts were the poorest in building stone, with estuaries like the Humber, Wash, and Orwell leading havens for trade with North-West Europe. So the eastern counties were well placed to make good use of this pioneer and king among prefabricated building materials. [21]

20 Glastonbury : the abbey barn, c.1290 and later
21 Little Wenham, Suffolk : the hall, c.1270
22 Caerphilly Castle, Glamorganshire, late thirteenth century

CASTLES

More exciting, and of note both historically and as architecture, were the Edwardian castles built in and round the conquered areas of Wales. Their geographical range was strictly limited by the political and

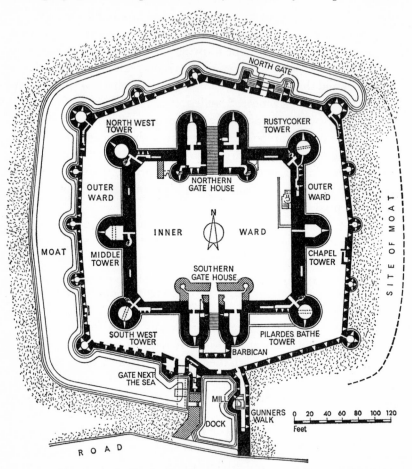

23   *Beaumaris Castle, Anglesey, c. 1295–1330: a perfect example of a concentric castle*

strategic needs of a new conquest. Though a few, like the particularly splendid fortress of the de Clares at Caerphilly, were the strongpoints of great marcher lords, they were mostly built, as part of a centrally directed policy, by the Crown.

Where these castles of the late thirteenth century differed from those of earlier dates was in their engineers' abandonment of the large tower keep as the predominant stronghold in a fortified ensemble. A castle's defences would be concentrated on one or more curtain walls, with round or polygonal projecting towers at suitable intervals, and with the main gatehouse a feature of particular strength. Where the nature of the ground compelled it, as at Conway and Caernarvon, these castles were irregular in shape, with the inner, or more important, ward at one end. Others were more symmetrical, as well as being highly scientific, in their plan. Harlech and Beaumaris are of this type. Caerphilly, apart from its tremendous eastern outwork, is very nearly so. The concentric plan, with outer defences running round an inner bailey of enormous strength, owed much to the great castles by now designed and built in Syria and elsewhere in the Crusader kingdoms. Parlours, halls, and other chapels tended to be more spacious and elaborate, whether in wholly new castles or in those that already existed. Such an improvement in the living quarters of an older castle was the great hall built at Cambridge between 1285 and 1299. The style of these non-military elements would usually be the geometrical used in churches of the time. But as the new castles in Wales were not started till after 1282 the tracery of their halls and chapels pointed, by the time of their completion, to the freer, more flowing, designs of what has come to be known as Decorated Gothic. [22, 23]

It was well settled, by the last decades of the thirteenth century, that most Gothic windows should be sub-divided into several 'lights', and that their arched upper parts should be filled with tracery; the same treatment applied to the small, but growing number whose heads were square. What was still, almost literally, in a state of flux was the design of the tracery itself. The time had come to break free from the stiff arrangements of basic geometrical figures such as circles, and parts of circles, and to burst through to a wider, more joyous freedom of interplaying curves.

THE MASTER MASONS

Every lover of our historic architecture has his own specially favoured period. For me, within the Gothic field of choice, nothing surpasses the lavish, inventive, and brilliant achievements of England's master masons and other designers between about 1290 and 1370. The master masons, moreover, were the men we have chiefly to thank for the buildings which the Middle Ages have left us to admire.

Much is known, for the thirteenth and fourteenth centuries, of the men responsible for the design and construction of the more important buildings. Chronicles and documents in growing abundance give valuable details of a type almost lacking for the great Anglo-Norman buildings. Thanks largely to the researches and writings of Mr John Harvey we now have a clearer knowledge of the names and achievements of the master masons and master carpenters who drew out (but did not always see finished) the main designs for new churches or parts of the same. Nicholas of Ely at Salisbury, Master Alexander at Lincoln in the nave, Adam Lock on the design for the wide western façade at Wells, William of Reynes at Westminster, Simon of Thirsk on the Angel Choir at Lincoln, William of Stow on the same cathedral's magnificent central tower, and William Ramsey on various early fourteenth-century masterpieces, all these carry on from such earlier known figures as William of Sens and William the Englishman at Canterbury. Master carpenters were also highly important, not only for wooden vaults like those in York Minster, and for timber ceilings over buildings of all types, but for the great baulks and beams needed for outer roofs built over the masonry of vaults fashioned in stone. So men like William Hurley, the royal master carpenter who put up the octagon at Ely and its supporting vaults with their specially long timber ribs, were as vital for the building of a major church as the master masons, fine or free masons, rough masons, and labourers who worked in stone, or the slowly growing band of 'red masons' whose concern lay with brick.

These master masons were the forerunners of the present architectural profession. They seem to have moved more from job to job than architects do now, with no fixed headquarters corresponding to a present day architect's office. Nor, in their own time, were the names of most of them so much publicised, in connection with their building commissions, as were those of their Renaissance or later successors. Patrons, whether kings, noblemen, bishops, or abbots, stood more in the public eye as the builders of castles, palaces, or great churches. One should not underrate the importance of these patrons, as sources of architectural ideas and still more of the money to pay for what was done. Sacrists like Alan of Walsingham at Ely in the years after 1323, and clerks of works like Elias of Dereham at Salisbury and elsewhere, were certainly of great importance. So too were such bishops as those of Exeter who commissioned the gradual rebuilding of their cathedrals. But they were no more the designers of those cathedrals than Bishops Henchman and Compton, or Dean Sancroft, were the real architects of Wren's St Paul's.

SPLENDOUR AND CURVATURE

Though tracery design is by no means the only leading feature of fourteenth-century building it is by window tracery that the work of that time is best distinguished. More plastic and sculptural impressions succeeded the stiff geometry of earlier windows. Flowing, beautiful curvature appeared in tracery and in the shape of archway heads. Not only did window tracery, and the cusping of the interior arches of screens and tombs, break out into the many fancies of 'curvilinear' and the net-like 'reticulated', but church and secular windows keep company with a generally bolder use of curves and plastic effects. For now is the time of the graceful S-shaped curve given to human figures in windows and embroideries. So too the attractive double curvature of the ogee often takes over from the simpler, two-centred arches of the earlier Gothic tradition. Panelling, niches, and mouldings above windows are apt to display the ogee, while in Ely Cathedral's gorgeous Lady Chapel the ogee-headed canopies of the wall recesses bulge out, two-dimensionally, in a second ogee-shaped bend. This flowing, plastic character of much fourteenth-century embellishment makes it akin to what was done, 300 years later, by such Italian masters as Bernini, Borromini, and their followers. If 'Early English' and 'Geometrical' are the Doric and Palladian of Gothic, Curvilinear is surely its Baroque.

The joyously unconfined spirit of early fourteenth-century architecture and decoration well fitted the temper of an age of splendid and triumphant chivalry. Architecture, painting, sculpture, glass, and textiles combined to produce interiors of great richness and splendour. Colour, in particular, was much more in evidence than it is now in most churches and halls. Painted carving and mural painting added their quota to the rich tints of the windows. No interiors of this period survive in their original state. We can, however, recall something of what they were like, about 1340, in the eastern Lady Chapel of Bristol

Cathedral, many-coloured with its partially original glass and Professor
Tristram's restoration of its painted stonework. More convincing,
because it has more original fourteenth-century work, is the splendid
presbytery of Tewkesbury Abbey as remodelled and rewindowed.
Chain-mailed knights are among the great figures in the ancient glass
of the windows, while below the complex lierne vault, with its numerous bosses and a radiating pattern of ribs in its midst, the surviving
Norman pillars support moulded and pointed arches which contain
Tewkesbury's rich array of tombs and chantries of the local nobility.
Here if anywhere one feels that this age of display and sculptural freedom was very specially that of the lords and ladies round whom later
ages cast the enveloping, distorting cloud of Romance. It is no cultural
accident that the ogee-shaped arch was much favoured by the neo-
romantic practitioners of Georgian 'Gothick'.

The earliest windows of this period were still 'geometrical', and not
yet 'curvilinear' in their tracery design. But their stonework, as in
such places as the chapel of Merton College, Oxford, the earlier windows of the eastern limb of Bristol Cathedral, and the Lady Chapel at
Wells, was a little sturdier and more massive than the thin bar tracery
of the late thirteenth century. Its plastic and sculptural possibilities
thus seemed greater, and out of those serried three- or four-lobed
tracery shapes the varied fancies of a more flowing manner could readily proceed. There followed, between 1320 and 1350, the full range of
Decorated window design. A few windows, like some in Derbyshire
parish churches, were square-headed, while the rarity of segmental
heads occurs in the Cambridge church of St Michael and at Over a few
miles away. The 'Bishop's Eye' at Lincoln has lovely curvilinear tracery
in a circular frame, while a most beautiful wheel window of the same
period is the chief glory of the old parish church at Cheltenham. But
the tops of most fourteenth-century windows are pointed, and fairly
acutely so. The range of their tracery designs, and of the rich cusping
applied to rear arches and to such features as doorways, screen openings, panelling, and the canopies of tombs, is far more than I can here
describe. The main outlines, and a few quoted examples, must needs
be enough.

The main idea behind the tracery of the fourteenth century's middle
decades was the infinitely varied curvature of its almost dancing stone.
Once the rigid geometry of plain circles had been abandoned there

were few limits on the possible range of designs and ornament. Tracery could recall leaves, tongues of fire, or the recesses of human eyes. Its narrowest, most acutely pointed sections could resemble dagger blades. Those most like flames resembled the 'flamboyant' tracery which in France and elsewhere on the Continent outlasted our English curvilinear, and which in Scotland blocked the acceptance of Perpendicular. More rigid in design, yet based on the regular repetition of ogee curves, were the reticulated, or netlike windows seen in many districts; Cheltenham, Holy Trinity at Hull, and Higham Ferrers provide good examples. In a class of its own, more angular and looking back to the Geometrical period with its eccentric, unusually laid out patterns, was the Kentish tracery found at Edenbridge and Chartham, and in one fair-sized window in Canterbury Cathedral.

The most notable windows put up in the first half of the fourteenth century were those whose tracery is curvilinear. As in Baroque, these windows are symmetrical as between the two balancing halves of the design involved, but within that limitation they show the wide range of exquisite patterns allowed by a new freedom in tracery design. Winterbourne Basset in Wiltshire, Little St Mary's at Cambridge, and Grantchester not far away are moderate-sized buildings with good windows of this kind. More splendid examples in parish churches are at Minchinhampton in Gloucestershire, Hawton in Nottinghamshire, and Snettisham in Norfolk. In Herefordshire, a county less rich than most in the architecture of the fifteenth century, this earlier period is well represented, whether in large parish churches like those at Kingsland and Ledbury or in the aisles, central tower, and eastern transepts of Hereford Cathedral. The East Midlands, and many churches in Lincolnshire, reflect the great prosperity of that region at a time when the wool trade, down slowly meandering rivers and so through the ports of the Wash, was at a notable peak. Stoke Golding, Kirby Bellars, and Claybrook are fine examples in Leicestershire, while Heckington and Sleaford are only two of the many curvilinear gems that Lincolnshire has to show. Towers and spires of great height and splendour remained a great fourteenth-century feature of the East Midlands, while on the other side of the country no lesser steeple exceeds the beauty of that at Lostwithiel in Cornwall on its octagon of miniature gables. These spires are the counterparts, for parish churches, of the superb stone steeple of Salisbury Cathedral which was built, about the 1330s, some

hundred years after the raising of its supporting piers. More noble still
were the curvilinear glories of some greater churches. Just as Tintern
Abbey and the slowly rebuilt fabric of Exeter Cathedral had shown how
the somewhat constrained patterns of 'geometrical' could evolve into
something freer and more ornate, so now the process was carried
brilliantly on. In the Midlands we have the eastern part of the choir at
Lichfield, and the apsidal Lady Chapel with its tall windows which was
neatly joined onto the new choir by William Ramsey. More spectacular
are some fourteenth-century masterpieces in the North. The new
eastern limb at Selby Abbey in some ways resembled that built at
Lichfield, but its windows are more curvilinear in character and end in
a superb east window of seven lights, with one in the gable above it
whose tracery is admirably reticulated. In York Minster the West
window of the nave is another great work of the curvilinear school.
Carlisle Cathedral followed the well established northern habit of a
magnificent eastern façade. Its great east window, of nine vertical
lights, with its complex tracery a dazzling display of virtuosity in curved
and writhing stone, may well claim to be the most beautiful window
in England. [24]
Architectural sculpture, like tracery, at the same time gave new
impressions of rich profusion. The canopies of tombs and niches, and
of such recesses as piscinae and sedilia and of a few Easter Sepulchres
like that at Hawton, were carved with a particular splendour of figures
and foliage. Even in its sadly battered state the foliate carving and muti-
lated statues on the wall arcading of Ely Cathedral's Lady Chapel give
some impression of how sumptuously its original craftsmen decorated
that most splendid of fourteenth-century interiors. Wall spaces, like
those behind some of the stalls at Southwell, were enriched all over
with the panels of diaper work, or carving in relief arranged in small
squares. Yet the sculpture itself, in this period of its richest application,
was much of it disappointing. The years about 1300 had seen brilliant
work in the naturalistic leaves worked in the chapter-houses at Southwell and York, and on many splendid corbels at Exeter, to succeed the
somewhat unbotanical foliage of the thirteenth century. Exeter Cathedral, and the new vaults put above the presbytery at Pershore and the
nave at Malmesbury, also showed foliate and figure carving of much
vigour and beauty. Yet the foliate carving of the next decades was much
of it lumpy and unconvincing; far better were the effigies on tombs,

24 *Selby Abbey, Yorkshire: the east windows, fourteenth century*

and the grotesque little animals or human heads of corbels and friezes.

Another important aspect of fourteenth-century carved decoration was a budlike ornament, known as 'ballflower' and thickly applied not only round the edges of doorways and windows but sometimes on tracery and mullions. The flowers with their carved piercing have a resemblance to rosebuds; they have also been likened to Brussels sprouts. This ballflower ornament, sometimes over-applied to the point of tastelessness, was specially popular in the counties of the Severn basin. Bristol Cathedral has some, and so have the windows of the south nave aisle at Gloucester as rebuilt early in the century. Leominster Priory and Ledbury church in Herefordshire have notable displays, but nowhere is this incrustation more spectacular than at Badgeworth church near Gloucester.

VAULT DESIGN

A new stage was now reached in the complication of vault design. Liernes, or connecting ribs, were thrown from one main rib to another. They thus added to the area of moulded stonework in the vaults where they occurred, while bosses at their points of intersection increased the quantity of sculpture. These liernes served little structural purpose. What they did, with their ramifications and numerous intersections, was to lessen the feeling that the structure of a church, within this period's larger and bolder buttresses and its wider intervening spaces of window, was a series of compartments and not a continuous unity. For complex lierne vaults, like those over the western part of the choir and over the Lady Chapel at Ely, over the apsidal presbytery at Tewkesbury (of about 1340), and over all the choir at Wells, gave a strong impression of a single pattern from one end to the other of the space concerned. It is the same whether the vault is in a greater church or in the lovely vaulted chancels of such parish churches as Bishopstone near Salisbury and Nantwich in Cheshire. From any point of vision the breaking down of architectural subsections is very clear; it is the more so when one sees the vaults, as their original users normally did, from an oblique angle and not by an uncomfortable backward craning of one's neck.

Another way in which some English vaulting of the fourteenth century broke from earlier conventions was when vaults over small spaces

25 AN ENGLISH HALL CHURCH *Bristol Cathedral: the choir, early fourteenth century*

were given 'flying' ribs, running clear with no masonry infilling between them. Bristol Cathedral's little sacristy and the screen passage at Southwell have vaults of this type; later still the collegiate choir at Warwick used flying ribs over a much broader space. More important, however, are those vaults of the Decorated period which draw attention to their designing mason's preoccupation with an almost plastic conception of unified space. Lierne vaults, as at Norwich, St George's Chapel, Windsor, and beneath the fifteenth-century towers of many parish churches, outlasted the fourteenth century. But it was in their earliest days, when much else was being done to enlarge and exploit the possibilities of interior space, that they mattered most.

It was in the opening out of spaces that England's designers of the years each side of 1300 were at their most daring and advanced. Polygonal chapter-houses had already shown how shapes other than rectangles could be used to frame brilliant architectural inventions. More were built soon before 1300 and in the next century. Those at Hexham and Bolton Priories were small, while at Wells the octagonal apartment, early Decorated with its canopied wall arcade and central pillar, stands on the vaulted undercroft of a century before. Most impressive of all, with its wide octagonal space uncumbered by any central pillar, and with its whole roof of timber, the new chapter-house at York Minster was started soon before the turn of the century. [18]

Octagonal space, vast, daring, and unconfined, appeared again when Ely Cathedral's Octagon was fashioned, at the main crossing point of the church, soon after the Norman central tower crashed down in 1323. Alan of Walsingham the sacrist, an expert master mason whose name remains unknown, and William Hurley the King's chief carpenter were the trio responsible for England's greatest architectural innovation since Abbot Wulfric commissioned his Rotunda at St Augustine's, Canterbury. To obtain the required extra space one ordinary bay was sacrificed from each transept, and one each from the nave and eastern limb. The octagon's other four sides were gained by cutting diagonally across the end of each transept aisle where that aisle met those of the nave and presbytery. The timber lantern was upheld by great cones of timber ribs, each group resembling in its function the pendentive of a dome. Tall arches led into the four main compartments of the cathedral, while large curvilinear windows, above rows of canopied panels, help to fill the remaining four sides of the stone-built outer octagon.

The whole impression is that of a great central dome. Wren well knew his uncle's cathedral at Ely, and could there have been drawn towards his obvious, fruitful, liking for a domed central space.

So far as we know, the Octagon at Ely was nowhere repeated in England. More frequent was the unification and widening out of the space contained in rectangular naves and choirs.

ARTISTIC UNIFICATION

I have shown how the ramifications of lierne vaults broke down the feeling that a great church's ceiling was made up of rigid compartments corresponding to the arches and pillars below. Unification was also carried out, lower down, on the three horizontal sections—arcade, triforium, and clerestory, which composed the side walls.

A notable point about mediaeval architecture is the way in which differing styles and details can combine, with the minimum of disharmony, into a single great church; disparities such as those between the Romanesque nave and early Gothic choir at Southwell were lessened by cutting the building up into the relevant liturgical centres and subdividing it by stone or wooden screens. Such architectural discords would have been out of the question for Graeco-Roman architects, as they were for those of the Renaissance. But a sense of incongruity and aesthetic discomfort does seem to have beset some master masons of the fourteenth century. Efforts were therefore made, where earlier work had perforce to be kept when new building operations were afoot, so to make the alterations as to create the impression of artistic unity.* This striving for uniformity is obvious in the nave of Westminster Abbey, and in some cathedrals, among them Exeter where the basic design of the late thirteenth-century choir was carried on, blind triforium arches and all, for some eighty years. So despite the interruption of the Black Death the western end of the nave is fundamentally akin to the choir, and was aesthetically out of date by the time of its completion.

More interesting was the master masons' handling of the choirs at Carlisle, Lichfield, and Wells; those at Selby and Milton were wholly new works replacing Norman predecessors.

* This was not, however, done at Ely, where the three new bays of Bishop Hotham's choir differ in many respects from the ornate thirteenth-century presbytery further east.

Carlisle had been given a fine new Early English choir; a chapel of this type remains intact off the southern transept. A fire gutted this choir in 1292. So when a new choir was fitted up, within the surviving aisle walls but with one extra bay to contain the glorious east window, a new, curvilinear triforium and clerestory were placed above the older arcades. But to complete the impression of a choir wholly designed in the new manner the simple capitals of the pillars were beautifully *recarved* in the style of the fourteenth-century sculptors.

At Lichfield the early Gothic choir of three bays was lengthened eastwards by five more bays, William Ramsey, the expert master mason employed by the Court, being asked in 1337 to carry out the task of joining the old choir to the western end of the slightly earlier Lady Chapel. Of the Transitional choir no more remained standing than the arches of its arcades. All else was pulled down. Above those arches, and those of the new section, a continuous clerestory and vault were built, but no triforium stage. But the new upper storey was given a passageway, just below the level of its beautiful Decorated windows with their panelled splays and a belt of panelling below them.* Along one side of that passageway a continuous parapet of cusped triangles reinforces the feeling of structural unity, at one time greater still because the older arches were masked by the solid backs and canopies of the choir stalls. It also reminds us that fine fourteenth-century tracery exists in parapets and balustrades as well as in windows.

In Wells Cathedral, provided at this time with its beautiful central tower, and with its three inverted arches to support a tonnage of stone never meant to rest on the older piers, a technique like that used at Lichfield was followed in the splendid refashioning of the choir. Three arches of the Transitional arcade were left standing on both sides, and were largely hidden behind the canopied stalls. Three new bays were added to the east, and as these bays were given a 'blind' triforium stage of rich, delicate niches and tabernacle work, somewhat similar rows of blind niches were placed, at triforium level, in the section of the choir built about 1185. A complex lierne vault was finally placed over the whole length of the choir. As at Lichfield a junction had to be made with a separate, polygonal Lady Chapel. William Joy the master mason achieved this brilliantly by a complex system of vaulting and slender

* With one exception, these fourteenth-century windows at Lichfield were replaced in the next century, by windows of 'Perpendicular' design which admitted more light.

pillars, so linking the two buildings that the space behind the High Altar was made a unity with the aisles and small eastern transepts. Here in the West of England the fourteenth-century builders seemed as happy to extend space sideways as to unify it from end to end of a great church's eastern limb.

Simultaneously with this new work at Wells, sideways space of another kind was being created, twenty miles away, in the new eastern limb of St Augustine's Abbey (now the Cathedral) at Bristol. From soon after 1306 till the 1330s a new choir and Lady Chapel, of a type unlike anything still surviving in England, was slowly built.* Its design is like that of the German hall church, the aisles being as high as the central alleyway, and the arcade arches being the tallest in England. All the side light comes in through the windows of the aisles, these being taller than the fourteenth-century average and horizontally transomed like many windows of the coming Perpendicular period. The Early English choir of the Temple Church in London had already given this broadly spatial, hall-church, impression. So too had most aisled parish churches, for these, by 1300, were mostly without clerestories, as Kentish churches like that at New Romney still are to this day. The fine church in the new town at Winchelsea was another of the same type. More notable, at Bristol, were the constructional devices made necessary by the fact that the new eastern limb was vaulted in stone. The vault itself, like that built about the same time over the choir at Ottery St Mary, was designed without a central ridge rib, and without clearly marked divisions between bay and bay. In the choir itself, though not in the eastern Lady Chapel, some compartments formed by the liernes were adorned by cusping, the whole effect being of unity, not of sharp subdivision. [25]

The aisles being as high as the central choir, the masons could not support the thrust of their main vault by flying buttresses high above the aisle roofs, or by transverse arches like those concealed in the triforium gallery at Durham. They did, however, fall back on transverse arches of another kind, running visibly across the aisles and supporting horizontal girders embellished with charming carvings. These arches

---

* In any study of the architecture of our greater mediaeval churches we have always to realise that much of the evidence was totally destroyed above ground at the Dissolution of the monasteries. Other abbeys, Keynsham for example, close to Bristol and another house of the Victorine canons, *may* have had similar work.

and stone girders lead to the outer walls, and to tall outside buttresses.
Unconventional devices thus appeared in an unusual design; unusual
also were the vaults of the compartments in the aisles. For each bay has
a ribbed vault *at right angles* to the main alignment of the church's
eastern limb, while on each side of each of these 'tunnel' vaults a
strange little cone of moulded ribs comes down to the middle point of
each transverse girder. Along with its spatial feeling this new building
at Bristol was unconventional in terms of earlier design in England's
greater churches. Likewise a novelty was the abbey's set of beautiful
tomb recesses, their half-octagon openings tricked out by delicate
cusping, and by a rhythmically waving pattern of outer decoration seen
also in some recesses which from about 1340 formed part of the slow
rebuilding of Bristol's great parish church of St Mary Redcliffe. That
church's hexagonal outer north porch is in itself spatial Gothic, on its
smaller scale as brilliant as the polygonal chapter-houses. The fantastic
outline of its outer doorway shows that the masons of the western
counties were not always confined within the usual Gothic shapes of
the two-centred arch and the ogee.* The hall at Berkeley Castle,
remodelled about 1330 by the family who were the chief patrons of the
abbey at Bristol, has work very probably by those who devised that
abbey's tomb recesses, while at Urchfont in Wiltshire the important
fourteenth-century chancel has a heavy, uncusped rib vault. The pattern of its ribs disregards its subdivision into six bays, and as at Bristol
and Ottery gives a unified impression.

CASTLES AND MANORS

Castles, apart from domestic work like that at Tiverton and Berkeley,
were for a time of minor note. Some peel towers and fortified manor
houses in the Scottish border country, and the single tower at Bever-
stone in Gloucestershire, with its two beautiful chapels, are exceptions
to a general rule. But splendid gatehouses, in monastic settings and
well in tune with the spirit which pervaded this age of display, now
begin to be of great architectural importance and decorative beauty.
The Great Gate at Bury St Edmunds and the Ethelbert Gate at Norwich

---

* It is possible, through Bristol's important trading contacts with Iberia, that the
more fantastic aspects of English decoration at this time may have had some influence
on such churches as Alcobaça and Bathalha in Portugal and S. Pedro Viejo in Madrid.

were both built as thief or riot-proof defences for the monastic precincts; both are nobly adorned with canopied and gabled niches, while
the flint and stone 'flushwork' of East Anglia adds to the effect at Norwich. Niches and flushwork also appear on the gatehouse of Butley
Priory in Suffolk, while Kirkham Priory in Yorkshire displays a specially good composition of niches, panelling, heraldry, gables, and complex tracery. St Anne's Gate into Salisbury Cathedral's Close is a much
humbler structure, but at Battle Abbey, and above the two fine fourteenth-century gateways of St Augustine's at Canterbury, tall battlemented turrets rise proudly aloft.

Manorial houses tended, by now, to abandon the compact, two-
storied design of earlier centuries, spreading out, on each side of their
dominant great halls, with a greater expanse of parlours, kitchens, and
other rooms. Penshurst Place in Kent, and Glastonbury's manor at
Meare five miles from the abbey, well show the new character of such
mansions in an age of increased internal peace. Their windows have
tracery like that seen in churches. Some however, as at Tiverton and
Meare, had their lower part cut off by a plain horizontal transom, the
resulting rectangular space being closed not by glass but by a movable
wooden shutter. The Glastonbury masons also showed, in the square-
built abbot's kitchen with its octagonal interior, lofty roof, and upper
lantern, that domestic planning could also enshrine new ideas about
the enclosure of space.

With monumental gatehouses, more elaborate canopied tombs and
sedilia (as at Beverley and Exeter), and more spacious manors the range
of architecture now started to expand. Stone bridges of the fourteenth
century are another type of surviving structure well worthy of notice.
Rivers were spanned by the requisite number of slightly pointed arches.
Between those arches the upstream side of the masonry piers would
have sharply angular cutwaters to deflect the current's force. The
undersides of some arches were given sturdy, simple, chamfered ribs
like those in cellars. St Ives in Huntingdonshire has one such bridge,
while between Cornwall and Devon Yeolm Bridge, over the river
Ottery near Launceston, is another. The beautiful Wiltshire town of
Bradford-on-Avon has two, for the upper side of the main bridge is of
this period, while a short way downstream a charming little packhorse
bridge made a transit point for sacks of wool on the way to safe storage
in the Abbess of Shaftesbury's noble barn.

Curvature, a pioneering treatment of interior space, and a new sense of the vertical were key points in the great hundred years of English architecture which started about 1250. Curves and space I have discussed. New ways had also been explored for giving emphasis to a great church's upward lines. These beginnings, and their copious fulfilment, are best taken together in a short survey of Perpendicular.

CHAPTER FIVE

Perpendicular Gothic

1350–1540

The great churches of France, and of countries under French influence, were apt to be higher inside than their English contemporaries. Their distance from floor to vault was usually greater, and their upward dimension was more, in proportion, than in the abbeys and cathedrals of England. Yet despite their impression of great vertical height the three horizontal elements—arcade, triforium, and clerestory—were clearly separate. Little was done, in thirteenth-century France, to eliminate the increasingly needless triforium, or so to decorate the walls and vaults as to mask a church's subdivisions or draw together the separate compartments of its interior space. It was left to English master masons, soon after 1300, to move slowly towards a style whose final works became an English speciality.

The process whereby the Perpendicular, or rectilinear, style came into being well shows how cautious the disappearance (above ground) of many notable mediaeval buildings should make those who seek to track an architectural story. Victorian scholars declared in honest confidence that the Perpendicular style was invented in Gloucester Cathedral's eastern limb, and that there it burst, fully fledged like Athena from Zeus's head, upon an astonished world. Yet the real story was more complex. There were certain important buildings, in London and elsewhere, in which many elements of the Perpendicular style were tried out before they appeared in the Severn valley. Though the relevant parts of the London buildings no longer stand, their convenient geographical location made it possible for certain engravers and antiquarians to record them with some accuracy before they disappeared.

Drawings and documents on St Stephen's Chapel in Westminster Palace, and on the new chapter-house started in 1332 at Old St Paul's, have given modern scholars like Dr Maurice Hastings vital chances not available when one comes to such vanished provincial buildings as Keynsham Abbey and the apsidal presbytery built by the Black Prince for the Cheshire monastery of Vale Royal.

Though an emphasis on the vertical (not always going with great loftiness) was a main point in the style dominant in England for two centuries after 1330, some earlier work foreshadowed what happened in the fourteenth century. Tall, cylindrical Norman pillars at Gloucester, Pershore, and Tewkesbury, and the virtual cutting out of the triforium stage in Cistercian churches, in Southwell's choir, and in Pershore Abbey's new eastern limb, all pointed to an architecture which favoured the upward glance. Tall, narrow lancet windows gave a similar impression. But then there followed such works as the long, unduly low interiors at Lincoln and Exeter, while the complex traceried beauties of Geometrical and Curvilinear windows arrested the eye's upward course above the long-drawn verticality of soaring mullions.

In the next century, however, new designs asserted themselves. The new patterns appeared not so much in the tracery of windows, but in expanses of vertical panelling, above and below windows, which continued the lines of those windows' mullions and so gave an appearance of vertical unity between sections which had previously been kept apart. The nave at York Minster, and the south side of the nave at Bridlington Priory, were early examples of this new technique, the lines of the mullions in the upper windows being carried downwards to form divisions between the openings of the triforium; the clerestory and triforium thus looked like a single composition. More important still were various buildings, in London and outside it, which were under the control and influence of William Ramsey, a master mason of much note in this formative period of English architecture.

The most significant of these London buildings was the splendidly beautiful, richly adorned St Stephen's Chapel in Westminster Palace. It was the English Court's deliberate answer to the Ste Chapelle in Paris; thanks to drawings and sketches we know approximately what it was like. Work started in 1292; it was over half a century before both the crypt and the upper chapel were finished and vaulted. The main building work was, however, complete by 1327; what we cannot certainly tell is how far any original designs were changed as building operations dragged on. In most parts of England these were the years of Geometrical, early Decorated, and then of Curvilinear tracery. But here at Westminster the tracery and panelling seem never to have followed the flamboyant fashion of the time. Wall spaces, moreover, were adorned with niches and panels whose dividing uprights often continued the lines of the mullions. From 1337 William Ramsey was in charge at St Stephen's, but he does not seem to have been responsible for these novel aspects of its design. Elsewhere, however, he did contribute to architectural innovations of a similar type.

At Old St Paul's a new polygonal chapter-house, raised on an undercroft and enclosed in a small cloister, was built, from 1332 onwards, under Ramsey's direction. The mullions of its windows were carried down to form exterior panelling of an even more Perpendicular character than that at St Stephen's; while although the basic design of the window tracery was reticulated, the sides of each traceried compartment were vertical in the manner one associates with the late fourteenth and fifteenth centuries. Then in the choir at Lichfield Ramsey's clerestory windows had the lines of their mullions continued as the dividing lines between panels which act as a slight substitute for the triforium. Their tracery, however, was still complex in the Decorated manner. The fuller logic of this stiffening and straightening of stonework in windows was first seen when the Romanesque eastern limb of the great abbey at Gloucester was so transformed as to give the impression of a wholly Gothic interior in the newest taste.

One reason for the reconstruction of the eastern limb at Gloucester was to make of the choir and presbytery a splendid chapel in memory of the murdered Edward II whose ornately canopied tomb lay beneath one of the Norman arches on the northern side. Edward III, of age and in effective control from 1330, was naturally much interested in the work. His money probably added greatly to the offerings of the pilgrims who visited the tomb. William Ramsey, as Court architect, may well have advised or directed the local masons. From about 1337, when the south transept was taken in hand, to about 1350 when the vast window which filled the whole eastern wall was glazed, the fullest, most logical use was made of the new style which gradually ousted Decorated in favour of a simpler, less elaborate idiom better suited to the mass production needs of a period when demand (largely from the rising middle class) was great, and when the Black Death and later outbreaks of plague had killed Ramsey himself in 1349 and had much lessened the supply of really skilled masons and carvers.

So the transepts and eastern limb of the Norman abbey, while remaining as the basic structure of this part of the church, were cut down above the triforium gallery. They made way for a new upper structure, distinguished by its large traceried and transomed windows, and by a lierne vault of great splendour and complexity which unifies the interior so created by running not only over the section east of the tower but also over the liturgical choir below the tower itself. The lierne vault in the south transept, being a little earlier than that in the choir, is simpler and without bosses. Here, moreover, were the beginnings of the spectacular masoncraft which made the side walls of this eastern limb seem as new as its east window and upper stages. For the whole interior of each transept, of the older part of the eastern limb, and of its short eastward extension, were covered with a pattern of panelling in the Perpendicular style. Nor do the dividing members of this panelling stop short at the arched openings which lead through to the aisles and Norman triforium gallery. Upright and horizontal stonework continues, in the form of thin transoms and mullions, across those openings, greatly masking their affect, though the actual arches keep their round or pointed outlines according to their dates. The impression of a delicate series of masonry screens was thus preserved; it was so admired as to be copied in a few more years at Malmesbury and Glastonbury. The Perpendicular style was now displayed in a full though early manner, while windows completed the proof that here at Gloucester the master masons had almost abandoned the older tracery designs. The south transept does retain some curvilinear survivals in its window tracery, but these tendencies are less in evidence in the choir. The great east window, designed as a shallow bow to strengthen it and increase its glazed area, and with two external buttresses to support an eastern wall almost all of glass and thin stonework, has tracery whose transoms and main mullions show a rigid grid pattern, and whose upper lights continue the mullions' vertical lines to the last possible point. Here about 1350 was a window of a type which soon became standardised to the point of tedium. [26]

Work in the Decorated tradition, with the acutely pointed arches of earlier Gothic and with various types of flowing tracery, lingered on in

26 ROMANESQUE TRANSFORMED   *Gloucester Cathedral: the choir, 1337–50*

some parts of the country. But the tracery of the newer, rectilinear kind had now got established. Many churches and other buildings were thus put up whose window tracery was transitional, combining lights of the straight-sided and of the flowing variety. Such windows exist at Cheltenham, in the east window of St Mary Redcliffe at Bristol, at Nantwich, and in Edington Priory in Wiltshire, built in his native village by Bishop Edington of Winchester. This bishop was also responsible for commissioning some important early Perpendicular work in his own cathedral. For his masons started a new nave to replace the Norman one, putting transomed Perpendicular windows into the short western sections of the aisle walls finished before Edington's death in 1366. More notably, they so designed the new western façade that the upright lines of its long, continuous mullions are most strongly marked, while severely vertical panelling, of a type which had its influence on some churches in the Low Countries, covers most of the wall surfaces below and above the windows and doorways.

York Minster was another great church where the new style was used soon after 1360. For as the present Lady Chapel and choir were slowly built the new idiom was clearly seen, though in the arches and in some other details much respect was paid to the slightly older nave. The upper windows and the triforium stage were thrown together by continuous mullions, and in the curious little false transepts two tall windows, specially large to admit all possible light to the sanctuary, are fully Perpendicular. Another vast glazed expanse is that of the main east window, Perpendicular like that at Gloucester but with its tracery more complex and beautiful. The whole eastern façade, with slight differences between its northern and southern wings, is a brilliantly decorative composition, a supreme masterpiece among the monumental eastern façades clearly popular in the North. Its side windows have tracery of a type also used in the aisles, a curiously awkward, unattractive blend of survivalist Decorated and new Perpendicular elements.

I can only mention a few major buildings of this period of Decorated–Perpendicular transition. The vogue for tall central towers, well started at Lincoln, Pershore, Salisbury, Wells, Hereford, and elsewhere* was

---

* We must remember that Salisbury, Lichfield, and Malmesbury were not the only towers of this period to be crowned with spires. Hereford and the Lincoln (the tallest of all) at first had lead-sheathed wooden spires.

PERPENDICULAR TOWERS

27   *Worcester Cathedral, c.1365–74*
28   *Huish Episcopi, Somerset, fifteenth century*

splendidly continued at Worcester where John Clyve's beautiful structure of the 1370s has a strong vertical emphasis but also a set of window
heads, and gables above them, belonging more to the style which was
then on the way out. Lincoln's two western towers were given upper
stages in the 1380s; these too are somewhat backward-looking in their
tracery and some other details, while at ground level their entrance
vestibules have panelling in the normal manner of their time, but also
some cusped arcading of an almost Moorish fantasy. [27]

More in tune with the new Perpendicular style was the work done
by William Wynford and Henry Yevele, two leading master masons in
practice between 1360 and 1400. Both of them, particularly Yevele who
worked largely for the Court and Government, were much helped by
their ability to impress masons from among the comparatively few
available men of this craft.

William Wynford's work lay largely in what he did at Oxford and
Winchester for Bishop William of Wykeham. New College at Oxford
and the College at Winchester were both built to his designs. Both are in
a rather severe early Perpendicular style, and their complete buildings
were regularly, systematically laid out so as to complete in one operation all the elements now thought proper in academic colleges. Here they
stood apart from the haphazard way in which older colleges like Merton
at Oxford and King's Hall at Cambridge had been thrown together.

In Winchester Cathedral the work commenced by Bishop Edington
was carried on in such a way that a severe and sturdy Romanesque nave
was almost wholly transformed into a particularly splendid one of the
late Gothic school; heraldry proves that the lierne vault and its bosses
were not finished till after 1405. What Wynford and his colleagues
did was to cut down the nave from three storeys to two, combining the
lower storey and part of the one above it into the noble arches of a
great arcade. The upper storey, representing the old clerestory and
the top half of the Norman triforium, was handled in the now accepted
Perpendicular manner, the mullions of the windows being carried down
to form panelling below them. But as at Gloucester the main structure
still rested on thick Norman piers. These, at Winchester, were not
masked by the thin falsity of a stone cage, but had their sturdy bulk
cased round with the clustered and moulded masonry of the late fourteenth century.

Henry Yevele designed and supervised the new nave of Canterbury

Cathedral at the very time when Chaucer wrote his *Canterbury Tales.*
One of the Norman western towers was left standing, but the rest of
the old fabric was demolished. Within the earlier area, and with its
slender pillars rising from Norman pillar foundations, this nave was
freer than that at Winchester to express the essential nature of a lofty
late Gothic church. So the vault is upheld not by the solidity of its walls
and pillars but by the tall buttresses of the aisles and their flying connec-
tions to the points where the thrusts of a beautiful lierne vault have
actually to be met. Canterbury's nave, with its comparatively thin
pillars, and with its lofty aisles having tall, doubly transomed Perpendicular windows, differs much from that at Winchester, though the two
are seemingly alike. Between them, these two naves proved convincingly that the new style had come to stay.

The vaults at Winchester and Canterbury, like that put over the
chancel, transepts, and nave of St Mary Redcliffe in Bristol, were all of
the lierne type; this lasted throughout the coming century for most of
the more important church interiors. But by 1400 a new, particularly
English form of vaulting had been used over a few spaces of modest
width. This was the fan-vault, whereby concave-sided cones of masonry,
strongly resembling fans as one looks at them from below, would rise,
from each side of the space concerned, to meet in the middle. The
cones themselves are richly decorated, though not wholly supported in
their structure, by stone panelling, while bosses or sculpture often em-
bellish the almost flat spaces left at the meeting points of the curves
which define the cones.

It seems that the earliest fan-vault was erected, soon after 1364, over
the ten-sided chapter-house at Hereford Cathedral, started much
earlier in the century. The cones of this vault rose from the sides to
meet the outer curvature of a complete cone springing from a thin
central column. This vault, of great importance in the story of England's architecture, was destroyed in the eighteenth century. It is yet
another pioneering structure whose appearance would now be lost but
for the drawing of a Georgian antiquary; like the chapter-house at Old
St Paul's it reminds us how many significant mediaeval buildings are
no longer visible. In a few years a start was made on the oldest *surviving*
fan-vault—that gradually placed over the much narrower space of the
cloisters at Gloucester Cathedral. It is brilliant, beautiful, somewhat
repetitive work; for about 100 years the fan-vault was only used over

such narrow compartments as cloisters, porches, tower spaces, and small chapels. Nor was its sway absolute even there. For complex rib-vaults, like those over the cloisters at Worcester, Canterbury, and Lacock, over the vestibule at London's Guildhall, and over the porches and tower spaces of many parish churches, were still built in the years just before 1400 and all through the coming century.

Some splendid castle and palace halls arose in the time of Richard II. Aisled halls had almost gone out of fashion, wide spaces being readily spanned by the daring ingenuity of the carpenters who designed their ever more splendid timber roofs. John of Gaunt's hall at Kenilworth Castle, now ruined but with transomed and traceried windows and remains of its interior panelling, must have been most splendid in its newly coloured glory. More imposing still, with cross arches, hammer-beams, and traceried spaces combined into a roof structure which sits low and heavy on the largely Norman walls, is Westminster Hall as refashioned by Yevele and Hugh Herland the royal carpenter. Except at the two ends the windows are small and of only two lights. The arcades and pillars of the ancient hall were swept away, and the new hall's main feature was its magnificent roof. This is of the hammerbeam type, with horizontal beams projecting from the side walls and support-ed from below by massive curved braces. These horizontal hammer-beams in their turn support great vertical timbers which run up to the rafters of the roof, while their ends are decoratively tipped by carved angels who hold shields of Richard II's arms. Such a roof can readily span a large rectangular space. Here at Westminster, and in the much smaller roof of the Booth Hall at Hereford, we see early specimens of the most spectacular among the many varieties of timber roofing which gave added glory to the somewhat unambitious architecture of many Perpendicular parish churches.

PARISH CHURCHES

By the last 20 years of the fourteenth century recovery had started from the worst effects of the Black Death and later outbursts of Plague. The prosperity of the wool and cloth trades, and of elements among the lesser gentry and the middle class, was steadily growing. All over the country many parish churches were being rebuilt or enlarged along what now became the standard lines. The cathedralesque rebuilding of

St Mary Redcliffe at Bristol was quite exceptional. More normal were the parish churches with simply planned rectangular chancels, more often than not provided with side chapels and special vestries. The naves of such churches often had clerestories of upper windows, while their aisles would be broader than those which might have existed since early Gothic or Norman times. The outer walls of these aisles were built, outside those of older aisles, while those earlier walls still stood; the older buildings could thus be used without undue disturbance while

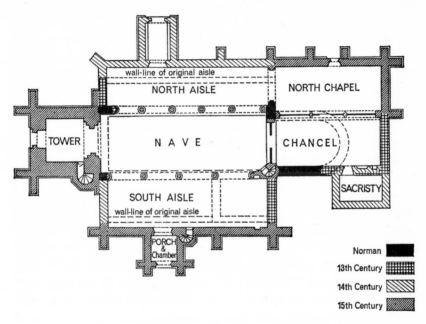

29   *The development of a typical parish church*

new work was in hand. Older chancels, particularly those built in the fairly new Decorated style, were often left standing. But new porches sheltered the main doorways, while western towers, like that built at Shepton Mallet as a foretaste of many others in Somerset, became much more common. Sutton in the Isle of Ely and Wellow near Bath are good examples of these early Perpendicular parish churches whose successors became a multitude. Though their masonry was often less ambitious than in the churches of half a century before they gained added splendour from the coloured magnificence of their roofs, screens, mural paintings, and painted glass.

CASTLES

The castles and town fortifications of the late fourteenth century were few, but were built to imposing, sophisticated designs. In some, their visual effect was improved, and made more 'romantic', by boldly projecting brackets, or machicolations. These supported parapets jutting out beyond the alignment of towers and walls, and so made it easier for defenders to drop missiles on attackers below. A few castles, like Warwick in its great gateway with a projecting barbican, had towers and other works built on squared plans. Several other places had round-faced towers used even more boldly than before. Great drum towers, of more than semicircular shapes, flank imposing gateways like that on the western side of Canterbury, and the fine entrance gateway of Cooling Castle near Rochester, designed by Yevele and built soon after 1380. When in 1373 the manorial lord of Nunney in Somerset got a 'licence to crenellate' his home he was not content with mere battlements or a small tower but built what amounted to a moderate-sized tower keep. A massive drum tower stood at each corner; so ponderous and rounded were these towers that they almost met on the narrow ends of the rectangular castle. In the next decade the beautiful castle of Bodiam in East Sussex, like Cooling built for the defence of a coastal area, was given a mixture of rounded and square towers. Earlier on, the magnificent Caesar's tower at Warwick had been built with a trefoiled ground plan, while at the end of the century the noble Guy's tower at another corner of the same castle is polygonal in shape and machicolated at the top; it completed a trio of features which made the northern side of Warwick Castle into England's finest sequence of late mediaeval fortification.*

More significant, and another important building now known to us almost wholly by the happy chance of an antiquarian's engraving, was the coastal fort put up in the 1360s at Queenborough in the Isle of Sheppey. Here was a plan which was concentric in the truly geometrical sense. For a circular outer wall, with a twin-towered gateway typical

* Old Wardour Castle in Wiltshire, started about 1392, is another example of a fortification with a polygonal plan.

of the time, enclosed a bailey and a fortified inner ring which rose well about the outer defences. This inner citadel contained the garrison's quarters, and was itself defended by a set of rounded, projecting towers, arranged as it were in the pattern of a flower. The influence of this fort was clear when Henry VIII discovered his need for a whole string of coastal defences.

ARCHITECTURAL MASS PRODUCTION

For over a century after 1400 Perpendicular Gothic had the field of English architecture to itself. The sheer quantity of what was built in the fifteenth and early sixteenth centuries would alone make this period as important as any in our story. For parish churches, Perpendicular is in many districts the overwhelmingly dominant style. Very few of our pre-Reformation churches are without some features due to the Lancastrian, Yorkist, or early Tudor periods, while many country manor houses join castles, town houses, and a few public buildings to make up the sum total of England's late Gothic achievement. The French wars and the Wars of the Roses hampered the building activities of the Crown and the greater nobility. But they had less effect on the life of the merchant class, and on the rising leaders of the wool and cloth trades. So the church-building urge remained strong and laid great pressure on the master masons and master carpenters, and on the less skilled craftsmen and labourers available for building work. Rivalry between parishes, ever anxious to have the most spacious naves and the loftiest towers that devotion could inspire and money buy, added much to the pressure. So the Perpendicular period became one of architectural mass production. The style itself, ornate and richly panelled in some of the greater buildings, and in fan-vaults wherever these were used, was also well suited to an age when large output and standardisation were the inevitable results of a flooding demand.

A certain stark austerity, particularly in window tracery and in the meagre quality of some sculpture on capitals, corbels, and elsewhere, is certainly noticeable in many buildings put up by about 1460. It even occurred in some of the more expensive and elaborate buildings, for it was in tune with a mood of matter-of-fact severity, or at times of asceticism, with which the fifteenth century reacted to the more unbridled splendours of that before it. This starkness in building fitted in

with the severe simplicity then current in men's hairstyles, and in the
civilian clothes shown in brasses and effigies. At the top level of patronage one notes it in Henry VI's commands against 'curious werkes of
entaille and besy moldyng' in the great chapels of his new colleges at
Eton and King's at Cambridge. But a new urge for the ornate, and
renewed flamboyance in tracery design, were apparent before the
Reformation closed the building history of the Middle Ages.

England has so many buildings of the fifteenth and early sixteenth
centuries that no full account of them is here possible. But some general points touch both on the basic nature of Perpendicular churches,
and on some distinct aspects of their style. That style itself divides
English churches of this period very sharply from their contemporaries
almost everywhere on the Continent. So too, the mediaeval churches in
such large towns at York, Exeter, and Norwich are generally numerous,
small, and very largely of this period albeit of older foundation. For
the towns themselves had usually been split into many small parishes,
thus making for many small churches rather than the fewer, far larger
late mediaeval churches in the ancient towns of North-West Europe.

English church designers of the Perpendicular period still opted
overwhelmingly for square east ends. Churches of this date whose
chancels end in apses are very rare; St Michael's at Coventry (the
cathedral bombed in 1940), and Westbury-on-Trym near Bristol were
two examples, while the apsidal termination of the easternmost chapel
at St George's, Windsor may have inspired the choice of the same shape
for Henry VII's superb chapel at Westminster Abbey. Where the
ground-plans of parish churches developed and became more interesting was in the building of many porches and vestries, and in the adding
of side chapels, with single entrance arches or complete arcades, not
only to chancels but also to aisled naves. The establishment of guild
and chantry chapels was a particular cause of these sideways enlargements. Cross-shaped churches often had their transepts absorbed into
broad aisles whose outer walls ran flush with theirs, while large town
churches like St Michael's at Coventry, the collegiate (now cathedral)
church at Manchester, Cirencester, Tavistock in Devon and St An-
drew's at Plymouth show how these enlargements could produce
churches with four, or even five, long parallel aisles. Fine central
towers, like those at Ashford in Kent and at Wedmore, Axbridge, and
Ilminster in Somerset were raised on the older crossing piers of some

cruciform churches. More important, all over the county from Lincolnshire to Cornwall and from Northumberland to London and Surrey,
were the splendid western towers which often made a new addition to
a church's ground plan, and were certainly the greatest single glory of
England's late Gothic architecture.* [1, 28]

STRUCTURAL POINTS

The logic of Gothic technique was still evident as most of England's
Perpendicular churches were built. Buttresses and pillars, not expanses
of wall, were usually the chief means whereby the main fabric of a church
or hall was sustained. Windows of even greater size, with shallow-
arched or even square heads to allow all possible light, filled the walls
of aisles and chancels with glass of a more silvery, translucent type than
that previously normal. Only in some hilly or mountainous districts, or
near the windswept expanses of Dartmoor and the West Country's
Atlantic coasts, were windows restrained in size amid the long lingering
solidity of sandstone or granite walls. Clerestories, away from the poorer and more windy areas, and in some southern districts like much of
Kent, became increasingly common; in East Anglia, and sometimes
outside it, many were so designed as to allow two upper windows
corresponding to each arch below. Though the timber roofs of these
clerestoried naves were massive and heavy, they were frequently
built at a low pitch or almost flat. Their outward thrust was thus reduced, so that flying buttresses, to transmit a roof's thrust to the aisle
buttresses lower down, are far from common. Timber roofs, richly
carved, in some cases adorned with the flying figures of angels, and
originally kept brightly coloured, are in many Perpendicular churches
more splendid, and of more interest, than the architecture below them.
The roofs themselves fall into several types. Hammerbeam roofs have
already been described. Less spectacular were the arch-braced roofs,
with curved wind braces to strengthen their rafters, which were much
used over the halls and more important private rooms of manor houses.
The post-and-beam roof, with horizontal main beams and upright
baulks above them to support the angled roofing, was perhaps the com-
monest of all. But down in the western counties, and particularly over

* A few towers, as in other periods, were polygonal in plan.

the long, low, unclerestoried churches of Devon and Cornwall, the favourite covering was the tunnel-like cradle or waggon roof, with panels of plaster to separate the lengthways beams, and bosses to mark the intersection points with beams running athwart the church. Nor were the roofs of naves, aisles, and chapels the only places for the continued display of timber technique. A few timber-framed churches or belfries survive in the eastern counties, or in such areas as Cheshire, Shropshire, and Worcestershire, which in those days were heavily wooded and also poorly off for really durable stone. More notable still, and even found in parts of Somerset and Gloucestershire where good stone was abundant, were the manors, yeomen's houses, or parts of houses like the upper frontage of the George Inn at Norton St Philip in Somerset. For timber framing, on lower courses of stone, and with some sort of plaster infilling, was still the normal practice. [30, 31]

The exteriors of many churches of the Perpendicular period gain variety and interest from their traceried or embattled parapets, from grotesquely sculptured gargoyles which often contain waterspouts as well as being decorative attractions, and from many pinnacles which are not only beautiful but which also perform an important structural task in that their downward-pressing weight adds stability to buttresses which might otherwise lean back beneath the thrusts they have to resist. The pillars which uphold the arches of a Perpendicular arcade are apt to be standardised to the point of dull repetition, while if their capitals are sculptured the carving is often somewhat meagre and without the boldness and variety of the earlier mediaeval craftsmen. The pillars themselves are often octagonal; concave sides like those at Rock and Kidderminster in Worcestershire and Northleach in Gloucestershire are a welcome variation on a widespread theme. Where columns of this period are clustered, four rounded shafts at the four main points of the compass are often parted by four intervening sides cut back in the concave moulding common in the architectural work of this time.

Much Perpendicular work, particularly the adding of clerestories above older arcades and the piercing of new and larger windows in Norman and early Gothic walls, was alteration and improvement, not new construction. Many towers, moreover, received new and lofty upper stages in the Perpendicular style, with niches, traceried windows, and pinnacles to give them a new feeling of grandeur and elaboration. Where the architecture of the Perpendicular parish church is

better judged is where the building was mainly or wholly new. The
urge for light, and for architecturally unimpeded space, was carried
far beyond the pioneering ventures of the fourteenth century. Pillars
were apt to be more slender than before, while chancels and naves ran
into each other without chancel arches or breaks in ceiling levels. Some
arches, as also in the fourteenth century, had no capitals. The whole
feeling of such churches, despite their subdivision by screens and the
richness of their colour, was increasingly unmystical and matter-of-
fact. [1]

The arches, doorways, and window-heads of the Perpendicular
period were apt at first to be fairly acutely pointed. Some, as in the early
Tudor clerestory at Bath Abbey, so remained till not long before the
Reformation and the temporary end of church building. But as a rule
they became flatter and less sharp. Some, with no striking display of
bold or deep mouldings, were continuously curved in the 'four
centred' design. In others the archway jambs ran straight from the curve
at each side to an obtuse-angled point at the top. Some windows, both
in churches and houses or public halls, exploited to its full conclusion
the prevalent craving for light, being square-headed with the least
possible elaboration of tracery, and with the mullions running, in a
workmanlike manner, very nearly to the top. Some arches were flat in
section, with the 'soffits', or undersides, attractively relieved with
panelling; this fashion was popular with the skilled masons of such
western counties as Somerset. Many pointed doorways were set in
square-topped frames; the spandrels, or spaces above the archways,
were pleasingly filled with sculpture or heraldry. Such doorways, in
churches, colleges, or manors, are among the most charmingly practical achievements of a prolific age.

I have shown how early Perpendicular windows were given tracery
whose designs provided for the greatest possible vertical extension of
the main mullions, and for the upright subdivision of most of the small
tracery lights. Where the windows built between 1400 and about 1520
were given tracery this fashion continued. Real beauty appears in the
tracery of the larger, more complex windows, while in some it is the
more interesting because tiny transoms run horizontally across some of
the upper lights. But standardisation and rigidity, particularly in some
country districts where individual masons must have been employed
by several parishes, were unhappily common. After over a century of

vertical lines some tracery designers seem, quite understandably, to have become bored with their work, so that an urge towards a new flamboyance, with less verticality and a freer flowing of the stonework in windows, crept in as the sixteenth century moved on towards the catastrophe of Gothic. At Crowcombe, Porlock, and elsewhere in West Somerset the new tendency is apparent in work known to date from the 1530s; it is even more pronounced in a porch at Stratford St Mary in Suffolk. The Lady Chapel at Rochester Cathedral and St Michael le Belfry at York show the new fashion in a modest way. It is more noticeable still in some of the woodwork of the time, for fully flamboyant tracery, or traceried panelling, enlivens the Spryng chantry at Lavenham, several bench ends of the 1530s in the West Country, and some stall ends a few years older in Bristol Cathedral. Canopied niches and sedilia, altar-pieces, and the fanciful delicacy of the side walls, window-like openings, and richly fretted roofs of cagelike little chantry chapels also showed that rigid severity was by no means the only distinguishing point of the style which so prolifically transformed the church and secular architecture of England.

The domestic output of the Perpendicular period was very great; despite the loss of many monastic buildings and the Georgian urge to replace Gothic with Palladian, large quantities of it remain and vie in quality with the architecture of the churches. Market crosses, moreover, particularly those with lofty central features, flying buttresses, and verandah-like, polygonal outer canopies, are another type of building once commoner than now, but still a glory of Salisbury and even more of Chichester.

REGIONAL VARIATIONS

The better-class houses remained largely as they had been. Great halls were still the main apartments of the residences built by landed gentry and prosperous clothiers on the upward social climb. In the districts of the stone belt they were usually of the local limestone; Great Chalfield and Westwood in the Wiltshire segment of the Cotswolds show how exquisite a manor house of such materials could be. In East Devon and West Somerset the dark sandstone walling would contain mullions, doorways, and other details in the golden stone of the Ham Hill quarries near Yeovil. In East Anglia flint rubble and warm red brick were often

PERPENDICULAR PARISH CHURCHES
30   *Blythburgh, Suffolk, mid-fifteenth century*
31   *Altarnun, Cornwall (showing the Norman font)*

the chief materials, while in the Welsh Marches, and in such Lancashire lowland houses as Speke and Rufford Halls the black-and-white pattern of exposed timber framing and plaster infilling eased the lack of good building stone. Where these manorial houses of the late Middle Ages differed from those of the preceding centuries was in the growing sprawl of the wings which contained private rooms at one end of the hall, and kitchens, pantries, and stores at the other. Haphazard irregularity, as at Compton Wynyates, may be lovably picturesque to some modern eyes, but was on all counts most unscientific and inconvenient.

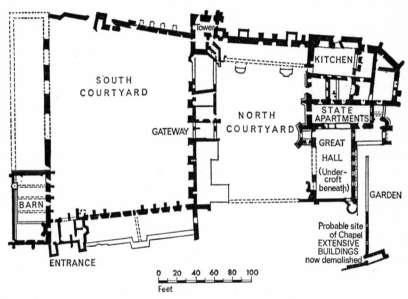

34   *South Wingfield Manor House, Derbyshire, c.1340*

So long were some of these wings, as at South Wraxall in Wiltshire, that they created three-sided courtyards. In a few houses, like Haddon Hall in Derbyshire and Cotehele in East Cornwall, the fourth side of a quadrangle was built, so that a gatehouse had to give access to the whole. The same secluded, quadrangular plan came naturally enough to more domestic academic colleges such as Lincoln at Oxford and Queens' at Cambridge. [32, 33, 34]

The style and detail of these houses was like that used in the churches; spiral stairways like those in church towers led up to the topmost floors. One feature alone was confined to halls and private rooms. The oriel window, bowed out in a half polygon, or sometimes in a set of triangular or rounded projections,* admitted extra light to the high table end of many manor or college halls. In a more exquisite version, the dainty little upstairs oriels, well seen at Thornton Abbey in Lincolnshire and at Great Chalfield, lit first-floor parlours and allowed a better view for ladies and others who spent much time secluded indoors.

Many houses in towns were now built to a different ground plan from that which had long prevailed. The more notable dwellings had at first been built lengthways to the street. Recent excavations have shown that a wooden house of the Saxon period was so aligned in Bristol; the same positioning was shared by Lincoln's Norman houses and by the Grevel house at Chipping Campden of about 1400. Now, however, the increasing congestion of urban sites caused houses to run backwards from narrow frontages. Their façades rose in two or three storeys. Such houses in the towns, like those of yeomen or clothiers in the timber-using districts of the Weald, East Anglia, and the West Midlands, made generous use of 'jettying', whereby the ceiling timbers of one storey so projected beyond its wall as to allow the storey above it to have more floor space. Only in their street frontages could the connected houses of a mediaeval, Tudor, or Jacobean street take advantage of this cantilevered convenience. As the streets themselves were narrow the upper storeys of opposite dwellings were far closer to each other than the actual width of the highway. Old prints and water colours show that such picturesque but darksome alleyways long survived the Renaissance, or in provincial towns like Norwich and Bristol the date of the Great Fire of London, while many of the houses themselves were of considerable size and spacious opulence. Despite many changes, the Shambles at York still convincingly shows these methods of urban building.

Stone bridges, of the same kind as those already erected, appeared in greater numbers during the fifteenth and early sixteenth centuries; they thus carried on a type of building work where civil engineering merged readily with architecture. Complementing the new manor

* The 'rounded' oriel was a feature of the early Tudor period. It occurs at Hengrave Hall in Suffolk and once adorned the hall of Michaelhouse at Cambridge. See Bryan Little, *Cambridge Discovered* (1960), p. 62.

houses and monastic living quarters the late mediaeval masons were also busy on dovehouses, and on more barns of great size and architectural merit. Ashleworth and Llanthony near Gloucester, and Tisbury in Wiltshire well show how large and important such buttressed and transepted structures had become. Grandest of all is the great barn, 300 feet long and only half of it now roofed, which is the best relic of the sheep-farming Dorset abbey of Abbotsbury. Some of its decorative details most strongly suggest that its designer also planned the hilltop chapel of St Catherine and the western tower of the nearby parish church.

So we come again, before dealing with military buildings and the more splendid church works of the Perpendicular heyday, to the parish churches which are overwhelmingly the most numerous buildings which still prove the skill and virtuosity of the masons and craftsmen who worked from about 1400 to the last years of Henry VIII.

With so much variety in England's climate and in the range of her building materials, and with such differences between the economic life of one region and that of another, it is no surprise that Perpendicular parish churches vary much from region to region. In many districts of the North, among them the valleys and plains each side of the Pennines, the buildings seem long and low, despite the clerestories of some churches in Lancashire and over such important West Riding buildings as Halifax and Bradford Cathedrals; a church like that at Thirsk, with a lofty clerestory, is more in the manner of the West. Where northern towers have pinnacles they are apt to be lower and less assuming than elsewhere. The finest parochial naves of the period are in East Anglia, with slender pillars and large aisle windows to admit ample light onto the soaring delicacy of their screens and the splendid carpentry of their ceilings. Panelled spandrels above the arches give added richness to their interiors. Lavenham in Suffolk, Saffron Walden in Essex, Great St Mary's at Cambridge, and St Peter Mancroft at Norwich are four among a host of splendid examples. Above some clerestories in this part of England single or double hammerbeam roofs, as at March in the Isle of Ely, Woolpit in Suffolk, and Blakeney on the Norfolk coast, are specially glorious with their winged host of angels poised, as if flying to heaven, on the tips of the beams projecting over the worshipper's heads. Many parish churches in Devon and Cornwall were rebuilt, with freestone or granite arcades, as the Perpendicular period

progressed. Clerestories like those at Callington, Cornwall and Tiverton in Devon were rare. More typical, indeed tediously frequent, is the
Devon or Cornish church of a nave and two aisles, all three being low,
unclerestoried, and of much the same height. Most of them have no
chancel arches, and they are roofed from end to end by the low tunnels
of their waggon roofs. The woodwork of those roofs, of pulpits like
that at Kenton near Exeter, and of their splendid screens is what gives
their chief merit to many of these churches. Devon in particular is still
fortunate in the survival of many of these feats of architectural carpentry, stretching all the way across the church in a dozen or more
compartments. Yet the humility of these naves often clashes with the
tallness of stately western towers. A few, as at Probus near Truro and
Cullompton in East Devon, are of an ornamented type more common in
Somerset. Yet many rely for their effect on simple masonry, windows,
and buttresses, breaking out at the top into ponderous pinnacles, crock-
eted and adorned with miniature battlements, and now after five centuries of Westcountry weather powdered over with yellow lichen
which glows burning gold in the dying sunlight of a summer evening on
Dartmoor or on Cornwall's coast. [30, 31]

But in towers the supremacy lies a little further to the East. Some
West of England churches, like Cirencester and Northleach in the
Cotswolds, Steeple Ashton near Trowbridge in Wiltshire, and Ilmin-
ster in Somerset, are distinguished in the design of all their parts. Yet
in others, Leigh on Mendip for example or Beaminster in West Dorset,
the body of the church fails to match the soaring dignity of Dorset and
Somerset's amazing wealth of church towers. Some are horizontally
divided into their component stories. In others, like St Cuthbert's at
Wells, verticality unites their stages in the truly Perpendicular manner.
Others are richly, fancifully pinnacled, decked out with a riot of niches,
gargoyles, and delicately fretted upper windows for the outpouring of
the pealed music of their bells. [28]

Though completely new greater churches were rare after the beginning of the fifteenth century much was done to finish and adorn buildings which existed already. Great towers, in particular, were very
much in favour. Some were central, or as at York new features of two-
towered western façades. In some monastic and college churches,
however, the existing central piers could not bear too much of a new
weight, so that new towers (sometimes to house parochial bells) were

built directly from the ground. Abbot Huby's northern tower at Fountains is among the best; with its relatively simple details it is clearly by
the master mason who ventured a short central tower on the crossing
piers at Kirkstall. Wymondham Abbey in Norfolk, Christchurch
Priory, and Wimborne Minster in Dorset, all boast fine examples of
this more cautious technique; the collegiate belfry of Magdalen at
Oxford is even more famous and successful. Of special interest is the
tower started about 1520, but never finished, at Bolton Priory in Yorkshire. For there we can see how a new tower would be started a few
feet west of an older nave, the end wall of that nave staying intact till
the tower was complete and the time came to pull down the wall and
open out the new tower into the body of the church.

The great central towers of this time are plentiful, and I can only
mention four. Solemn dignity distinguishes that built over the main
crossing at Durham, while at York Minster the sturdy central tower,
with its long-drawn windows, looks sterner than William Colchester
its designer intended because its corner pinnacles, to save weight on the
piers below, were never built. More elaborate, richly panelled and with
its 'openwork' pinnacles linking it to towers at Wrexham, Bristol, and
elsewhere, is the brilliant central tower at Gloucester. Stateliest of all,
with its great corner turrets, two tiers of transomed windows, and
bands of panelling between them, is the Bell Harry tower at Canterbury
Cathedral. The important master mason John Wastell was its designer;
it was in progress as Columbus sighted the Bahamas in 1492.

Many splendid lierne vaults were also placed over earlier structures.
Those at Norwich Cathedral are the best, while the two transepts at
Bristol Cathedral were given new vaults of considerably varying designs,
one unifying the building's length, one emphasising its division into a
pair of bays. More ambitious works were the completions of naves at
the abbey (now the Cathedral) at Chester, and at Westminster where
the western wall, but not Hawksmoor's towers above its upper portion,
shows strongly Perpendicular traits. Great Malvern Priory was another
church where important refashioning, inspired by Gloucester, was done
in the fifteenth century. The new nave at Ripon, strongly simple, without a triforium, and never quite finished, was a northern equivalent to
the architectural happenings in the South and West. New Lady Chapels
also remained in favour in this last fully mediaeval century. That at
Gloucester is perhaps the most lavish of all such buildings, a delicate

cage of glass and finely masoned Cotswold stone, repeating on a smaller scale, without having to consider older work, the pattern set a century earlier in the choir.

Additions were also made to the buildings of many monasteries, while academic colleges like Eton, All Souls and Magdalen at Oxford, and the early Tudor Christ's and St John's at Cambridge added to the Perpendicular achievement. Cloister walks like those at Durham and Chester Cathedrals resemble, in their architectural nature, the aisles of churches. But much other work was domestic in character. New refectories like that at Cleeve in Somerset, and new priors' and abbots' halls or houses like those at Watton in Yorkshire, Forde and Milton in Dorset, and Castle Acre in Norfolk all contained features we have noted in the manor houses of the laity. The ecclesiastical tradition of vaunting gateways was brilliantly continued, with niches, panelling, turrets, battlements, and miniature oriels adorning those at Thornton in Lincolnshire, Kingswood in Gloucestershire, Montacute in Somerset, and that built about 1520 as the main entrance from the busy city outside to the calmer monastic precinct of Canterbury Cathedral. Colleges, moreover, were strong competitors in this field, with Cambridge at last drawing ahead of Oxford in the turreted splendour of two at King's Hall (now Trinity), and one each at Queens', Christ's, and St John's; that at Jesus rose without turrets but with attractively stepped battlements.

Sophisticated, small-scale Perpendicular work also occurred when special aisles and chapels were added to collegiate and parish churches; most of these were planned to contain the chantry chapels of private families and guilds. Much money was often available for such extensions; only in their window tracery and in some of their figure sculpture did they fall far behind the decorative masterpieces of Gothic's peak period. Panelling, heraldry, carved devices, and in some cases rib or fan-vaults added much to the rich effect of their coloured glass and of the tombs, brasses, and effigies of the founders. A few surviving examples must suffice to illustrate my point. Halifax in Yorkshire has one such chapel. At St John's, Devizes and not far away at Bromham ornate early Tudor chapels are clearly by the same designer. The Greenway chapel at Tiverton and the Lane aisle at Cullompton have carved ships and other references to the clothier founders' sources of wealth. The Cullompton aisle, and one added to the nave at Ottery St

Mary, are alike in the splendour of their fan-vaults. Noblest of all, with one of England's most magnificent tombs, is the Beauchamp chapel at Warwick, enshrining the memory of the lordly Earl of Warwick who died in 1439. The sheer splendour of this brilliant addition to a fine collegiate church reminds us that it was under the patronage of the very highest in the land that the Perpendicular style found its best expression.

Great buildings of the late Perpendicular period were as a rule commissioned by royalty, or by patrons in touch with the Court. Several, though not all, involved the use of fan-vaults, not merely in aisles like those of St George's, Windsor, but on a grand scale over the main compartments of naves and choirs. Basic points of late Gothic were still as in somewhat earlier buildings. Vast transomed and traceried windows occurred between deep buttresses which upheld the great thrust of the vaults. Triforia were still absent, while vertical panelling was popular as a mural decoration. Magnificent lierne vaults were planned, but never carried out, over the great chapels at Eton and King's, Cambridge.* But at Windsor lierne vaults of great complexity and beauty, and of a shallow-arched daring and virtuosity almost that of some railway bridges by Brunel, were placed in the early sixteenth century over both nave and choir; the latter had attractive panelled pendents in the manner which had already graced the brilliant lierne vault of Oxford's Divinity School. For a long time the master masons of our late Gothic age seemed chary of trying fan-vaults over spaces of great breadth. Their first venture of this kind was not over a royal building but in a Dorset monastic church.

The almost complete rebuilding of Sherborne Abbey was among the leading architectural feats of its time. Older (perhaps Saxon) pillars in the nave were cased, in the Winchester manner, with beautifully panelled masonry, and a short new eastern limb was built from the ground upwards. Over both choir and nave splendid fan-vaults conclusively proved that such ceilings need no longer be confined to aisles and small chapels. As the cones did not quite meet along the centre line of the vault a central belt of the ceiling was filled with stone patterning of the ribbed variety.

The Sherborne lesson was soon applied elsewhere. Three designers

---

* They appear, however, in the earlier side chapels at Cambridge; at Eton a simplified *fan*-vault has recently been built.

much employed by royalty were those most associated with the continued use of fan-vaults on their larger scale. One was John Wastell, who
may have designed the attractive scheme of low altitude fan-vaulting,
with no clear demarcation of bays, over the New Building which about
1500 replaced the Norman eastern chapels at Peterborough. In a similar
style, but with its great cones bisected by cross arches, and with the
interior space somewhat harshly split up into its 12 compartments,
was Wastell's tremendous fan-vault which was finished, along with an
antechapel ornately vaunting its Tudor heraldry and badges, at King's
Chapel, Cambridge. This, perhaps, is the famous of all fan-vaults. But
its beauty and virtuosity are no more than in those devised, about the
same time, by Robert and William Vertue. [35]

From 1499 onwards the large Norman cathedral at Bath was replaced by one which extended over little more than the length of the
older nave, reusing the foundations of its piers for its pillars but
achieving the usual cruciform plan. Bishop King, who urged on the
work, had been a prominent official at Court. Robert and William
Vertue the master masons had already worked for Henry VII, and were
now summoned to design this new cathedral. The work was unfinished
when in 1539 the cathedral monastery was dissolved; had the church,
and some necessary changes in the monastic buildings, been completed
a new landmark in England's cathedral and monastic architecture would
have been reached. The west front, with its angels on Jacob's ladders
and much Tudor political stonework, is very well known. More important are the Vertues' vaults. The main one is in the choir, and as at
Sherborne and Peterborough the upper parts of its cones uninterrupt-
edly overlap the divisions between its bays. Those in the aisles have
their flat central compartments adorned by beautiful panelled pendents
which foreshadowed, and much resemble, some of those designed by the
Vertues for the elaborate fan-vaults in Henry VII's chapel at Westminster. The structure of these vaults combined elements seen in more
than one of the others by Court designers. Cross arches are some of
them partly hidden above the masonry of the main vault, but they
serve to subdivide the chapel's ceiling into its bays. Yet this subdivision
is confused, and the whole structure is fantastically enriched, by a proliferation of pendents along the centreline and towards the sides of the
main vault. The cones, and the undersides of the cross arches, are enriched by cusping and carved detail of lacelike delicacy. So overpower-

35 FAN-VAULTING *Peterborough Cathedral: the retrochoir*
by John Wastell, c.1496–1508

ing is the whole riot of decoration that it seems, in an almost Oriental manner not seen again in England till the domes of Brighton's Pavilion, to have some kinship with the even stranger contemporary fantasies of Manoeline decoration in Portugal.

Some aisle windows in Henry VII's Chapel are not flat-surfaced, but are curiously arranged in groups of triangular projections. Other windows of this many-angled type occur in Henry VII's Tower at Windsor. Some more, as well as some with rounded projections, appear in the one domestic wing of Thornbury Castle in Gloucestershire which the Court designers finished, before his execution in 1521, for the royally descended, dangerously ambitious Duke of Buckingham. Thornbury Castle, had it been completed, would readily have surpassed the splendour of Wolsey's brick and stone mansion at Hampton Court. Enough survives of its entrance façade to display a new tendency in design more akin to ordered architecture than to the picturesque jumble of the past. For the semi-polygonal towers of that frontage were so planned as to balance each other in a symmetrical composition. The same tendency had earlier appeared in such castles as Bodiam, and at Bolton in the North Riding, being repeated in the brick-built, moated and partially fortified country houses of Hurstmonceux in East Sussex and Oxburgh Hall in Norfolk. Symmetry and ordered balance were also shown, under Henry VIII, in such wholly unfortified manors as Barrington and Poundisford in Somerset. Now at last it seemed that the drawing-board planning of complete mansions was replacing the more haphazard processes of architectural accumulation.

CASTLES AND FORTS

Not many castles of the fully military variety were built in the fifteenth century. Even the brick-built Lincolnshire tower of Tattershall, though as imposing in its massive silhouette as any late Norman keep, has comfortable rooms and many traceried outer windows of an unwarlike type. The most impressive fortification of this period is in the Monmouthshire castle of Raglan. Its two gate towers and its numerous curtain towers project on partially polygonal plans, while gunports pierce them at various tactical points. Supreme among them all is the sturdy, isolated, semi-ruinous Yellow Tower of Gwent, a superb hexagonal keep, once taller than its present ruins and in its design akin to Guy's

36 *Raglan Castle, Monmouthshire, fifteenth century*
37 *Deal Castle, Kent, c.1540*

Tower at Warwick. Artillery was now a commonplace of attack and defence, so small gunports were also provided at the brick-faced, moated castle of Kirby Muxloe near Leicester, like Thornbury unfinished through the political debacle and execution of its owner. [36]

By 1500 the building of serious fortifications was almost extinct. But in 1538 the policies of Henry VIII embroiled him with the great Continental powers of the Empire and France, plunging England into a short spell of invasion scares. So the Government took steps to guard against attacks on harbours and roadsteads along the section of England's coast most exposed to the Continent. A string of regularly garrisoned coastal forts was built between the Humber and the Fal. Dissolved monasteries supplied abundant materials; the church at Beaulieu, for example, was grubbed down to its foundations so that its stone could go down river to build the Solent forts of Calshot and Hurst.

These forts of Henry VIII are of interest for their scientific, geometrical planning, and for the many splayed cannon ports which pierce the thick masonry of their walls. Concentric planning, with a central tower and rounded outer defences, is common to most of them, and though a Continental engineer named von Haschenperg was employed on some of their building they seem to owe more to the example of Queenborough than to any work done abroad.* Deal and Walmer Castles, built to guard shipping in the Downs lying close inshore off the steep shingle beach where Caesar's legionaries first struggled ashore, are perhaps the finest, and certainly the least altered of these buildings, low and squat but powerful with their two rings of defences and short central turrets. The architectural details of these castles are late Perpendicular, of a wholly utilitarian plainness not uncommon in the dying Gothic of the next hundred years. [37]

By the late 1530s some signs had appeared that new things in the visual arts were under way. But in England, as in most of North-West Europe, Spain and Portugal, and early colonial Mexico and Peru, little as yet assured the eye that rediscovered architectural fashions were now normal in Italy. Perpendicular Gothic, despite the Renaissance intellectual

---

* But the pointed 'arrow-head' bastion at Yarmouth Castle, Isle of Wight, foreshadows Continental practice.

culture of a Colet or a More, was still entrenched this side of the Channel. King's Chapel at Cambridge had been started in the same year as Alberti's classical S. Francesco at Rimini, while the fan-vaults at Bath and Westminster were being built as Bramante finished his delightfully domed and Doric *tempietto* in Rome. Yet the Renaissance, Italian or Franco-Italian in its initial motivation, was beginning to be seen in England. Wolsey and the Crown both patronised designers from Italy itself. Terracotta busts in roundels appeared on frontages at Hampton Court and in Whitehall, while at Hampton Court the Cardinal's arms were supported by naked *putti* and flanked by Corinthian colonnettes. Pietro Torrigiano, a Florentine designer in stone, bronze, and terracotta, carried out the purely Renaissance tomb of Dr John Young in the Rolls Chapel,* and in Westminster Abbey those of Henry VII and his Queen, and of Lady Margaret Beaufort his saintly mother; the king's tomb has classic architectural detail as well as its splendid sculpture in bronze. Close by that tomb, a small altar had a flat canopy architecturally upheld by small classical columns. In a few more years, while Anne Boleyn still flourished as Henry VIII's second Queen, the newly completed chapel at King's, Cambridge saw the installation of its great wooden screen. French as well as Italian in its wholly Renaissance artistry, it was, and is, a great contrast to the building itself. Like the little altar canopy at Westminster it came as a stylistic slap in the face to the exponents of a dying Gothicism.

* Now in the Museum of the Public Record Office.

CHAPTER SIX

Renaissance Infiltration

1540–1660

By about 1550 England was becoming better aware of the return of Antiquity. The Palace of Nonsuch at Cheam in Surrey, with strong elements of the French Renaissance in its fireplaces and other decorations, was traditional in plan and construction, yet was closer, in some details, than most previous English buildings to a revived and diffused classicism. At Wells, so it seems from what we know of his pillared Market Hall, and certainly from the style of his simply designed stone pulpit in the Cathedral, Bishop Knight was a Renaissance advocate late in Henry VIII's reign. Though Italian designers were now less employed than in Torrigiano's time, English builders and decorators continued to take ideas from the French sources, in many ways so promising, which lay nearest at hand. It was not these early experimenters' fault that, as the century progressed, and as 'Elizabethan' merged into 'Jacobean', there came so sad an aesthetic decline.

Some newly risen magnates in Edward VI's short reign were important as architectural patrons. Some of their buildings have disappeared with nothing but pictures to recall them, or survive only in fragments. Among them was the original Somerset House, built for the Protector Somerset on its fine Thames-side site. As Sir John Summerson has pointed out, the derivation of its windows, of its gateway, and of other non-structural items in its decoration, was decidedly French. Another notable figure, not only for what he did on his own house and tomb but also as the chosen adviser on the design of some other mansions, was Sir William Sharington, the new owner of the attractive Wiltshire property of Lacock Abbey. His balustrade, octagonal turret, and other alterations at Lacock, showed a sensitive awareness of French

Renaissance taste. He directed some important work done at Dudley Castle, and the first building put up at Longleat by Sir John Thynne. His ideas may also have affected the great house (now destroyed) which the Wroughton family built at Broad Hinton in Wiltshire; the slightly pre-Elizabethan tomb of Sir William Wroughton in the church combines late Perpendicular with pure Corinthian, and with some specially French elements of Renaissance design. Yet other buildings still stayed within Gothic confines. Such a structure, among many imposing gateways still erected, was that which alone survives from the mansion, with its central courtyard in the mediaeval manner, built on the site of the great nunnery at Wilton.

But neither lingering Gothic nor the fairly pure classicism of the French Renaissance long withstood the rivalry of ostentatious, more confused versions of Renaissance design. Before touching on the unhappy architectural bastardy which made much Elizabethan work the ugliest and least significant before the Victorians one must mention certain historical facts of patronage, and some basic points of structure and design which distinguished this period, or kept it in line with mediaeval traditions.

Most of the more important Elizabethan and Jacobean buildings were country houses. The Crown, short of money and parsimonious, dropped out as a leading patron of architects. Industrialism, for another two centuries, made no demands. Public buildings of major note remained few, though Gresham's Royal Exchange in London, with its main block and a colonnaded courtyard like that of the famous Bourse at Amsterdam, was a leading exception. Another was the projecting façade, with its pillars, transomed windows, and upper balustrade, which was added in the 1590s to the older Guildhall at Exeter. But pillared market halls now became an agreeable adornment of many country towns. Their material—brick, half-timbering, or stone—reflected the great variety of materials still found in England. An upstairs room, as a rule rectangular but polygonal at Newent in Gloucestershire and at Wymondham, served as a public meeting place. The space below it gave shelter from rain and sun to those who sold such goods as butter or cheese. Ross-on-Wye, Chipping Campden, and at one time Bath and Hereford, all proved how pleasant were these manifestations of Elizabethan or Jacobean civic pride; the type lasted, as one sees at Reigate and Monmouth, for over a century after 1600.

More important than civic building was the architecture of learning and benevolence. Elizabethan parish churches are extremely few, though at Standish near Wigan in Lancashire Gothic and classical work were well blended in the 1580s. The chapels of colleges and almshouses were almost the only new places of worship put up at this time. Their style, as at Trinity, Cambridge and Jesus at Oxford, unexcitingly continued the late Perpendicular of the sixteenth century, while the untraceried, plainly subdivided windows of the bald worshipping room at Emmanuel, Cambridge gave an early hint, about 1584, of the long Puritan blight on the visual arts. More stylish were the domestic quarters of these colleges, of 'hospitals', and of grammar schools like the fine Jacobean range of Blundell's at Tiverton, with its mullioned windows, shell-headed niches, and spacious hall. The quadrangle was now considered the most fitting collegiate plan; it was a rarity when Dr Caius of Cambridge enforced his physician's views about fresh air and insisted on an open-sided court for his augmented college. The chosen style, as one sees in the domestic ranges of that court of the 1560s, in several charming almshouse courts or single ranges, and in the important work of Ralph Symons at St John's and Trinity at Cambridge, was the simplest of late Perpendicular. Only in the central, monumental feature of a principal range, in the tricking out of oriel windows and doorways, and in the rich strapwork plaster ceilings now increasingly popular, did English builders and their decorator colleagues find a place for Renaissance decoration of the type now generally accepted.

None of these buildings really departed, in planning, structure or predominant style, from those long familiar. Nor, in many respects, did the new country mansions. Their Renaissance features, largely derived from imported pattern books like those of the Frenchman Philibert de l'Orme, the Italians Serlio and Barbaro,* the Flemish Vredeman de Vries, and the German Dietterlin, were apt to be a stylistic veneer on earlier methods of construction. Yet some points of domestic planning, if not of construction, were comparatively new.

The exterior grouping, and the varied silhouettes, of an Elizabethan or Jacobean mansion were apt to continue certain trends well in evidence in the early years of Henry VIII. Very often the wings of such a

---

* It also seems likely that Sir John Harington's mansion at Kelston near Bath (long since destroyed) was based on plans or drawings by Vignola, perhaps those contained in his treatise of 1562; Harington was a well known Italophile.

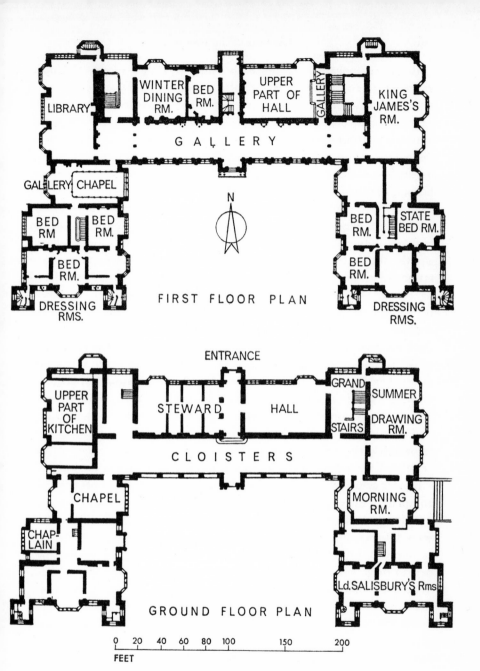

FIRST FLOOR PLAN

LIBRARY

WINTER DINING RM.

BED RM.

UPPER PART OF HALL

GALLERY

KING JAMES'S RM.

G A L L E R Y

GALLERY CHAPEL

BED RM

BED RM.

N

BED RM.

STATE BED RM.

BED RM.

BED RM.

DRESSING RMS.

DRESSING RMS.

GROUND FLOOR PLAN

ENTRANCE

UPPER PART OF KITCHEN

STEWARD

HALL

GRAND

SUMMER

STAIRS

DRAWING RM.

C L O I S T E R S

CHAPEL

MORNING RM.

CHAP-LAIN

Ld. SALISBURY'S Rms

| 0 | 20 | 40 | 60 | 80 | 100 | 150 | 200 |

FEET

38 *Hatfield House, Hertfordshire, 1607–11 : the symmetrical, yet traditional,*
plan of a great Jacobean house

house symmetrically balanced each other on either side of the main range which contained the great hall. The porch which led to the principal doorway, and so to the 'screens passage' between the hall and the pantries, projected and sometimes had one or two rooms above it. Such projections gave houses the E-shaped plan supposed to have paid a deliberate compliment to Elizabeth I; however, I doubt that such a gesture would have impressed so hard-headed a sovereign. In other houses, the flanking wings projected both ways, thus making the shape of the ground plan that of an H. Above the roof tall, elaborate chimney-stacks, of a type already pioneered, in brick, by many East Anglian builders and by the Duke of Buckingham at Thornbury, arose to diversify the silhouette. The end walls and wings of such houses might have attractive gables. On a smaller scale ornamental gables were also placed over many intermediate windows, while in the seventeenth century they appeared, particularly in Oxford or Cambridge colleges, over the dormer windows made necessary by the provision of extra rooms among the timbers of the roof. The shapes of these gables vary, and give much of their undeniable charm to many architecturally insignificant houses of this period. Some, in the mediaeval manner, are simply triangular. Others, like those of the brick-built library of Trinity Hall at Cambridge, are 'stepped', while those of the most interest look to Dutch or Flemish examples and are curved in a variety of shapes. Many are crowned with carved finials or saucy little balls, while some of the grander houses have their windows, gables, or parapets crowned by elaborate cresting, or else, in an ostentatious 'conceit', by balustrading comprising the capital letters of an inscription.

Windows, though divided vertically by mullions, and often cross-ways by transoms, had almost abandoned the cusping and tracery of earlier Gothic; the most one can expect is that the top of an Elizabethan or Jacobean light may not be rectangular but simply arched. Where the more ambitious Elizabethan windows most fully expressed the late Gothic spirit was in their enormous size; 'more glass than wall' was as true of Wollaton or Hardwick as of the Lady Chapel at Gloucester. Such expanses were well suited, as at North Cadbury Court in Somerset, for the vaunting display of heraldic glass. Doorways were sometimes round-arched in the Renaissance manner. But where, like fireplace openings, they were still Gothic in outline, the points of their shallow arches were so slight and feeble that they hardly belong to the

39   MID-TUDOR BLACK AND WHITE: *Moreton Old Hall, Cheshir*

great art which produced the acuteness of thirteenth-century arcades and the lovely sinuosity of the ogee. [40]

Inside the Elizabethan mansions and manors the halls were still the largest, most ceremonial rooms. In the greatest houses, as also in the Middle Temple, and at Trinity, Cambridge whose new hall of about 1600 closely imitated that of the London lawyers, they were still of great size; those at Longleat and elsewhere absorbed the height of two storeys or more. Yet their status had somehow changed. They were used for such great occasions as banquets and masques, but they seem to have served less as ordinary living rooms. The sixteenth-century surveyors and masons made experiments in changing the positions of the great hall in relation to other rooms; when at Wollaton the great clerestoried hall was put in the *middle* of a quadrangular house it became a lobby or central circulating space. The feeling of the hall as a vestibule, with genteel living carried on in the 'great parlour' to one side of it, occurs in some smaller manors. In these the hall, though long, is of only one storey, with its windows no different from those elsewhere on the ground floor.

Where the Elizabethans made real changes and improvements in house planning was in their increasing provision of wide wooden staircases. Mediaeval builders had never advanced on external steps, or on the spiral stairways by which one climbs church towers. But in the sixteenth century the square-planned staircase, with its sequence of miniature landings and a real feeling of grandeur, became much more normal. As such staircases need more space than 'vices', special projections, or staircase towers, were often built to hold them. In some houses, particularly where the existence of two staircases gave designers their chance of adding character to already balanced compositions, two staircase turrets with cupolas rise high above the roofline.

Another Elizabethan novelty, practical and picturesque but of proportions which denied it real beauty, was the Long Gallery found in most country mansions. These galleries were narrow, comparatively low, and very long. They were provided upstairs, and were planned for the indoor pacing and exercise of weatherbound occupants. Galleries of this type exist in the half-timbered President's Lodge at Queens' College, Cambridge, at Hatfield House in Hertfordshire, and at Knole in Kent. One sees in the last-named (like Hatfield a Jacobean example) how such a gallery could be used for the display of pictures and curios.

40 *Elizabethan: Hardwick Hall, Derbyshire, completed 1597*
41 *Jacobean: Hatfield, the Long Gallery, c.1607–11*

Some, like great parlours and other important living rooms, or halls
like that of Collacombe Barton in West Devon, have the elaborately
worked plaster ceilings much in favour with Elizabethan and Jacobean
patrons. Strapwork in shallow relief, floral patterns, and moulded
panels of religious or mythological scenes were all frequent tricks of
decoration, while some ceilings both of the sixteenth century and of
the early seventeenth have bold plaster pendents recalling those in
Perpendicular fan-vaults. [41]

The Elizabethan age was not only one of new fantasy and competitive
display. Modes of thought and its expression often entered into new com-
plexities. The period was the time for 'conceits' and strange artificial-
ities. So some buildings defied pedestrian practicality, aiming at unreal
plans and elevations. Wollaton Hall near Nottingham was one such
house, with its great corner turrets and many-windowed sides all dominated by the rising central block of its clerestoried hall. Robert Smythson, the eminent 'surveyor' and draughtsman, was its designer in the
1580s; some drawings in his great collection are for houses (including
one with a narrow main block and four rounded bay windows) little
less strange. The cruciform 'New Building' of Lyveden in Northamptonshire, never finished but started by the devoutly Catholic Treshams,
had its plan chosen for its religious symbolism. A triangular shape, to
symbolise the Trinity, appears at Longford Castle near Salisbury, where
Sir Thomas Gorges's surveyor seems likely to have been John Thorpe,
who also made drawings for a mansion on a plan of his own conjoined
initials.

Smythson and Thorpe were leading figures among the 'surveyors'
who worked for wealthy Elizabethan patrons. They are the best known,
thanks to the survival of many of their drawings, several of these being
of unexecuted projects or of buildings designed by others. They did,
however, carry out considerable original work. With them and others
like them we come to what some modern scholars have hailed as the
originators of the modern architectural profession. There was at this
time no architectural training of the modern type, and for another
two centuries the frontiers between architects, land surveyors, and
mason-craftsmen remained hazily drawn. Nor can we easily tell how far
these late Tudor and Jacobean 'surveyors' differed from mediaeval
master masons. There was, however, less of a tendency to attribute the
design of buildings to those who commissioned them, so that the sur-

veyor or architect got the credit once given to bishops, abbots, or sacrists. Yet we also have the rise, among the more enlightened lay patrons, of the 'amateur architect'. Gentry like Thynne, Sharington, or Lord Burleigh were apt, by using the foreign design books now available in England, to take an informed interest in architecture, the more so if they had seen new Renaissance buildings in Italy and France. So some of them made 'platts' or 'uprights' (i.e. ground plans and elevations) of houses and their internal features, passing these to the masons for execution. As Renaissance stylistic features were in the main a structurally inessential decorative veneer the results were unlikely to involve them in disaster. For another two centuries the 'amateur' or 'gentleman' architect played an honourable, at times distinguished, part in England's building history.

THE DECLINE IN TASTE

Yet despite the initial acceptance of Franco-Italian Renaissance detail, and the genuinely cultured leanings of some notable patrons and their surveyors, the Elizabethan age and the early seventeenth century witnessed a sad measure of aesthetic tragedy. When one looks at some architecture and some of the less tasteful tombs of this time,* and still more at the furnishings, panelling, and other fixtures in some outwardly seemly buildings, it is hard to recall that this was the age of Shakespeare, Spenser, Raleigh, and Nicholas Hilliard. For the years between about 1580 and 1620 saw the construction and fitting out of some of the ugliest buildings (also the ugliest clothes and furniture) before the dire time of the Great Exhibition; one must admit, in all fairness, that things were equally bad elsewhere in Europe.

Much of the damage was done by the wide acceptance of style and detail from Germano-Flemish, not Italian sources. In the architecture of Germany and the Low Countries the use of the Renaissance style was long halting and confused; as in England a clumsy union between Gothic

---

* Church monuments and tombs, whether free-standing and canopied or built against church walls, were now more important even than in the Middle Ages. Their artistry was divided between the sculpture of their effigies (sometimes most noble, crudely ridiculous in such horrors as those shown reclining on one elbow) and the architectural composition of their setting and canopies. This, at its best, could be convincingly of the classical Renaissance, Netherlandish influences being due to the origin of many of the carvers.

and Classic produced some unhappy artistic bastardies. The pattern
books of Dietterlin, de Vries, and lesser artists from the same cultural
area became standard reference-works among England's builders and
joiners. The results were often disastrous, and worse inside houses than
on their exteriors. A house such as Montacute in Somerset has a dignified, unfantastic severity about the masonry, gables, and demure niches
of its exterior, yet the best thing about that exterior is the very early
Tudor porch transferred in the 1780s from the demolished mansion of
Clifton Maybank not far away. It belongs fully to the best of the late
Gothic tradition; the main house is in standing water between two
great streams of artistry. There is also much appealing charm about the
increasingly extravagant carving and timber patterns of such 'black and
white' houses as Moreton Old Hall in Cheshire and many others in the
West Midlands and Welsh Marches. But other buildings of the period
are artistic failures. Either they jumble or misapply Franco-Italian
Renaissance detail as at Bramshill in Hampshire and Kirby Hall in
Northamptonshire, or else they indulge, in porches, screens, panelling,
and ostentatious chimneypieces, in a riot of ill-digested, romantic
motivation from across the North Sea. The Elizabethan fireplace and
plaster ceiling put in to 'improve' the late mediaeval parlour at South
Wraxall well show this cross-bred decadence, while town houses in
London, York, Bristol and elsewhere greatly multiplied these unhappy
trends. Curiously contorted strapwork and cartouches, pleasant little
obelisks supported on small balls, bulbous pedestals, herms, and strange
male or female caryatid figures blended in with heraldry, personal
devices, symbolic figures, and more orthodox classical features to produce strangely barbaric ensembles. Away from the areas near London
the provincial time-lag meant that such decoration, like peaked gables,
mullioned windows, and Gothic-style fireplaces, dragged on, under
local and vernacular designers, till far into the generally more enlightened period of Charles II. [39]
   The large-scale architectural fantasies of the Elizabethans and Jaco-
beans were so inept and confused that the more modest efforts of provincial masons and craftsmen often give a more lovable impression of
the great building talent then available in England. These were the
houses of the smaller gentry, of yeoman farmers and clothiers. Except
for their doorways and main fireplaces they sometimes lack the stylistic
eccentricities of the great mansions. Masonry, brickwork, mullioned

windows, and sturdily effective timber framing—all these, however, are well in evidence. Many such houses exist in the counties of the stone belt, in the granite areas of Devon and Cornwall, in East Anglia and East Kent where rounded or fancifully curved gables in mellow red brick give great character to many houses of this time. The West Midlands and Welsh Marches have their timber-framed houses and stone-built chimney-stacks, while in the Pennine country one can admire the solid, honest masoncraft of the low-built, profusely mullioned manors which were the originals of the wind-swept, doom-laden upland homes portrayed by the Brontës. Inside, the low parlours of these middle-class homes are often darkly panelled with woodwork whose carving is aesthetically confused yet decently restrained, giving a cosy, pleasing atmosphere of *biedermaier* charm.

England's architecture was unusual, in Renaissance Europe as a whole, for its long and lasting survival of Gothic. But by about 1600 Gothic had so far waned, and Renaissance decoration was so much in fashion, that the time was ripe for the slow infiltration of the past six or seven decades to make way for the country's first essays in full Renaissance design as this was understood at its Italian fountain-head. There had, by now, been some important forerunners of the next century's more complete acceptance of Continental practice. Among them were some Elizabethan fortifications at Upnor, where a sharply projecting battery was built across the Medway from Chatham Dockyard, at Castle Cornet in Guernsey, and in the new town walls of Berwick-on-Tweed. All these were an advance on the rounded bastions of Henry VIII's coastal forts, for they had the sloping masonry walls and the triangular, projecting bastions and ravelins familiar at Malta and in other fortresses then built by Italian military engineers. In the next century, when the Dutch engineer Sir Bernard de Gomme was employed by the Crown, designs of the same kind, as improved by the school of Vauban, were used at Tilbury Fort and in Charles II's splendid new citadel at Plymouth; in the Civil War de Gomme had tried them on the magnificent Royal Fort which briefly dominated Bristol.

There were also several English buildings of a non-military character (as well as many canopied tombs and mural monuments) where Renaissance style and detail were applied uncloyed by Flemish or Germanic glosses. Early in Elizabeth I's reign Sir John Thynne had made a sensitive use of chaste Italian decoration, of an almost Palladian stamp, on the outside walls of his quadrangular but essentially Gothic mansion at Longleat. In the 1560s Dr Caius of Cambridge, a Padua graduate who had sojourned in the Palladio country and may even have met Palladio himself, used fully Palladian detail, somewhat oddly blended with late Perpendicular planning and some Gothic detail, on two of the gateway façades of his new college court. Some Smythson drawings, particularly one for a two-tiered screen with its round arches, Roman Doric columns, and balustrade in the Italian manner, show that English designers were now well versed in the external niceties of Renaissance Italy.

INIGO JONES AND PALLADIANISM

As on many previous occasions in English architecture, it was from Court circles that the impetus came for the next decisive forward move. James I and Anne of Denmark his queen, Charles I and the designer and architect Inigo Jones were those most responsible for giving English eyes their first sight of some buildings not only decorated but also planned in the full manner of the Italian Renaissance. The early career of Jones himself largely explains what happened.

Inigo Jones was a Londoner, born in 1573 and early in touch with cultured circles at Court. He was a joiner's apprentice, and decided to make his career among the visual arts. To this end, under noble patronage, he paid several formative visits to Italy and one to France. His journeys were much more than the somewhat amateur perambulations of a dilettante, for he made serious studies not only of Italian buildings he saw but of the theories of design which lay behind them and the published works of leading Italian architects. Of all the Renaissance architects who had lately worked in Italy Andrea Palladio of Vicenza, and Scamozzi his pupil whom Jones actually met, were those whose idiom had the most influence on the true pioneer, among English architects, of the full Renaissance. Nor were Jones's intellectual interests merely those of the aproned mason or carpenter. Though of humble origin, he readily made friends with the highest in the land. He read, and spoke Italian, and his books at Worcester College, Oxford, show his interests were those of a man of wide-ranging curiosity and intelligence.

The Palladian architects of the Venetian hinterland derived their somewhat rigidly antique Roman style from Palladio's own careful study of ancient buildings still standing in Rome, and from the precise, mathematically expressed instructions, on planning and proportions as well as on detail, of the Imperial Roman architectural author Vitruvius. Palladio himself, in his *Quattro Libri dell' Architettura*, drew heavily on these classical examples. Though by no means the only Italian master-pieces of their time (as one well sees in Genoa, Tuscany, and Rome) the Palladian buildings of the Veneto were among the most seemly and attractive of those built in Italy about 1600. They, and the English buildings derived from them in the forty years before the Civil War, were original and up to date; what was a much less fortunate anachron-ism was the way in which the style was enthusiastically readopted, in the England of the eighteenth century, when it had been superseded in most of its homeland. Though in Italy it included churches, villas, and public buildings, Palladianism was a style most suitable for a country like England where architecture was now almost wholly concerned with buildings other than churches.

Little is known for certain of Jones's early life. He worked in Den-mark (the native country of James I's queen) as well as in England. Like other designers of his time he lacked a modern architect's training. His executed work included designs for the costumes and scenery of masques as well as the construction, repair, and alteration of buildings. The design of temporary structures like scenery, triumphal arches, and catafalques was a common activity among Renaissance and Baroque architects; from surviving drawings it seems that Jones's work of this kind was more exciting, and much less Palladian, than the buildings he saw completed, or designed without their being built. Completed and projected work must, incidentally, be taken together if one wishes to assess the mental processes and talents of Jones, Wren, and other English architects prominent from now onwards. The seventeenth cen-tury, in particular, was one when political troubles and financial stresses affected Court and private building activity as the Wars of the Roses had long frustrated King's chapel at Cambridge. Unexecuted designs, and completed buildings now pulled down, are an essential part of the story of Inigo Jones and of what he did to bring his country's architec-ture to new realms of vision and taste.

Soon after the turn of the century, and his return from Denmark, Jones worked on some masque designs. Then in 1611 he obtained the promising post of Surveyor General to Prince Henry, the cultured young heir to the Throne. But late in 1612 the Prince of Wales died, and in 1613 Jones was again in Italy with the Earl of Arundel, the most important of his noble patrons. In 1615 came his key appointment, that of Surveyor General of the Royal Works; it was under Court auspices that most of his really significant work was done. Palladianism, with some lesser borrowings from other Italian sources, was his ruling style. But he was genius enough to adapt it considerably (most notably in the size and spacing of his windows) to English conditions of climate and taste.

Inigo Jones's chief surviving buildings are at Greenwich, in the Court quarter of London, and at Wilton. His alterations at Somerset House, among them a large, internally ornate Catholic chapel for Queen Henrietta Maria, have disappeared, as have various monumental gateways and an important pedimented lodge built, early in his architectural career, as an addition to the Palace at Newmarket. His ambitious plans for a new Whitehall Palace, with additional drawings by John Webb his nephew by marriage, never got beyond the paper stage. His alterations at Old St Paul's, among them a vast, unpedimented Corinthian west portico, did not survive the Great Fire. His beautiful Palladian screen in Winchester Cathedral was found obnoxious by early nineteenth-century Gothicists; some pieces are down in the crypt, while the central element is in the Archaeological Museum at Cambridge. There are also many unprovable Jones 'attributions'. Among them, fairly plausibly, is the central element of the mansion façade at Castle Ashby in Northamptonshire. Others, of less likelihood, include a wing at Ashton Court near Bristol, and interior fittings at Forde Abbey in Dorset and elsewhere. As with Wren, the posthumous reputation of Jones has been enough for his authorship to be a desirable, and indeed marketable, feature. Though a pure classicist he is also claimed for a few imitation Gothic works like the tower of Calne church in Wiltshire.

Jones's first full demonstration of Palladianism, and of planning in the manner of the Renaissance villa where the hall is a central vestibule with other rooms leading out of it, was the Queen's House at Greenwich; it was started in 1616, the year in which Shakespeare died. Anne of Denmark's death in 1619 caused the work to stop, but early in the 1630s Jones supervised the house's completion for Henrietta Maria. Not for nothing, in view of what had been normal in the planning of

42   *Wilton House, Wiltshire: the double cube room, by Inigo Jones, after* 1647

English mansions, was it dubbed by a contemporary as a 'curious devise'. The Palladian nature of its planning is distorted by the strange fact that the house was built athwart a public road, so that the hall, with its balustraded gallery carried on cantilevered brackets, occupied more space, in the northern section, than a Renaissance hall would normally do. But symmetrical balance between the rooms was preserved in each section of this truly innovating house, and although it is lower, in proportion to its other dimensions, than a Palladian designer would have made it on the banks of the Brenta, the first-floor loggia facing the Park is a pure Renaissance delight with its Ionic columns and dainty balustrade.

A finer, more truly Palladian masterpiece by Inigo Jones is the Banqueting House in Whitehall. It was built, as the Pilgrim Fathers sailed, between 1619 and 1622, a pure Palladian *palazzo* amid a mediaeval and Tudor Gothic jumble which it put culturally to shame. Its internal proportions are that Vitruvio-Palladian beau ideal, a double cube; Rubens's superb painted ceiling is more Baroque than its setting, a precedent for what happened in many Georgian Palladian interiors. The main façade, with its rusticated wall spaces, large rectangular windows,* Ionic and Corinthian pilasters and half columns, bold cornice, and crowning balustrade, was first to have had a pediment over its middle three 'elements'. But this, as Jones revised his ideas, was cut out. What we now see, refaced in Portland stone but in essence as Jones saw it, is a serene, monumental composition, its details deriving from Palladian villas and from palaces in Vicenza. Sculptured masks and garlands form a stately frieze between the Corinthian capitals of the upper storey. Had Whitehall Palace been rebuilt this noble hall would have been kept in the vast total layout. It remained as England's best exemplar of an architectural fashion whose full acceptance did not come for another century. [43]

Two places of worship, one rebuilt in the 1790s, are the rest of Jones's surviving achievement in London. A simply pedimented, unassuming exterior was all that in 1623 was politically possible for the Catholic chapel started at St James's for Charles I's intended Spanish bride and used instead by Henrietta Maria. Inside, it was far more

---

* They now have sashes, but at first had four compartments, split up by mullions and horizontal transoms and fitted with casements. Had this not been so in 1649, Charles I's walk to his execution would have lacked its much applauded dignity.

JACOBEAN CONTRASTS
43 *The Banqueting House, Whitehall, by Inigo Jones, 1619–22*
44 *Oriel College, Oxford : the hall quad, c.1620*

lavish, and a rich segment-shaped coffered ceiling still proves Jones's competence at fully Italian decoration. More barnlike, and indeed called by its architect a 'Tuscan barn ', was St Paul's, Covent Garden, of the 1630s. The piazza itself, arcaded in the Italian manner and geometrically laid out as a regular square, was novel in London as a fine piece of what the Renaissance Italians called *sistemazione*; Jones's collaborator here was a French designer named Isaac de Caux. The church, in its late Georgian reproduction, is the least Palladian and the least attractive of Jones's designs, deliberately Tuscan with its heavily overhanging eaves, overwhelming pediment, and crudely spaced columns; the more primitive Romano-British temples, unbeknown to Inigo Jones, had achieved much the same effect.

Jones's latest work, commenced in 1647 and finished under his nephew John Webb's supervision, is the Palladian block which makes up the southern wing of the quadrangular mansion at Wilton; it replaced a Tudor building wrecked by a fire. The exterior had features which now and in the eighteenth century were characteristically Palladian— pedimented pavilion turrets at each side, and in the middle a fine 'Venetian' window with its central light round-headed and higher than the other two. The Roman severity of the exterior belies great sumptuousness within; as in the Whitehall Banqueting House the finest room is a setting for paintings (in this case by Vandyck) which are older than the building and in a tradition more opulent and ornate than that of Palladio. The two principal rooms have extremely rich doorcases and chimneypieces, more Baroque than antique Roman in taste. But Palladian proportions are observed in the rooms built as a cube and a double cube. In the latter, widely held to be England's loveliest room, the double cube shape is modified by the curved cove which gracefully links the walls to the ceiling's central panel. [42]

Inigo Jones died in 1652 during the Commonwealth, which was not, on the whole, a fruitful period in our architecture. But in some buildings Palladianism continued under the guidance of John Webb, and of Sir Roger Pratt, a 'gentleman' or 'amateur' architect. Their work overlapped the Restoration of 1660. But Webb designed the partially Palladian Lamport Hall in 1654, while the 1650s also saw Pratt at work on the country house which, rather than the bisected Queen's House or the single block at Wilton, gave England its best early demonstration of the Italian 'villa' plan. This was Coleshill in Berkshire, a mansion most sadly burnt down in 1952. Its plan was a vital example of the new dispensation. The entrance hall, with roundels filled by classical busts, also contained the noble double staircase, while out of it there led the central saloon and, in reasonable symmetry on each side of these ceremonial spaces, the living quarters. The exterior presented a solemn frontage of carefully spaced, unpedimented main windows; the more dignified decoration of pediments occurred only over the entrance doorways. More English touches were seen in the high-pitched roof with its pedimented dormers, and in the tall, symmetrically balanced chimney-stacks. A balustrade ran round the crest of the roof, while in its midst Pratt placed a bold cupola like that which he later poised on the surviving, much altered Kingston Lacy in East Dorset. Here at Coleshill, however, there was the assurance that, even if Palladian detail was not long to outlast its pioneer, the traditions of design which Jones had notably pioneered in England had come to stay.

SURVIVALIST GOTHIC

But for some buildings of the first half of the seventeenth century another tradition proved itself to be deeply rooted. English Gothic, like Charles II, was an unconscionable time a-dying; unlike the Merry Monarch it never quite achieved that feat. It long lingered, not only in buildings where it remained the dominant style, but in others where it occurs in odd, intellectually confused partnership with Renaissance, 'Jacobean', or even Baroque.

A few parish churches were built in the first forty years of the seventeenth century; their style was mostly simple, unexciting late Perpendicular. Groombridge in Kent and Wyke Champflower and Low Ham in Somerset display the trend, while at Keynsham the masons of the stone belt proved that when an earlier Perpendicular tower fell down they could replace it much as before. The best of these churches, in its arcades and east window more akin to the Gothic of about 1330, was St John's at Leeds of 1632–3. But its pews and screenwork, as at Abbeydore in Herefordshire where 'Laudian' church furnishing abounds, are in the comfortable barbaric 'Jacobean' idiom handed on by the less tasteful Elizabethan designers. At the same time the important London church of St Catherine Cree combined rounded arches and Corinthian columns with a Gothic shell whose east window had a clear antiquarian reference to that of Old St Paul's.

Romantic antiquarianism, as well as a merely survivalist conservatism, lay behind much of the 'academic' Gothic built, early in the seventeenth century, in Lincoln's Inn Chapel, and in the two Universities. Oxford is the main stronghold of this lovably muddled architecture. But much of it was also put up at Cambridge, though there, as in Clare and in Nevile's Court at Trinity, the buildings have been much changed by Georgian alterations. This academic architecture is apt to be a strange blend of late Gothic and theatrical Baroque, while at Wadham College, Oxford the main feature of the original quad piles up the Roman orders as Philibert de l'Orme and some Italians had taught the Elizabethans to do. Fan-vaults blend with Baroque settings at Clare College, Cambridge and in the famous porch of St Mary's at Oxford, while in Canterbury Quad at St John's, Oxford the juxtaposition of tame late Perpendicular with ornate Baroque suggests a very English unwillingness to draw firmly logical lines. Elsewhere, as in the east windows of Peterhouse chapel at Cambridge and that of Lincoln in Oxford, and in the fan-vault built in the 1630s over the hall vestibule at Christ Church, Oxford, college Gothic of this age is more strictly Perpendicular. Yet other windows, like some in the fine library of St John's at Cambridge, and at Wadham and Oriel in Oxford, bring back the waving tracery lines of Curvilinear, and so look forward to that romantic recovery of the past which for another three centuries meant so much in English architecture. [44]

Some Gothic Survival work, and some architecture which blended Gothic and Baroque, was achieved in the lean years of the Commonwealth. At Staunton Harold in Leicestershire the new church resembled an aisled and clerestoried fifteenth-century parish church with a pinnacled western tower. But at Oxford the chapel of Brasenose has a plaster fan-vault, and some fanciful tracery, along with Corinthian pilasters and other Baroque detail not unworthy of the first Oxford and Cambridge buildings (in progress as this chapel was nearing completion) of a young mathematician and astronomer named Christopher Wren.

CHAPTER SEVEN

Renaissance Acceptance

1660–1700

Though building activity increased after Charles II's Restoration the range of architecture was still limited outside the circles of the Court, the Church and the Universities, and the aristocracy. Though several public buildings of this period have disappeared, the total of such architecture, apart from work in London made necessary by the Great Fire of 1666, was strangely small. But Abingdon's Town Hall with its striking 'giant' order, the Customs House at King's Lynn with its Dutch Renaissance inspiration, and noble almshouses like the College of Matrons at Salisbury, Morden College at Blackheath, and Colston's at Bristol all show how accomplished, in this field, were the achievements of the 'Restoration' and 'William and Mary' periods. The last forty years before 1700 were among the greatest in English architecture, remarkable not only for their dominant genius but for moves forward both in planning and style. [45]

Two provinces of taste we can set on one side when dealing with the period dominated by Wren. Though the Gothic style, and mediaeval methods of plannning and house-building in the streets of towns, tenaciously survived, the Gothic idiom was clearly outmoded. There could be no question that Renaissance planning, and some version of revived classic decoration, were what most patrons would instinctively choose. Some churches, indeed, were still conservatively built to mediaeval plans and in the late Gothic tradition. Monnington-on-Wye in Herefordshire is one such church, and in Somerset the tower at Midsomer Norton replaces a Perpendicular fabric with as much accuracy as the local masons could achieve without photographs to copy. The same thing happened, at Berkeley and Dursley in Gloucestershire and at Sherston in Wiltshire, where fine Perpendicular towers had to be replaced in the coming century. Where Wren himself built in Gothic, as at St Mary Aldermary in London where he added nice Baroque touches to a basically neo-Perpendicular fabric, it was because the parishioners so insisted. Tom Tower at Christ Church, Oxford, was another case where he both humoured his patrons and paid the respect of a sensitive mind to Wolsey's earlier substructure.

The other idiom still normally eschewed in the architecture of Restoration England was full-blown Baroque of the lavish, curving, 'sculptural' type pioneered in Rome by Bernini and still practised there by Borromini his successor. For religious reasons, and because of the sober temperament of a largely Puritan England, it was impossible for English buildings too openly to express the favoured style of lands which were Papist and which also seemed, to the staid English, to be unbalanced in their emotions; even more impossible was the Churrigueresque of Spain and her great Empire in the Americas. Internal decoration, and the applied arts, were another matter, so we find that in these smaller-scale, more hidden artefacts both Englishmen and artists from Baroque Europe could happily luxuriate in realms of taste which were taboo for exteriors and denied to the furnishings of conventicles and meeting houses. But Baroque exteriors were rare except in a few gateways like Wren's Temple Bar, and such fancies as the temporary triumphal arches put up in the City of London (perhaps under the aegis of that flamboyant, somewhat eccentric immigrant Sir Balthasar Gerbier) to celebrate the Coronation of Charles II. The fine Baroque gateways of Tilbury Fort and of Plymouth's Citadel are the best survivors of this rare exuberance. Both probably owe much to the Continental taste of the engineer Sir Bernard de Gomme.

JOHN WEBB AND ROGER PRATT

The first few years after 1660 saw the final achievements of John Webb and Roger Pratt. They were mostly country mansions, and as Wren never had the chance to work much on such private commissions these houses by his immediate predecessors helped greatly to establish Renaissance design and planning in a class of English building of immense future importance. So while Webb followed his earlier work in

Wiltshire with the now destroyed Amesbury Abbey, and as Pratt designed Kingston Lacy to compare with Coleshill, Pratt's Clarendon House, a London building with projecting wings, a high-pitched roof, bold dormers, and a central cupola, was closely followed at Belton House in Lincolnshire. In their style, moreover, these early Restoration mansions were less indebted to Palladio than were the pioneering buildings of Inigo Jones. The heavier severity of the French Renaissance, as displayed at the Court of Louis XIV, was now in evidence. It appears, along with predominantly Palladian elements, in the long, low, handsome block designed by Webb to start a new Palace projected by Charles II to replace rambling mediaeval buildings on the splendid riverside site at Greenwich. The giant Corinthian half-columns of its central feature, and the equally large pilasters of its end pavilions, have Palladian precedents, yet the building seems akin to comtemporary Paris. It would seem that had Wren never lived, or had he, like Milton, been of Puritan sympathies (which would have amounted to much the same thing), England's more monumental architecture would anyhow have turned towards Continental precedents of its own time. [46, 51]

CHRISTOPHER WREN

Sir Christopher Wren was a great and varied genius, and has had much written on his work. So this short survey of the whole range of England's historic architecture can do no more than recall his main achievements, while noticing a few strictly historic factors which some have minimised. Not only was Wren an architect whose completed buildings are among our greatest national treasures; he also proved how deeply an architect's career can be swayed by events little connected with architecture or its attendant arts.

Wren's architecture, and the constructional virtuosity of such works as the ceiling of the Sheldonian and the dome of St Paul's, were much conditioned by his intellectual training as a mathematician and a scientist. His chance, as Surveyor General or Court architect, to prove his talents came largely, indeed decisively, from his intensely royalist family background. His genius transcended the politics of his time, and Wren was as ready to design for William and Mary as for Charles II and James II. But his first opportunities came not from Dutch William or Whig lords but from Restoration divines and from the restored monarchy of Charles II. The son of a Dean of Windsor who had been deprived under the Commonwealth and died before the Restoration, and the nephew of a Bishop of Ely whom Cromwell had long kept in the Tower, and who lived to reassume his bishopric, had the right background for employment by Church and Crown. Notwithstanding many ups and downs, Church and Crown were Wren's main paymasters for the whole of his architectural career.

Yet despite Wren's great benefits from his royal and ecclesiastical patrons, and despite the great chances given him by London's Great Fire in 1666, it was from the vagaries of politics that he also had his greatest sadness and frustration. It has been well said that architecture is frozen history; England's history in the years between 1660 and 1714 was also such that politics often effectively froze architecture. Charles II, as his ideas for Greenwich, Windsor, and Winchester showed, had many of the ambitions and tastes of a Baroque monarch. His years of exile, and his close knowledge of Louis XIV's Court, drew him strongly towards the pomp and flamboyance of the French monarchy whose favoured style in building was in any case chosen by architects in Restoration England. Yet he was never, least of all in the realms of finance, enabled like his cousin Louis to assume that he himself personified his half Puritan realm, or that all its resources were ready at his disposal. The Duchesses of Cleveland, Castlemaine, and Portsmouth, and to a lesser, less aristocratic extent Nell Gwynne, were an English equivalent to one pattern established at the French Court. But the Stuarts, with Parliament holding the purse-strings tight, with many dynastic and political uncertainties, and with the changes of royal inclination inevitable in three short reigns, never went far towards an English Versailles. Charles II, James II, and William and Mary may all have dreamed of some truly monumental setting for their Courts. But the grand designs for such palaces very largely remained on paper—as conceived and drawn by the brain and pencil of Christopher Wren. The surviving buildings by Wren are a noble group, though none of the greater ones was built as the architect really intended. But alternative designs for those buildings, and drawings of masterpieces never even started, are almost more important for an insight into the splendour of Wren's mind. A few hours' study of the volumes brought out by the Wren Society can be just as valuable as a perambulation, between Cambridge, Oxford, the London area, Lincoln, and some other provincial districts, of the buildings

45 *Salisbury: the College of Matrons, 1682*
46 *Belton House, Lincolnshire, c.1680*

which certainly or probably owe all or most of their structure to Wren's designs.

Heredity, inclination, and his Oxford career first drew Wren to the career of a mathematician and a scientist. He was a leading member of the Royal Society and in 1681 was its President. He was Professor of Astronomy at Gresham College, London, and later in his own University of Oxford. His achievements as a scientist were considerable; it was from applied science, and as a man versed in constructional engineering, that he moved on to his second career as a designer of buildings. He might, indeed, have spent many crucial years of his life as Surveyor of the fortifications which were slowly erected at Tangier. Like Inigo Jones and the other builders of this period he had nothing of what we should call an architect's training; his architecture came from his own observation, genius, and commonsense, from books and prints, and from his long personal experience. He was, however, successful in creating a splendid team of building and decorative craftsmen. Edward Strong and Christopher Cass were among the senior masons who long worked for him, Grinling Gibbons achieved fame as his collaborator over brilliantly carved woodwork, and in Nicholas Hawksmoor his faithful Clerk of Works he trained an architect very nearly as gifted as himself.

As Wren seemed a promising building designer he got some interesting commissions before the peak years of his career. His two buildings of 1663—the Sheldonian Theatre at Oxford and Pembroke College Chapel at Cambridge—are unlike many other Wren projects in that both were built (as their architect always best liked) on empty, unimpeded sites. Both, moreover, were completed as Wren designed them; no political changes or shortage of money brought frustrations. Pembroke Chapel, like that at Emmanuel in the same University,* is a delightful, straightforward rectangular building. Both are talented works which would not, in fact, have been past the capacity of some other contemporary designer. Its pedimented façade, with simple giant Corinthian pilasters and a cupola perched above the pediment, was an early, uncomplicated work of its young designer, respectful of Renaissance precedents and in better taste than the exterior of the Sheldonian

---

* The grouping of Emmanuel Chapel, with its arcaded loggias on each side, derives from earlier Cambridge work at Peterhouse.

which was, because of its unusual construction, a building of more novelty and importance.

The Sheldonian 'Theatre' was built for public University ceremonies rather than for the performance of plays. But its D-shaped plan, with its pit and galleries inside, made it a building of the same general type as Wren's later playhouse at Drury Lane. It was inspired, from illustrations in a book by Serlio, by open-air theatres like that of Marcellus in Rome. As these had been covered, in sunny weather, by awnings drawn aside by ropes the Sheldonian's painted ceiling rather preciously includes imitation ropes in a criss-cross pattern across its surface. What mattered more, however, was what one does not see—the ingenious and novel arrangement of special timber trusses designed to sustain an unusually wide flat roof.

By 1665, with good royalist patronage behind him, Wren must have realised that his future career might well lie in architecture. So in that year, and early in 1666, he spent valuable months in and near Paris which in that heyday of Louis XIV was full of important recent buildings and current architectural activity. This was his only trip abroad. Unlike Jones he had no personal knowledge of Italy; as his career progressed, and as he widened his quest for models to follow, he relied on what he could glean from Dutch, French, or Italian prints and illustrated books. His short Paris encounter with Bernini seems not to have helped him. But his meetings with French architects, and his close observation of buildings by le Vau, Mansart, and other leading exponents of France's severe, unemotional Baroque were long a leading influence on his work. They were specially fresh in his mind when he planned the renovation, and then the complete rebuilding of St Paul's.

ST PAUL'S AND THE CITY CHURCHES

Despite Inigo Jones's repairs and alterations, the cathedral was in a wretched state by the 1660s. The central tower, though no longer supporting the weight of its steeple, was a particular worry. A commission was established to consider action. To this Commission Wren presented plans a few days before the Great Fire. He proposed to case the interior of the Norman nave with stonework in a Renaissance idiom. More important still, he suggested a great dome, with a hideously elongated pineapple on top, to replace the Gothic central tower. To make the required central space the ends of the aisles were to be cut away as in the Octagon of his uncle's cathedral at Ely. The young designer had lately seen and admired some important domed churches in Paris, and his other drawings clearly show that he much favoured domes and monumental cupolas. Many of those he designed, but never saw built, are more fancifully Baroque than the few he completed.

Wren's long connection with St Paul's is well known, well documented, and fully chronicled. It was nine years after the Fire before building work started on a new cathedral; in the meantime its architect had become deeply involved in other aspects of London's restoration.

A few days after the fire Wren produced a bold, imaginative, politically risky plan for rebuilding the burnt area of the City. Wide, straight streets and several piazzas and open spaces were to supersede the narrow, twisting streets and alleys which had previously abounded. Many gutted churches were to be replaced, though not always on their old sites. Wren's plan, better suited to a royal or governmental quarter than to England's commercial capital, was soon turned down. Despite important improvements in house design, and brick construction instead of mediaeval timber framing, the merchants soon reoccupied their old sites and the City's street plan stayed much as before. So such churches as were due for replacement had mainly to be rebuilt on cramped and often irregular sites. The City churches rebuilt under Wren's aegis splendidly show how their designer could fit new Renaissance buildings to difficult mediaeval sites, making clever adjustments to conditions forced upon him; this very English gift of the constant modification of earlier paper plans was among Wren's strongest points.

His parish churches, and his initial schemes for St Paul's were Wren's main concern for some fifteen years from 1670. Actual building operations first started on some City churches; on a few (as in the steeple and cupola of St Magnus) it continued early in the eighteenth century. Many Wren churches have perished by nineteenth-century demolition or under air attack in the 1940s, the Victorians being more effective destroyers than the Nazis. From the survivors, and from what we know of the others, we can see how varied and brilliant was this part of Wren's achievements. He never failed to fit a church successfully to its available ground. His plans were well conceived in that they did not look back to mediaeval naves and long chancels, but set a lasting fashion for 'auditory' interiors well suited to Anglican worship which laid more stress on the sermon than on the Eucharist. The bodies of his churches, bar Palladian features like the Corinthian half-columns and garlands of St Lawrence Jewry's east end, are seldom of exterior importance. But inside they presented a fascinating variety. Some, like Christ Church, Newgate Street and the 'pattern' Wren church of St James's, Piccadilly on its virgin site, were rectangular in plan with aisles, pillars, and galleries. St Mary le Bow was basilican in that it directly followed the plan of Maxentius' basilica in Rome. A few of the lesser buildings were unaisled rectangles, relying for splendour on rich carving in their altarpieces, pews, organ cases, and pulpits. A few, like the vanished St Mildred's, Bread Street, were square or rectangular with shallow domes (hardly visible from the street) to give added height and dignity to their simple spaces. Others combined domes with more complex interiors. Those of the demolished St Antholin's and St Benet Fink had sets of slim supporting pillars attractively arranged in an elongated polygon. Best of all, and among Wren's finest buildings, is the splendid church of St Stephen, Walbrook. For there the dome is upheld by a set of twelve Corinthian pillars, arranged in a square but with the nave, chancel, and transepts opening out from the dome-covered central space to give a cruciform effect within a rectangular ground plan. [49]

The exterior glory of Wren's churches mainly lies in their towers and steeples. The towers, whether conservatively Gothic or Renaissance in their artistry, were the successors to a lasting English tradition; some include earlier masonry that was solid enough to withstand the Fire. More important and exciting are the steeples whose stages, like spires, diminish in size as they approach their summits. Partly Italian in their inspiration, they also drew on the examples, nearer home and known to Wren from illustrations, of the lately completed church steeples of Amsterdam.

Wren's steeples well displayed his resourcefulness in design; the later ones showed him moving from High Renaissance and Palladian artistry to the greater fancy of Italian Baroque. Among his earlier steeples is the splendid composition at St Mary le Bow, with its topmost spirelet rising from a lantern which is itself above a circular, pillared *tempietto*. At St Martin, Ludgate a slender spire rises high above a lantern and a bulbous cupola in the Dutch manner, while a charming cluster of miniature columns supports other Baroque details at St

James's, Garlickhythe. Christ Church, Newgate Street has three varied square compositions in a sharply diminishing sequence, while the graceful steeple of St Bride's has its spirelet perched above a set of simple octagonal stages. Of special note is the late steeple of St Vedast's. For there the main stage below the spirelet is concave-sided, looking clearly to Roman Baroque designing by the great master Borromini; so too, with differences, do the two western towers of St Paul's. [47]

London's present cathedral is unique in England, without predecessors or followers of its own scale or style. It has a complex background of alternative schemes, and of great changes in the design officially approved in 1675. It is not what Wren really wished to erect on the cleared site. Yet when in 1710 he saw it finished he could look with pride on a great achievement of design, and of skill in suiting the requirements of his clients and meeting the demands of a structure new to England's architectural scene.

Wren's favourite design was that of 1673 of which a large model survives. Apart from a western vestibule and an entrance portico of giant Corinthian columns, this 'model' plan was the mathematical intellectual's ideal of the Greek cross whose arms are all equal. The splendid dome above the main worshipping area was to cover a great circular space. But the clergy, respecting what the Middle Ages and the Anglican church have required as the setting for choir services, rejected this plan; Brasilia and Mount Pleasant in Liverpool are now experimenting with the virtues of a round cathedral. What the Restoration divines obtained from Wren was a mediaevally planned church with a long eastern limb to hold its choir, and with a slightly longer nave beyond the dome retained from the pre-Fire scheme and from the 'model' design. The flanking chapels off the nave may derive from Lincoln Cathedral where Wren had lately worked in another connection.

The 'Warrant' design of 1675 established the main plan of the new St Paul's. Yet the actual building is much unlike it. Wren showed great skill in so altering his neo-mediaeval design as to make the cathedral seem a wholly Renaissance masterpiece, with many details drawing less on the Palladians and seventeenth-century France than on the more recent examples of Roman Baroque.

The new cathedral was started in 1675; then and later Wren made many changes for the better in the supposedly approved design. Among his new features were the screen walls, pilastered and with pedimented niches instead of windows, which rise above the aisles and hide from all but aerial view the flying buttresses which sustain the main vaults. The curved porches of the transepts freely copy that designed by Pietro da Cortona for Sta Maria della Pace in Rome, while the comparatively slender pillars of the two-storeyed western portico replaced Wren's giant Corinthian order because his favourite quarries at Portland could not send huge enough blocks of stone. The splendidly fanciful western towers are a Borrominian touch, partly inspired by pictures of S. Agnese in Piazza Navona. The superb central drum, dome, and lantern are immeasurably nobler than the strange composition, capped by a steeple like that of St Bride's, shown in the 'Warrant' drawing. Like much else in St Paul's the dome blends Italian and French elements with stylistic touches and building devices which are all Wren's own. Its main interest is constructional. For the stone lantern and its surmounting cross rest not on the outwardly visible dome of lead-sheathed timber, but on a great brick cone concealed by the outer dome, and from within by an inner dome upholding nothing but the railings round its central opening. Lesser domes, shallow and saucer-shaped in the manner of a few city churches, and of some later churches not by Wren, cover the main bays of the choir and nave. The piers of the arcades are square in the Renaissance manner, with beautifully rendered, non-structural pilasters to stand below the arches and mark off the cathedral's bays.

Though it must have fallen short of its architect's hopes, St Paul's was Wren's greatest masterpiece.* I cannot deal here with all his other works and projects, or with the many 'attributions' to the second great English architect who became a legend. Three libraries, four palaces, and two splendid charitable buildings must illustrate his versatility and power.

By Wren's time the long, rectangular plan, with presses projecting at right angles from the walls, was well established for the libraries of learned bodies. In 1674 Wren designed such a building for Dean Honywood at Lincoln Cathedral. His simple rectangular block is at first-floor level, being supported on a round-arched arcade of Roman Doric columns on one side of the mediaeval cloister. Similar in conception,

---

* One should not overlook Wren's Deanery; it is one of the few houses authentically by him and proves how splendidly he could handle the masses and profiles of brickwork.

though grander in scale and more splendid in detail, was the library started, in 1676, to close the riverward side of Nevile's Court at Trinity, Cambridge; Wren's original idea had been for a circular, domed building. Sansovino's Venetian library may have suggested some stylistic details, particularly the Ionic three-quarter columns which face the court. More revealing for Wren's sense of architectural sympathy was his treatment of the library floor over its open piazza. For the floor comes down to the level of the first storey of the neighbouring buildings, being supported not by Wren's arches, whose upper parts are blind, but by a set of transverse beams level with the crowns of the older arches on each side of the court. Another fine library with an open space below it was that of Queen's College, Oxford, debatable as between Wren and Hawksmoor, and with its lower space enclosed in the 1840s. [50]

COURT COMMISSIONS

From 1669 Wren held the post of Surveyor General (with consequent work on such buildings as a storehouse in the Tower of London). But it was late in Charles II's reign before he got his chance to design a palace. That at Winchester was started in 1683. After Charles II's death it was left unfinished, became barracks, and was pulled down in modern times after a serious fire. Its plans allowed for considerable dignity. A three-sided court would have had a fine portico and above it a dome. The Palace also showed, as did many other mansions of this time, how well Wren and his contemporaries could handle the beautiful mixture of red brick and dressings of silvery stone. Had Wren's full ideas been realised a broad street, in a ruthless stroke of monumental planning, would have led down from the Palace to the Cathedral's west front.

The design and building of palaces and royal residences was the part of Wren's work most often at the mercy of short reigns, political vicissitudes, and the veerings of royal taste. His ambitious schemes for Windsor Castle remained on paper; it was his rival Hugh May, like Wren an important official in the Royal Works, who actually made important changes in the castle's living quarters. For Westminster Wren planned a splendid new Parliament House, but in fact only made adaptations in St Stephen's Chapel, already long in use for the cramped sittings of the Commons. At Whitehall Palace he achieved nothing for

Charles II, but for James II he built the wing which contained the lavishly Baroque Catholic chapel whose carvings by Gibbons and Arnold
Quellinus of Antwerp astonished Protestant observers. The whole
Palace, bar Jones's Banqueting House, was burnt in 1698. For William
III, who still expected a long reign and had no anticipations of the
Little Gentleman in Black Velvet, Wren designed a new Palace whose
extent and Baroque splendour would have far exceeded all his surviving
works; the scheme included some unhappily insensitive alterations to
the Banqueting House which Wren actually fitted up as Whitehall
Chapel. Only at Kensington and Hampton Court did the Crown's
Surveyor General carry out work which has lasted.

Kensington Palace's southern side ranks among Wren's less spectacular works. But its brick, in the Dutch manner, displays a beautifully
handled group of surfaces, well showing how well this material was
now understood in eastern England. Brick and stone were chosen for
the two wings, very dignified and finely adorned if a little tame with
their flat silhouette, which Wren built for William and Mary as additions to the Tudor Palace at Hampton Court. Here again an attractive
reality fell short of a superb Baroque plan which could have given
Dutch William a rival to the Versailles of his great Continental adver-
sary. Largely French Baroque in its inspiration, this courtyard Palace
would have had a superb main entrance with great Corinthian half-
columns, and with an attic storey crowned by a bell-shaped dome.
Wren's drawings for this unachieved Palace well prove how many of his
noblest conceptions never arose in brick or stone. His actual blocks at
Hampton Court were none the less a considerable success. Their decoration by Wren's team of craftsmen, and the brilliant garden ironwork of the Huguenot smith Tijou who also worked at St Paul's, help
to make this Palace as important a shrine of England's Baroque as it is
of her late Gothic and early Renaissance.

Of Wren's two hospitals for superannuated warriors that at Chelsea
was started in 1682. It is the simpler of the two, a dignified, severe
building in brick and stone; its layout resembles that of many almshouses
and colleges. Its central cupola, and two simple Roman Doric porticoes,
are its main monumental features. More grandiose, and reminding the
beholder that its oldest buildings were once those of a waterside Palace,
is the Seamen's Hospital (now the Royal Naval College) at Greenwich.
Best seen from the Isle of Dogs across the Thames, it succeeded, in the

last decades of Wren's active life and at a time when both Hawksmoor and Vanbrugh had a large hand in its completion, in being Wren's one fulfilled scheme of monumental planning. Yet here too there is a background of frustration and of favoured plans turned down. [51]

Queen Mary II was the founder of Greenwich Hospital; its main details were settled a few weeks before she died in 1694. She insisted on the retention of Webb's block, and that the great courtyard enclosure of the Hospital should be open at the top to allow a view of the Queen's House. At the top of the hill Wren's Observatory of 1675 appeared in the distance. Wren himself, however, had more monumental ideas. While sparing the Queen's house he wished to veil it from the river by a splendid main range containing the pensioners' hall and chapel. This block was to be graced with a grand portico, and by a dome artistically closer to St Peter's at Rome that to St Paul's a few miles upstream. Again Wren had to use his brilliant powers of adaptation, producing so monumentally successful a layout that one hardly worries over the frustration of something even more splendid. The lower court, with a replica of the Charles II Building facing Webb's block, gave Wren no trouble, for Webb's work of the 1660s was like much of his own. But the upper portion was narrowed to the width of the Queen's House which closed the vista. The noble Painted Hall and the chapel ran at right angles to the upper court, while that court was lined with Roman Doric colonnades which lead the eye to the Palladian simplicity of the Queen's House. More elaborate features crown the entrance bays of the hall and chapel. For we see an admirable pair of domes, the only monumental ones, apart from St Paul's, that Wren actually saw built. Their supporting cornices and colonnettes recall Roman Baroque; the domes themselves derive freely from Michelangelo at St Peter's. [51]

The building of Greenwich Hospital involved some of Wren's important successors and brings us well past 1700. By 1700 the work of Wren, and of other English architects of his time, had been thoroughly done. Wren himself worked little on private mansions, and the style of the country houses of his time owed more to the examples of Pratt and Webb, and to Dutch Palladian borrowings (as at Eltham) by Hugh May and others, than to the Surveyor General's more ambitious visions. By May and his contemporaries, both in London and in the provinces, the pattern was now set for solid, compact houses built in the Dutch manner by middling squires, merchants, and gentleman clothiers. Downton

50 *Trinity College, Cambridge: the library, by Wren, 1676–84*
51 *Greenwich Hospital, by Webb, Wren, and others;*
the Queen's House, by Inigo Jones, is in the centre

in Wiltshire, South Shoebury in Essex, Nether Lypiatt near Stroud, and the similar fronts of Tintinhull in Somerset and the Palace at Lichfield, all show delightful domestic work of the 'Restoration' and 'William and Mary' school. High-pitched roofs with bold dormer windows, projecting eaves, and doorways, windows, and fireplaces edged with bulging 'bolection' mouldings were common in such houses. So too were principal doorways crowned by 'shell-pattern' hoods, or by pediments segmental in shape or broken in the middle to receive an urn or a Baroque heraldic cartouche. Gothic, except in some churches or academic buildings, was now regarded as antiquarianism or whimsy, nearly everything being designed and built in idioms unmistakeably of the Renaissance. All over England seemly, solid, decorative buildings arose to prove the skill of unrecorded masons and craftsmen or of such known provincial designers as Sir William Wilson in Warwickshire, Robert Grumbold at Cambridge, and Henry Bell of King's Lynn who seems also to have worked on the reconstruction of Northampton. Their work, like that of such famous architects as Hawksmoor, Vanbrugh, and William Talman, overlaps the chronological division between the seventeenth and eighteenth centuries.

CHAPTER EIGHT

The Eighteenth Century

1700–1800

The hundred years from 1700 to 1800 are on any count of tremendous importance for a chronicler of England's architecture. The country's economy was steadily expanding, and the rise of a much larger educated middle class increased those who had the means and taste to patronise architects. From about 1760 the Industrial Revolution encouraged a swift population growth, particularly in the towns of the North and Midlands. Though many new dwelling houses were too unpretending to come easily under our 'architectural' heading the sheer quantity of the more notable buildings was impressive. The range of architecture was, moreover, much widened so as to include buildings made necessary by new economic events. From the naval dockyards to imposing mills in the Stroud Valley and Lancashire, and from canal viaducts and tunnels to iron bridges the architecture of industry and transport became newly significant. New materials (cast iron in particular) joined stone and brick in Georgian building technique; so notable were some of these structural novelties that the Shropshire Iron Bridge is more important than many staid Palladian mansions. But in buildings of the more traditional type, especially in country mansions and formal urban compositions, style and structure remained divorced. Main walls, of brick or stone, were the load-bearing elements; it did not really matter whether the decorative veneer was Doric, Ionic, Corinthian, or all three at once as in the Circus at Bath. Porticoes and pediments became optional features, and often 'status symbols' in buildings which aped the dignity of temples or palaces, while Georgian terraces, like theatrical scenery and the west fronts of Continental or Latin American

Baroque churches, displayed a certain dishonesty in their architecture of façades. A walk round the back of an outwardly splendid Georgian terrace or crescent can often bring sad disillusionment.

From now onwards we know the names of far more designers to whom buildings can safely be attributed. Traditional mason-craftsmen still abounded, but well-known architects like Hawksmoor, Vanbrugh, Gibbs, Kent, Flitcroft, the Woods of Bath, Chambers, Taylor, Robert Adam, Henry Holland, and Soane, tend to dominate the scene. Local figures like Wing of Leicester and the Bastards in Dorset are important in their own areas. Yet the architectural profession was still embryonic, and architects' training was haphazard and rudimentary. James Gibbs, with his four years in the Rome 'office' of Carlo Fontana, was unusual, and rarely qualified, among England's early Georgian architects. But by 1800 the system of training by pupillage, already justified by Hawksmoor's relationship to Wren, was well established. Academic training also made its entry, though England still had little to compare with the highly organised system of France's Academy of Architecture. Yet the Royal Academy Schools now gave lectures on architecture, and when in 1806 John Soane (who had learnt his architecture from his builder father and then under George Dance the younger and Henry Holland) became Professor of Architecture he restarted the lapsed architectural lectures and steadily continued them. The new status and competence of the architectural profession led, in 1835, to the founding of the Institute of British Architects.

In most of England's eighteenth-century buildings the main principles of design were those of the symmetrical, well-balanced classical tradition. Even those whose outward appearance was Gothic were apt to follow those rules; much Georgian Gothic, as late as the 1830s, is Renaissance architecture in a pseudo-mediaeval dress. The general tone, if unexciting, was one of poised and rational good taste. Architectural good manners, with urban buildings tending to respect the scale, style, and height of their neighbours, were normally observed. Georgian 'Gothick' was almost unique to England. But in its classical aspects this country's architecture of the eighteenth century lay strongly under Continental influence, though some exuberant aspects of Continental architecture were rejected, and much of what was adapted was substantially modified. From about 1770 neoclassicism looks back, as the English province of a great international art movement, to a rediscovered

Antiquity. It led, in the early nineteenth century, to the Greek Revival. This was even more international, differing little whether its buildings were in Germany, France, England, or the United States. Within eighteenth-century England one could distinguish the three classical phases of modified Baroque, Palladian, and 'Adam'.

ENGLISH BAROQUE

It has been said that England never had any real Baroque, and that the style's drama and emotionalism (linked to the visible expression of Catholicism) were alien to the English temper and unacceptable in late Stuart and Georgian religious and political conditions. Religion and politics certainly had their restraining influence, and the full exuberance of Baroque is better seen in England in church monuments and interior decoration than in actual buildings. Much sculpture, wood-carving, and metalwork of fully Baroque character was done not by Englishmen but by immigrants from Flanders, France, or Italy. Yet there was a short and promising period when unexecuted plans and finished buildings proved that English designers could participate in the great art movement which flourished more freely in Catholic Europe.

Sir Christopher Wren was the truest pioneer of the English Baroque school. His influence, and some of his unexecuted designs, had a great effect on the work of those who immediately followed his peak years. Vanbrugh's Castle Howard, for instance, owes the notion of its dominant block to the palatial central section intended by Wren for the top side of the courtyard at Greenwich. After Wren himself our leading Baroque figures were Hawksmoor, a Wiltshireman named William Talman, Sir John Vanbrugh, the man of the theatre who turned architect and never lost his taste for the dramatic, and the Warwickshire 'gentleman architect' Thomas Archer whose foreign travels included Rome, and whose work showed directly observed Borrominian influences. Provincial areas also had their Baroque practitioners, so that in the West Midlands, the North, and the western counties many buildings with strongly Baroque details long vied with the more stylish, socially accepted Palladianism.

Of the leading figures William Talman is of the least consequence. Yet the giant order and bold voussoir blocks of his windows in the south wing at Chatsworth make it a striking composition; added drama comes from his device of a horizontal, unpedimented silhouette with its balustrade and a skyline picked out with fine Baroque urns. The same effect appears, more modestly, on the eastern half of Dyrham in Gloucestershire, designed by Talman in 1698.

The main greatness of English Baroque lies in the interconnected work of Hawksmoor and Vanbrugh, inspired by Wren, continuing his achievement, yet with its own fantasy, ingenuity, invention, and faults. One cannot yet say for certain how far Castle Howard, Blenheim, the continuation of Greenwich, and some other buildings were of Hawksmoor's designing, and how much was contributed by Vanbrugh's unaided brain. Both men had talent amounting to genius; their combined work ranks with Wren's buildings, those designed by Inigo Jones, and the churches planned by the leading mediaeval master masons, among the greatest treasures of England's architecture. Hawksmoor may claim credit for some late buildings attributed to Wren. He participated in the work done at Kensington Palace, while at Christ's Hospital the pilastered, segmentally pedimented Writing School of 1692 seems really to have been his. Then from 1699 at Castle Howard, and after 1705 when Blenheim was being built, he was certainly the experienced *éminence grise* behind Vanbrugh the nominal designer. For John Vanbrugh was still an architectural novice, and must have learned much from his more modest, supremely competent colleague. In Vanbrugh, we find another brilliant English designer whose architectural training was haphazard. One must, however, remember that the builders and masons of those times knew much about structures and the technique of actual building, and the Georgian 'architects' needed to know little of what we require by way of plumbing, lighting, and ventilation.

Hawksmoor's earliest independent commission seems to have been the Northamptonshire mansion of Easton Neston, designed before 1700 and completed without its intended wings; in the manner of Wren, and of Talman at Chatsworth, it was adorned round its main block with a most dignified giant order of Composite half-columns and pilasters. Next come the two great palace-mansions on which Hawksmoor and Vanbrugh worked together. Both of them, particularly Blenheim, are very well known. Castle Howard had the more striking skyline, with a dome which must have pleased Wren when he knew of it, and which covers a nobly spacious central hall. Taken together, these vast, unrepeatable and unrepeated houses well show the main characteristics of English Baroque as practised by their two architects. They both have the central block and balancing wings which were also dear to the Palladians. Though their upright and horizontal lines reject the curves and sinuosities of Mediterranean Baroque they are full of drama and paradox in the bold grouping of their architectural masses. A noble solidity of masonry, much favoured by Hawksmoor and Vanbrugh (as by Wren and Gibbs), reinforces their impression of triumphant grandeur. The giant order, in halls and staterooms as well as on the exterior, is part of the same technique. At Blenheim, too, we see the horizontal, deeply scored rustication, of wall surfaces and heavy Doric pillars, which Hawksmoor used on the London church of St Mary Woolnoth, and which Vanbrugh dramatically displayed at Grimsthorpe, Eastbury, and Seaton Delaval. [52]

Hawksmoor, like Wren, had his experience of frustrated projects. His plan, of about 1713, for the remodelling of central Cambridge showed a sweeping vision like that of Wren when planning a new City of London. He also got out more than one ambitious scheme for the remodelling of central Oxford, with important new buildings but with more respect for existing ones than Wren needed amid the charred desolation of London. Moreover it was Hawksmoor, not Gibbs the actual architect, who first envisaged a circular Radcliffe Library set spaciously in a specially cleared square. As Gibbs was eventually chosen for the new buildings at King's, Hawksmoor built nothing at Cambridge. At Oxford his screen at Queen's, with its graceful pillared cupola over the foundress's statue, is an admirable work,* while the Clarendon Building is dignified though less moving than most Hawksmoor designs. But his Gothic quad at All Souls lacks the light charm of some later Georgian Gothic, and its two towers are among the less happy elements in Oxford's skyline; their upper stages are a mediaevalised version of those in Hawksmoor's fine pair of churches in East London, and are even closer to the lantern which he designed for the tower of Greenwich parish church. His grandiose ideas for Worcester, Brasenose, and Magdalen Colleges were never even attempted.

---

* But one of Hawksmoor's alternative projects, with a dominating entrance tower supported by gargantuan Doric columns, would have produced one of Oxford's most hideous buildings; there were times when 'fancy' and megalomania could lead Hawksmoor astonishingly astray.

Hawksmoor's most compact and successful achievement lies in the six London churches built to his designs between 1712 and 1730. All bar St Mary Woolnoth were on unencumbered sites. So Hawksmoor could plan, more freely than Wren, for the precise requirements of Queen Anne High Anglicanism. Their plans vary from the markedly basilican Christ Church, Spitalfields, with its noble Corinthian arcades and transverse barrel vaults, to the square main compartments at Bloomsbury and St Mary Woolnoth; the church at Greenwich and the two in the East End are more rectangular. Unusual, impressive features abound, notably the *westwerk* and lanterned steeple at Limehouse, the four silhouetted cupolas of St George's, the unusual portico and patterned tower at Spitalfields, and the Borrominian niches on one side of St Mary Woolnoth. Hawksmoor shone as an inventive handler of the masses and contrasting surfaces of what Dr Downes has called the 'cubic geometry' of masonry. In his parish churches (except for his inept steeple at Bloomsbury) he may fairly be said to have equalled his master. [48]

Hawksmoor outlived Vanbrugh, and his domed and pillared circular Mausoleum at Castle Howard was unfinished when he died. Vanbrugh's later houses were an anticlimax after Castle Howard and Blenheim. But Seaton Delaval, with its bulky, powerfully masoned main block and the flanking wings of its vast forecourt, showed that he never lost his stagecraft. At Kingsweston, moreover, the spacing of his great pilasters recalled the main entrance of Blenheim, Townsend of Oxford's masonry is superb, and the arcade of chimney-stacks added drama to the skyline of Severnside.

No less Baroque in spirit, and aided by having seen Borromini's work in Rome, was Thomas Archer. He designed less than Hawksmoor, and nothing on the Vanbrugh scale, but enough to give him real importance. Corinthian columns with inturned volutes, windows at Heythrop copying those of a Borromini palace, and dramatically split pediments at Monmouth House and on St John's, Smith Square, proclaimed his aesthetic allegiance. So too did some cartouches and other external details on his excellent church (now the cathedral) at Birmingham. His most famous works are two 'centrally' planned churches. The brilliant St Paul's at Deptford was started in 1712; it has a curved entrance porch, and a steeple very much in Wren's manner. St John's at Westminster, most striking with its good masonry, Roman Doric order,

52   *Castle Howard, by Sir John Vanbrugh, started 1699*
53   *Cambridge: the Senate House, by James Gibbs, 1722–30*

and four corner towers like a quartet of Athenian choragic monuments, is as dramatic and challenging as anything by Hawksmoor.

Our English tradition of modified Baroque was also carried on by many provincial designers; their buildings coincided with the more fashionable mansions of the Palladians. Bell's pair of twisted Corinthian columns flanked a doorway in King's Lynn, while in Hereford, Birmingham, and some western clothing towns other craftsmen produced their attractive 'swan's neck' pediments. In these, the two sides rose in sinuous double curves towards the central break, turning over at their ends in decorative volutes. Inturned volutes of the Archer–Borromini type occur on capitals put up after 1731 by the Bastards in Blandford, and in the work of the Somerset builder Nathaniel Ireson. Thomas White of Worcester worked in Wren's manner when in 1719 he started Worcester's new Guildhall, ornate in its decoration of sculptured panels and window aprons, and with its large segmental pediment richly filled with George I's arms and a vaunting trophy of weapons. A similar pediment once graced the middle of the long terrace of officer's houses in the dockyard at Devonport. For now was the time for urban groupings as well as separate houses. So in Queen Square, Bristol, Minor Canon Row at Rochester, and Maid of Honour Row at Richmond Queen Anne and early Georgian masons, bricklayers, and joiners built simple rows of houses demurely picked out with Baroque embellishments. Almshouses, as in Liverpool's Blue Coat Hospital and in the superb Yorkshire grouping at Kirkleatham, partook of the same trend. These buildings carried on the sober traditions established in Wren's time; it was extraordinary when in 1735 John Strahan of Bristol built Rosewell House at Bath with its ornate frontage imitating South Germany's fanciful Baroque. For more elaborate Baroque impressions, whether Flemish or Italian, we must turn to interior decoration in carved wood or plaster, and to church monuments and mural cartouches. Roman Baroque, as he knew it at its fountain-head, was thus superbly recreated in the Duke of Newcastle's monument set up, in Westminster Abbey in 1723, to the architectural design of James Gibbs.

JAMES GIBBS

Gibbs's training and tastes set him apart from his contemporaries who worked within the rigidly bookish discipline of Palladianism. Though

54 St Mary le Strand, London, by James Gibbs, 1714–17;
behind, St Clement Danes

some of his clients insisted on Palladian designs Gibbs's own preference was for the restrained Roman Baroque of his master Carlo Fontana. His years of Roman training, and his Scottish thoroughness and tenacity made him an outstanding figure. He was less of a genius than Hawksmoor or Vanbrugh, but his sheer talent put him ahead of nearly all his competitors. Yet his Scots birth was a disadvantage, and though he hid his Catholicism his Jacobite politics lost him his New Churches Surveyorship and Burlington's patronage. Nor did the tastes of the dominant magnates dispose them to architectural Baroque. The career of Gibbs, like those of Wren and Hawksmoor, was also conditioned by the premature deaths of some patrons and by other external factors. So Gibbs, like Wren, is as well studied in unexecuted plans as in his famous buildings. But those buildings, and his books, gave him a leading place in a century well supplied with good architects. Gibbs's earliest building was St Mary le Strand. It was started in 1713, a narrow, unaisled church on an island site, considerably Baroque but also with strong elements of sixteenth-century Italian Renaissance design, and with a steeple in Wren's manner for which Gibbs made five alternative designs. Then in 1719 he added a particularly brilliant steeple in Wren's idiom to Sir Christopher's nearby church of St Clement Danes. **[54]**

A few of Gibbs's later buildings were Baroque in character. The octagonal music parlour, added about 1720 to Orleans House at Twickenham, has a severe brick exterior but is resplendent inside with Corinthian pilasters, sculptured busts, and ornate plasterwork by Gibbs's favoured Italian *stuccatori* Artari and Bagutti. In such a building, as in miniature temples and 'follies' dispersed in parks and formal gardens, a Georgian architect was freer to indulge his fancy than in the main structures he designed. At Sudbrooke Park, Petersham, Gibbs created a splendid cubical room of about 1726, with a giant order of Corinthian pilasters and Baroque decorative touches. Then in 1737 he started his un-Palladian masterpiece, the Radcliffe Library at Oxford. The idea of a circular library had been Hawksmoor's, but Gibbs's noble building, with its rusticated lower storey, an imposing rotunda of paired Corinthian columns, rococo plasterwork by Artari, and a ribbed dome which owes much to St Peter's in Rome, looks clearly to Italian precedents other than those of Vicenza.

Church monuments apart, most of Gibbs's other work stayed soberly within Roman classic conventions. In his country houses this point is evident at Ditchley (despite some Baroque touches both within and without) and at Bank Hall (now the Town Hall) in Warrington. So too the restraining hand of a patronage inclined to Palladianism is evident in Gibbs's unexecuted design for a finely porticoed Lowther Castle, in many of his drawings, and in the plans printed in his *Book of Architecture* of 1728. Of his other buildings the Senate House at Cambridge, dignified and Roman with its pediments and giant Corinthian order, owed something of its design to James Burrough, like Dean Aldrich at Oxford both a don and a notable amateur architect. The Senate House and the Gibbs Building at King's are both mere fragments of larger projects never wholly carried out; their date range is 1722 to 1731. St Bartholomew's Hospital in London, a fine quadrangle whose blocks were built separate to lessen the risk of fire, is more satisfactory in that the whole design was eventually carried out, a dignified enclosure of severe, well composed buildings, the lower windows being edged with the rustication blocks much favoured by Gibbs. Elaboration was, however, admitted in the administrative block, with Baroque decoration in the Committee Room, Italian rococo plaster work in the Great Hall, and mural paintings by Hogarth on the grand staircase's walls. [53]

More famous, and more influential than Hawksmoor's highly individual designs, were some of Gibbs's plans for churches. At St Peter's, Vere Street (designed in 1721) and St Martin-in-the-Fields (of 1722–26), and in 1724 at All Hallows (now the Cathedral) at Derby Gibbs rationalised, in a manner easy to take as a universal model, the body of a new Anglican church which Wren had pioneered on some of his varied sites. The steeple of St Martin's, though awkwardly placed above the fine Corinthian portico, is itself a graceful, sophisticated essay in Wren's manner of successively diminishing Baroque stages and a crowning spirelet. Here too, as at St Mary le Strand, Gibbs made some alternative designs for the church as a whole. His plans for a circular building were followed by George Steuart in the neoclassic St Chad's at Shrewsbury, and about 1790 in the brilliant All Saints', Newcastle-upon-Tyne. The actual church had many followers, among them St John's, Waterloo Road a century after St Martin's was built. Some of Gibbs's six alternative designs for St Martin's steeple were adapted not only in this country but by overseas builders, especially in North America, who studied the prints in the *Book of Architecture*. For designs were now diffused by lavish pattern books produced in England. A few years before London admired the Roman classicism of St Martin's this new aspect of architectural tuition had been steered back to Palladianism by the titled example and faithful entourage of the Earl of Burlington.

THE PALLADIANS

The Hanoverian dynasty appeared in England in 1714. The first Jacobite rising occurred next year; so too did the publication of Colen Campbell's *Vitruvius Britannicus* and Giacomo Leoni and Nicholas Dubois' English edition of Palladio's *Quattro Libri dell' Architettura*. For once a new political phase almost coincided with an architectural revolution, and 'Georgian' is a reasonable title for the architecture whose Grecian period outlasted the four Georges.

A few tentative returns to Inigo Jones's Palladianism had been made under Queen Anne. But it was after 1715 that fashionable England settled down to the balanced, dignified neo-Romanism of the Palladian revival. The two books of 1715, and others in following years, helped greatly to spread the style. So too did the example of Lord Burlington the amateur architect, and the fact that antique Rome and Vicenza were essential stages on the Grand Tour which became an ever more important cultural influence among the young gentlemen of England, enlarging their minds and giving them hints for the rebuilding of ancestral homes and the embellishment of parks and formal gardens.

The young Lord Burlington was himself most significant in Georgian Palladianism. Returning from Italy he threw himself with zest into the diffusion of the style, making it known to patrons and builders by his sponsorship of the English edition of Palladio and by his own activity (especially in his villa at Chiswick and in the admirable suite of the York Assembly Rooms) as a designer in the style whose influential apostle he had become. Along with architects like Campbell, Leoni himself at Moor Park and Lyme Hall, Flitcroft, William Kent and Isaac Ware, he established a virtual dictatorship of taste. Provincial masons might cling for some years to a Wrennish Baroque. But among the dominant aristocracy, mainly Whig or moderate Tory, Burlingtonian Palladianism became the chosen style; it was also used by such Tory diehards as the Duke of Beaufort who employed Kent at Badminton. So the careful proportions of Vitruvius became those which an English gentleman had to follow in his hall and in the saloon leading out of it, and in his front portico if he could afford one. Wings, which often contained stables and kitchens, were neatly balanced on each side of a central block. Some, as at Wanstead and Wentworth Woodhouse, or in the 1740s on a smaller scale on Clifton Hill House and Clifton Court above Bristol, abutted directly on the central mass, their walls combining with it to form a continuous façade. Elsewhere, as at Holkham, short vestibules connected these wings and the main mansion. The all-important balance and symmetry of the Renaissance were thus maintained. The construction of the load-bearing walls, and of roof timbers

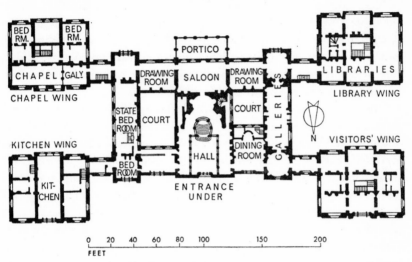

55   *Holkham Hall, Norfolk, designed by William Kent, 1734: a Palladian plan with a double set of flanking wings*

or floor joists, was much as in the century before. Some exteriors were of brick with stone dressings, but most aristocrats preferred the greater dignity and ambition of stone.

The best display of Palladianism, and of the antique Romanism expressed by its opulent rustication, by its columns and pilasters, and in its friezes and pediments, lay in the monumental exterior treatment of mansions and of palace-like terraces in London or Bath. The great work of the Palladians was to standardise, for some fifty years, an architecture of great dignity and restrained repose, the style that in early Hanoverian conditions had the best chance of fashionable acceptance. For it suited an educated class which prided itself on its Latin culture and Roman *gravitas*, whose Whig politics followed the guiding lights of Reason and Enlightenment, whose decorous Anglicanism rejected Enthusiasm, and whose good taste sought a discreet, universally accepted uniformity. As the Palladians had steeped themselves in a great tradition their buildings inevitably displayed admirable proportions, fine balance and an ornamentation never risky, excessive, or out of place. So great mansions like Houghton or Holkham in Norfolk, public buildings like the elder Wood of Bath's Exchanges at Bristol and Liverpool,* the same architect's pedimented northern terrace in Queen Square at Bath, and his mansion of Prior Park looking down on the city, are inspiring architectural adornments of the English scene. In them Palladianism reached its monumental best. At its most standardised and least inspired, as in some London houses by Ware and Vardy, and in some lesser streets in early Hanoverian Bath, it had much of the dullness pilloried in the *Dunciad*. [56, 57]

Among Georgian England's more striking Palladian buildings were those closely copying some by Palladio himself. The Villa Capra (or Rotonda) at Vicenza was a house whose domed circular hall and four porticoes enthralled the Burlingtonian imagination. It became the model, in Kent, for Colen Campbell's Mereworth Castle and a mansion at Foot's Cray, and for Burlington (with one portico) in his summer villa at Chiswick. More playful, among park embellishments, are the covered Palladian bridges at Wilton and Prior Park, while at Stourhead in Wiltshire Flitcroft's beautiful lake-side Pantheon derives from that in Rome. The idea of the formal terrace was splendidly continued in Grosvenor Square, London and in Queen Square, Bath, while fine individual houses like York's Mansion House also enriched England's urban architecture. But the churches of the period, despite Venetian windows in St Julian's, Shrewsbury and in some by White of Worcester or the Woodwards of Chipping Campden, were less indebted to Palladio than to Wren or Gibbs. More notable still was the loose link of the severe symmetries of Palladian architecture with interior adornment. For the Italians' plasterwork, and the Baroque sculpture of the immigrant Rysbrack or Scheemakers and of Sir Henry Cheere the Englishman, were like Paul Lamerie's silver and the furniture of the walnut period in their adherence to Baroque conventions which were

* The latter of these two (now the Town Hall) has been much altered since it was built.

accepted indoors but shunned for exteriors. The full co-ordination of building and decorative art had yet to arrive. [57]

By about 1760 the first impetus of Palladianism was exhausted. But for a few more years a severe version of the style continued, with even less exterior adornment than that favoured by the Burlington school. Sir Robert Taylor, James Paine, John Carr of York, and the younger John Wood of Bath were among the important architects, along with many local and provincial designers. They designed houses and public buildings of massive size and imposing Roman gravity. Stone Building at Lincoln's Inn, unusual in that it has pedimented and pillared ends but no central feature, is a dignified work by Taylor, while Carr designed the great block of Harewood House in the 1760s and the arcaded Crescent at Buxton later in his career. Paine's Mansion House at Doncaster is an early work, with its façade in the full Palladian manner making it one of provincial England's best public buildings.* More typical of Paine's later work is Wardour Castle in Wiltshire, a magnificently dignified work of the 1770s whose Corinthian pilasters and unevenly spaced three-quarter columns look south to the chalk downs over a park not formally laid out but landscaped, with studied clusters of trees, in the manner of 'Capability' Brown. Wood the younger's Royal Crescent at Bath is his best known work, simple and stately with its unbroken sweep of Ionic half columns above a plainly masoned lower storey. Some interiors here provide a strange decorative dissonance; the same thing happens in some houses by Bridges of Bristol and other West-of-England designers. For although some Royal Crescent houses have ceilings or fireplaces of the neoclassic designs which became normal by 1775 when the building was finished, one has a ceiling by some member of Bristol's group of rococo plasterworkers. Rococo plasterwork, and Georgian Gothic decorations, occur also in some houses in this Bath–Bristol district whose exteriors are demurely late Palladian, while at Claydon House in Buckinghamshire a severe exterior conceals an inner riot of rococo chinoiserie. Ornately chased silverware and rococo mirrors also co-existed, in these first two decades of George III's reign, with Palladian or neoclassic architectural design. The full assimilation of building and interior decoration was the main achievement of the period generally known by the name of Robert Adam.

The years between about 1760 and the outbreak of war in 1793

* Its attic storey is of a later date.

were full of architectural activity, not only on town and country mansions but on such varied buildings as town or shire halls (as at Bath,
Chelmsford, and Chester), hospitals and county infirmaries which continued a great movement of philanthropy already well established,
churches and Nonconformist chapels, barracks, and elegantly designed
bridges such as Richmond Bridge by Paine, Atcham Bridge near
Shrewsbury and Magdalen Bridge at Oxford by John Gwynne, and the
particularly splendid structure at Hexham by Robert Mylne who was
both a civil engineer and an architect. Churches, as one sees in St Paul's
at Birmingham, tended to be aisled and rectangular; among those without aisles, and of a novel, 'spatial' design, is All Hallows, London Wall,
a delightful, delicately plastered early building by the younger George
Dance, an architect who outlived both the eighteenth century and
the full transition to the 'Grecian' revival. Other churches, like William Paty's two buildings of the 1780s at Badminton and Christ Church,
Bristol were still much indebted to Gibbs at St Martin's. But a few,
like the splendidly detailed Holy Trinity, Halifax of the 1790s, were
'centrally' designed with almost square plans. Theatres were now apt
to be more ambitious and important than before. None of those built
in London have survived, so that apart from a small one in the Yorkshire Richmond and a larger, much altered auditorium of 1787 at
Margate the chief survival is Bristol's beautiful horseshoe-shaped
Theatre Royal. It was finished in 1766 on the pattern of Wren's Drury
Lane, and though its auditorium was greatly changed about 1820 and
later in the nineteenth century it seems, in large measure, to re-present
its original.

The architects of this early phase of the classical revival were very
numerous. None were of the genius of Wren or Hawksmoor, but many
were highly competent technicians, and talented in the tasteful handling
of accepted elements of design. Robert Adam, Sir William Chambers,
Thomas Leverton, Henry Holland, Robert Mylne, and James Wyatt (in
the classical aspect of his work) were leading designers based mainly on
London, while the early career of Sir John Soane also falls into the last
years of the eighteenth century. In the provinces one found such men
as James Essex in Cambridge, Thomas Harrison of Chester and John
Johnson of Leicester, Thomas Baldwin and John Palmer in Bath, the
Paty family in Bristol, and many other masons and craftsmen who could
rely on the increasing flow of 'directors' and pattern books to produce

THE PALLADIANS
56 *Holkham Hall, Norfolk, by William Kent, begun 1734*
57 *Queen Square, Bath (north side), by John Wood the Elder, 1728–35*

admirable brick or stone houses. The streets of expanding Liverpool and Manchester, small towns like Pershore, and villages such as Mountsorrel and Church Langton in Leicestershire, proved how admirably these humbler late Georgian designers could adorn a variety of scenes. The period saw a clear stylistic evolution from late Palladianism, through the varied experiments made famous by Robert Adam, to an elegant, but sometimes insipid neoclassicism.

THE 'ADAM' SCHOOL

The dominant late Georgian urge was to go back, behind the Renaissance, to genuine Antiquity. As many architects, by now, had studied carefully in Italy their sources of inspiration were extremely varied. Nor were Roman buildings, in Italy, Dalmatia, or Syria, the only ones of which they took account. Greek decorative art, as revealed in Graeco-Roman versions at Herculaneum and Pompeii, was increasingly followed, while the genuinely Grecian architecture of South Italy, and of Greece itself, was becoming known to English draughtsmen and designers.

Robert Adam's earliest buildings and interior decorations were still partly Palladian. But later on, with work at Bowood which displayed his close knowledge of Diocletian's palace at Spalato, and with many richly applied ideas in splendid interiors like those at Syon House, and on the boldly pillared south front of Kedleston, he moved on to an opulent, richly coloured neoclassicism. He pioneered the close correspondence of architecture and decorative art. All his details, even grates and door furniture, were within the same artistic tradition, and the patterns of his ceilings sometimes corresponded to the designs of the carpets below them. Sir William Chambers, as one well sees in his great riverside block of Somerset House in London, was more restrained and closer (as also was Henry Holland) to current neoclassic practice in France. But Chambers, like Adam, achieved a close correspondence between his main design and his interior decoration. So too did other neoclassic architects of the time. Severely plain exteriors, especially by Mylne and Wyatt, masked interiors which boasted most of a house's decoration; the most interesting rooms were those whose ends were semicircular or whose whole shapes were oval or round. What decoration was allowed was often sparingly applied, with plasterwork

58 *Syon House, Middlesex: the hall, by Robert Adam, 1762–70*

and carving thin and in shallow relief, aiming mainly at the over-sensitive, delicate elegance found also in contemporary silverware and ceramics or in Sheraton or Hepplewhite furniture. Some interiors, like Wyatt's early masterpiece of the Pantheon in London or Baldwin's Banqueting Room in Bath's Guildhall, had a truly sumptuous effect. But in general it was a far cry from the robust spirit of Vanbrugh's buildings or from the Baroque interior decoration still countenanced by the Palladians. More exciting than most domestic interiors were the spatial effects created in the domed interiors, with much of their light admitted from above by lunettes or by windows in the actual domes, created at Wimpole and in the Bank of England by the innovating genius of Soane. With him, moreover, as with other architects whose careers long outlasted the year 1800, the fully Grecian revival became an accepted source of style and decoration. [58]

While Palladianism succeeded Baroque, and as the Palladians gave way to neoclassicism, Georgian Gothic persisted and grew as an import-ant part of England's eighteenth-century architecture. The Continent had few equivalents to a phenomenon which seems the product of a very English turn of mind, romantic, escapist, and then antiquarian in its recreation of an imagined mediaeval past. At first it was fairly rare outside churches, and college buildings like the Radcliffe Quad at University College, Oxford, where patrons insisted on reasonably close copies of what already existed or had fallen down. But with park follies, mock ruins, and sham castles a fancifully romantic Gothic made head-way. Somewhat strangely a pioneer of the style was William Kent the Palladian; the ogee arches of his now vanished screen at Gloucester Cathedral recalled the most fanciful pattern available from English mediaeval design (see p. 79). This romantic, almost rococo Gothic appears in Shobdon church in Herefordshire, on some buildings in and near Bristol, and on Sanderson Miller's important hall of the 1750s which well suited the genuinely mediaeval surroundings of Lacock Abbey. The contemporary Gothic designs and fancies of Batty Langley were often so confused and bizarre that they only make sense when taken as a joke, while other designers oddly blended 'Gothick' with a no less escapist chinoiserie. The whole movement, with its more scholarly exponents sometimes concerned to make accurate renderings of mediaeval detail, was much encouraged by Horace Walpole, the creator of Strawberry Hill and the would-be Burlington of Gothick. But Kent and Miller achieved more in the style; so too did Henry Keene, with his delicate plaster imitations of fan-vaulting at Hartwell near Aylesbury and in the Bishop of Worcester's chapel at Hartlebury Castle. Here, as also at Arbury near Nuneaton, were the signs of a more scholarly and respectful approach to the mediaeval past. Antiquarians encouraged the trend, and the new spirit was apparent in Francis Hiorn of Warwick's splendid church at Tetbury in Gloucestershire, erected between 1777 and 1781 and a herald of things to come. By these last decades of a fruitful century the lines were being drawn for the great contest of the styles. [63]

CHAPTER NINE

The Battle of the Styles

1800–1840

The late Georgian Gothic Revival in part continued the use of a style which had never become extinct. But the employment, for the first time in Britain, of architectural forms directly drawn from genuine Greek work of the fifth century B.C., originated as a conscious act of artistic rediscovery.

The idea that classical Greece, South Italy, Sicily, and western Asia Minor might properly supply inspiration to English designers first appeared about the middle of the eighteenth century. Between 1751 and 1755 the young 'gentleman architect' Nicholas Revett and his companion James Stuart were financed on their sojourn in Greece by the Society of Dilettanti. The first volume of their important book of drawings and designs, *The Antiquities of Athens*, came out in 1762; seven years later Revett was partly responsible for a work on Greek buildings in Ionia. Now at last English patrons could have good knowledge of classic Greek design. Should they so desire, they could take Hellenic masterpieces as patterns for churches, houses, or buildings in their parks. Revett's church at Ayot St Lawrence in Hertfordshire, Greek Doric in the manner of a small temple but with pavilioned and colonnaded loggias, was one such building of the 1770s; the same designer added Grecian porticoes to the mansions of some of his antiquarian-minded friends. James Stuart, in 1758, designed the Doric temple in the park at Hagley. More important were his strongly Athenian park buildings at Shugborough near Stafford, and the brilliantly decorated interior which he and William Newton his Clerk of Works contrived, after 1779, within the gutted walls of the chapel at Greenwich Hospital.

But work by these two Grecian pioneers is scarce. The more Italianate neoclassicism of Adam and his contemporaries long held the field, and the effect of *The Antiquities of Athens* was not fully felt till after 1800.

The main impetus of the Greek Revival coincided with a general enthusiasm for Greek culture, and with a new interest in the Greek, as distinct from the Roman, aspect of the classical heritage. Its English expression was but part of a great international movement, as strong in Germany, Poland, France, or the United States as in the British Isles; its more romantic side was seen when Byron died in the cause of Greek independence. The Grecian movement in architecture was much encouraged by some rich men of taste, and by the appearance of lavish volumes and design books which helped those of Stuart and Revett to spread knowledge of 'Grecian' architecture and interior decoration; localisms and regional idioms were at a discount in such a climate of taste. Thomas Hope, the rich, leisured connoisseur who owned Deepdene near Dorking, was influential among the amateur arbiters of strict Grecianism, while among the new books William Wilkins' *Antiquities of Magna Graecia* of 1806 made known the details of the temples at Paestum and in Greek Sicily. Wilkins himself, with his important, pioneering Ionic work (of the years just after 1800) at Downing College, Cambridge, and at Haileybury College where the East India Company's Directors chose him because of his experience at Downing, was among the chief figures of the frigidly correct Greek Revival which now competed with Gothic. One must, however, recall that Wilkins, along with such other contemporary architects as John Foster of Liverpool, Thomas Hopper (who also worked in neo-Norman and mock-Jacobean), and Jeffery Wyatt, was 'bilingual' in Greek and Gothic. For in addition to his Grecian academic buildings, the National Gallery and the Masonic Hall of 1817 in Bath, he designed such Gothic mansions as Tregothnan and Pentillie Castle in Cornwall, also much Cambridge academic architecture which included the neo-Perpendicular New Court at Corpus Christi and the hall at King's which likewise imitates English mediaeval Gothic's final phase. For these years between 1800 and 1840 were a time of tense artistic conflict, each style revealing a movement in educated minds. We may compare this struggle with that which gripped England about 1620, the time of Inigo Jones's Palladianism and of survivalist Gothic, when mediaeval artistry and incipient Renaissance taste overlapped and conflicted.

Other classical architects of this Regency period were more rigid, as Holland had been, in their Grecian allegiance. Sir Robert Smirke and C. R. Cockerell were among them; only rarely did either architect design a building whose stylistic veneer was anything but Greek. So Smirke's British Museum and his various churches, his Shire Halls of the Regency decade at Gloucester and Hereford, and his Covent Garden Opera House were all Ionic or in the Greek Doric now prevalent, with its thick abaci, its columns without plinths, and its Athenian proportions to distinguish it from the Etruscan, Roman, or Renaissance versions of the style. C. R. Cockerell, despite a scholarly use of Greek detail which came naturally from his close study of many Hellenic buildings, could none the less break away from the strictest Greek conventions of basic design. His Philosophic and Literary Institution in Bristol, and Holy Trinity Church at Hotwells in the same city were neither of them over-rigidly bound to Greek structural precedents, and in his standardised, early Victorian Bank of England offices in Manchester, Bristol, and Liverpool he displayed a massive, ponderous severity more Roman than Hellenic in spirit. Yet Cockerell may be placed among the leading figures of the Greek Revival. More individualist in their approach, using Greek detail yet treating it as one element alone in a wide vocabulary of decoration, were the widely differing Soane and Nash. The former is best known for the great brilliance with which he handled the domed and top-lighted spaces of his late eighteenth and early nineteenth-century interiors, while the incised lines with which he often enlivened plain exterior surfaces performed something of the decorative task which the Greeks gave to their famous key pattern. John Nash, a more wayward designer with a real genius for the lay-out and scenic handling of such urban areas as Regent's Park and the great sequence of streets leading south to Carlton House Terrace, was never a fully correct Grecian even in his classical buildings. His taste for the dramatic and the romantic made him equally at home amid his Gothic and castellated expressions of the great cult of the Picturesque which disputed the field with cool Greek rationalism in those early decades of last century. [59]

The Greek Revivalists' output was impressively large, especially in London which now blossomed as the rich, victorious capital whose plundering potentialities were so quickly sized up by Blücher. Nash's delayed, extravagant work on Buckingham Palace at last solved the old problem of a grandiose royal residence in London, while elsewhere in the capital new head offices of professional bodies, churches, some City halls, and the splendid monumentality of Regent's Park all adorned an expanding metropolis. Elsewhere an outburst of new public buildings, and a few mansions to add to the great accumulation of the earlier Georgians, gave many architectural opportunities. The structure of buildings was sometimes such that Greek columns and pilasters were only a stylistic veneer on fabrics which could as well have supported Roman, Romanesque, or Gothic decoration. But in some dignified porticos, and in the peristyle and splendid interior completed in 1830 by John Forbes in the Ionic Pittville Pump Room at Cheltenham, impeccably Greek columns bore loads as their forbears had done in Athens, Syracuse, or Ephesus. Grecian columns, whether derived from the Parthenon, the Theseum, the Erechtheum, or the now vanished temple by the Ilissus, were therefore important in the porticos of the Shire Halls at Durham, Devizes, and Worcester. They occurred in numerous Athenaeums, or Literary and Philosophic Institutions, whose whole *ethos* demanded a revived Greek style, and on the monumental frontages of Infirmaries of the 1830s like that at Huddersfield, and at Stockport where the architect was Richard Lane of Manchester. His dignified Greek Doric Town Hall at Salford (unlike Goodwin's noble Ionic one of 1819 in adjacent Manchester) survives to prove that municipalities could also give fine chances to late Georgian designers. **[60]**

Churches seemed a poor field for the Greek Revivalists, for the narrow cella of the genuine Greek temple was never meant for indoor congregations. Yet Smirke, Forbes, Soane, and others applied Greek porticos to the boxlike, galleried bodies of many Anglican buildings. The Inwoods' famous, brilliantly detailed St Pancras church of the 1820s was even supplied with two highly inappropriate replicas of the Erechtheum's caryatid porch. A happier, splendidly rendered Greek Revival church was George Basevi's St Thomas, Stockport of 1822–5. It has a severe steeple, of basically Gibbsian composition, at one end, a Corinthian galleried interior, and at its eastern end a grand Ionic portico. Many Nonconformist chapels displayed entrance porches or complete façades in the Grecian style long preferred to the Establishment's increasingly chosen Gothic, while some of the Catholics' now numerous churches adopted a Grecianism not uncommon in their stronghold of Lancashire, and favoured (as at Hereford and Clifton) in his western

Vicariate by that redoubtable, passionately anti-Gothic prelate Bishop Baines. [62]

No less notable than public buildings and churches were individual villas and ambitious urban compositions. Spa and seaside towns were specially distinguished in the general rise of elegant urbansim, but the process was evident elsewhere. In Plymouth and Devonport the local architect John Foulston designed some splendid Grecian embellishments. The best, in Plymouth, was the combined building, with Ionic porticos on one side and at one end, which once housed the Theatre and the Royal Hotel. Foulston's main work in Devonport (first called Dock and laid out as a Georgian new town outside the Dockyard gates) was the civic centre, with Ker Street leading up to a Doric Town Hall and a tall column of the same order which commemorated the town's change of name in 1824. Among many growing seaside towns the leader was Brighton, with its great sequence of urban features between Hove and Kemp Town. Others shared in the general trend, and at Teignmouth and Hastings fine crescents of houses were glorified in the middle, not merely by pedimented and pilastered centrepieces but by separate buildings. So Teignmouth's Den Crescent of 1826 had the Assembly Rooms in its midst, while at Hastings Pelham Crescent contains the fine semi-circular, porticoed church of St Mary in the Castle which was built in 1825–8; its architect was Joseph Kay who in Bloomsbury had designed the monumental side of Mecklenburgh Square. Cheltenham and Leamington are the best of the inland spas. The former started modestly enough, with its Royal Crescent and earliest terraces unadorned in their Regency simplicity. But from the 1820s, under Papworth, Forbes, and other designers, a stylish Grecian town was quickly built; for the Greek Revival it was as fine a demonstration as Bath had been for urban Palladianism. Along with squares and terraces individual villas of great refinement also arose in such towns to satisfy their growing crowds of permanent residents. Other towns joined the rush for sophisticated urban improvement. The patrician area of Liverpool shows Grecian streets as good as many in Brighton or Leamington, while across the Mersey no other late Georgian square in England can rival the massive dignity of Hamilton Square, the first great element in a new town created by the shipbuilding Lairds. Its order is Doric of the Roman variety, and although Gillespie Graham of Edinburgh designed and started it in 1826 its style comes nearer to that of Adam in Edin-

THE GREEK REVIVAL

59   *London: the British Museum, by Sir Robert Smirke, started 1823*
60   *Cheltenham: Pittville Pump Room, by John Forbes, 1825–30*

burgh than to the Grecian of Wilkins or Foster. Individual villas, like modest terraces, also arose on the fringe of expanding industrial towns. Edgbaston at Birmingham has many such, but northerly centres like Huddersfield, Halifax, Burnley, and Bradford contribute their modest quota. The 'Regency' domestic idiom outlasted Victoria's accession in 1837, and in Clifton there are eschato-Georgian terraces, built as late as the 1850s, which coincided with some of the most objectionable efforts of the Victorian Gothicists.

GOTHIC REVIVED

Like its Grecian competitor, early nineteenth-century Gothic was often scholarly in its approach. It was more respectful of late mediaeval precedents than most work by Langley, Sanderson Miller, and the earlier Romanticists. For this was the period when Thomas Rickman brought out the studious book which first contained the terms, from Norman to Perpendicular, by which England's mediaeval styles have since been generally known. His own work, as in the 1830s at Holy Trinity and St Matthew's in Bristol, was apt to imitate Perpendicular, with occasional Decorated idioms in St Mary's, Birkenhead and St George's, Edgbaston, both started in 1819. Neo-Norman was also occasionally favoured. But Norman Romanesque reproduced less well than Gothic, and such buildings as Hopper's great castle at Penrhyn in North Wales impress more than they convince. Nor was scholarship the only idea among architects who chose, or were asked, to put up buildings of a mediaevalist stamp. For these years of the literary Romantic Revival were also, under the influence of Payne Knight, Uvedale Price and others, the period of the Picturesque and studied rusticity. Along with the many mock abbeys and bogus priories which followed Fonthill and were satirised in *Northanger Abbey*, numerous leisured gentry turned, very profitably for their architects, to a charming though intellectually empty profusion of rustic aviaries, *cottages ornées*, and thatched homesteads for idyllically contented rustics. Many such buildings arose in the hilly, 'romantic' scenery of the Lakes, of Wales, and of the Welsh Marches, or in the Isle of Wight and some Devon coastal resorts which abound in 'picturesque retreats'. Plaw, Papworth, Lugar and others published illustrated books which gave many ideas for such fancies, often with thatched roofs, ornate chimney stacks derived from rural

ECCLESIASTICAL CONTRASTS
1 London: St Luke's, Chelsea, by James Savage, 1820–24
2 London: St Mary's, Bryanston Square, by Robert Smirke, 1823–24

East Anglia, and verandah pillars made of unshaped and unstripped tree trunks. On a more substantial scale these Gothic tastes found expression in Smirke's Eastnor Castle, in Wyattville's reconstructions at Windsor Castle, and in Nash's castellated achievements. Nash himself, as his charming Blaise Hamlet of 1811 proves, could readily design romantic cottages. But his castles and Gothic mansions were a more serious matter. Despite references to Alnwick, Warwick, Raglan, and other genuine baronial strongholds their antiquarianism need not deceive those versed in truly mediaeval military architecture. But their basic planning, domineering circular towers, and Gothic decoration which includes Perpendicular tracery and well imitated fan-vaulting, made Nash's 'castles', like the Gothic 'gentlemen's seats' by other late Georgian architects, an important part of the architecture of their time. [64]

The Gothic of the early nineteenth century also occurred in many schoolhouses and colleges, in almshouses, and in asylums for the blind, deaf, or dumb like the long range of 1834 designed in Manchester by Richard Lane. Many churches were also built; Roman Catholic and Nonconformist buildings joined those of the Establishment in growing numbers between 1800 and 1840. Many of the Anglican churches were built by the Commissioners set up by the Church Building Act of 1818, and as Gothic was now thought 'more ecclesiastical' than the classical styles a strong Gothic trend got firmly rooted. Yet the issue was still open enough for some architects to submit alternative plans, Greek Revival or Gothic, for particular churches. Many Nonconformist chapels concentrated the 'stylistic' effect of doorways, windows, and pinnacles on their entrance façades. [61]

Despite their mediaevalist style these pre-Tractarian Anglican churches adhered to the standardised Protestant plan. Boxlike, galleried naves comprised most of the structure. Western towers, as in R. D. Chantrell's Leeds churches, Charles Dyer's St Paul's, Bedminster in Bristol, and in many Lancashire Commissioners' erections, were battlemented and pinnacled Perpendicular but were often slimmer than their genuine originals. Slender pillars and window tracery were sometimes of cast iron; one sees them in Goodwin's fine nave at Walsall with its ceiling of pendents and rich plaster ribs. Chancels or sanctuaries were only just deep enough to contain the Communion table; even pre-Puginesque Catholic churches like those at Hexham and St Patrick's,

Huddersfield, and the Regency Gothic pro-Cathedral at Liverpool, were often content with shallow apsed sacraria, often pleasant period pieces with the thin-ribbed plaster vaults which were widely favoured in this period. Styles varied considerably within the field of Gothic selection. Imitations of lancet Gothic were conveniently cheap, and thus popular with the Commissioners, and such unambitious works as St Paul's, Stonehouse at Plymouth are among England's baldest and least attractive places of worship. Late Georgian Early English could, however, be more ambitious, so that Theale church in Berkshire and Goodridge of Bath's Catholic church at Lyme Regis looked forward to the better Victorian achievements. More notable still, in this 'first pointed' style, were Goodridge's chapel and monastery commenced in 1822 for the Benedictines of Downside. Some churches, like St Paul's and St Patrick's at Huddersfield, blended lancet and Perpendicular Gothic in a manner rare in genuine mediaeval churches. Chantrell, Goodwin, Rickman, and others occasionally used tracery in the Decor-ated tradition. But accurate Perpendicular, far more than in the Victor-ian period, was the favourite idiom. The elder John Pinch of Bath, in St Mary's Bathwick of 1814–20, showed how well the style of the great Somerset towers could live again. The next twenty years saw churches built in this late mediaeval, yet also functionally Georgian, vein. Holy Trinity, Bolton of 1826 well typifies many others. J. P. Pritchett and Thomas Taylor at Huddersfield, Francis Goodwin in St George's, Hulme, John Palmer who started what is now Blackburn Cathedral in 1820, and Charles Barry at Brighton and Manchester where he freely blended Perpendicular design with fourteenth-century touches, all showed how adaptations of carefully studied late Gothic could meet a greatly swelling demand.

Though Grecian and Gothic had held the centre of the stage in the contest of the styles, some other vagaries also fluttered in the wings. Britain's Indian commitment, and a knowledge of Indian buildings drawn from the water colours of Thomas Daniell and others, created a passing fancy for an Indian style. This was first seen at Sezincote in northern Gloucestershire, where from 1805 onwards a retired 'nabob', Sir Charles Cockerell, got Samuel Pepys Cockerell his architect brother to design a mansion whose conservatories and other outbuildings have an Indian character, and whose main block is boldly crowned by a dome in the manner of the Taj Mahal. The interiors, however, are rigidly in the Grecian taste. Sezincote seems largely to have inspired the Prince Regent's far more drastic handling of the Royal Pavilion at Brighton. Some pseudo-Indian stables were built there about the time of Sezincote's commencement, and then after 1815 Nash spoilt Holland's elegant classic mansion by a weird proliferation of domes and slim minarets, with much Oriental decoration inside and a riot of Chinoiserie to disconcert Prinny's guests in the Banqueting Room.

This period's other eccentricity was neo-Egyptian, connecting with a new enthusiasm for Egyptology and the Nilotic motivation of much First Empire and Regency furniture. So bizarre Egyptian façades arose, about 1830, in London, in Penzance, and at the top of Ker Street, Devonport. More imposing was the scheme for the pylon towers of the Clifton Suspension Bridge. But the hieroglyphic panels and paired sphinxes of Brunel's design were never carried out, and, though the actual pylons have a Pharaonic flavour, what mattered was not the bridge's stylistic idiom but its engineering. **[66]**

63   *Lacock Abbey: the hall, by Sanderson Miller, c.175*
64   *Ashridge, Hertfordshire, by James Wyatt, started 1808*

CHAPTER TEN

The Enlargement of Architecture

c. 1750–c. 1860

Whatever their style, the Georgian buildings so far noticed did not exploit many new methods of construction or incorporate untried materials. Some churches had roofs whose spans were wider than those normal in the Middle Ages, while the industrially produced material of cast iron occasionally appeared in window tracery and in pillars which supported galleries in churches or upper floors in factories and mills. At St Alkmund's, Shrewsbury of 1795, and in some other churches conveniently near the famous iron works at Coalbrookdale, cast iron had been used in the windows, and we have seen how Francis Goodwin fairly often employed it. Delicate, many-patterned iron-work was also displayed in the porches and balconies of villas and terraces in Cheltenham, Gloucester Spa, Leamington, and elsewhere. Another new material, much used for the sculptural adornment of buildings, was the durable artificial stone produced late in the eighteenth century by the London firm of Coade (later Coade and Seely). More notable than this tentative use of new materials was the extension, to new types of buildings, of conscious architectural design.

Industrial expansion and pioneering means of transport lay behind the new uses of architecture; new types of buildings and fresh production techniques both arose from the late Georgian manufacturing and transport revolutions. Some examples of the extension of architecture and the builder's craft had indeed been seen in the comparatively few places where one found industrial plants of the modern type. Glass and pottery works had furnaces and kilns whose conical tops, though works of civil engineering and not in any accepted architectural style, were

PIONEERING BRIDGES
65 Ironbridge, Shropshire, by Pritchard and Darby, 1779
66 Clifton Suspension Bridge, Bristol, by Brunel, started 1836, completed 1864

none the less striking, picturesque elements in the skyline of Bristol and other early industrial centres. On the lower Thames, and at Chatham, Portsmouth, and Devonport, the Royal Dockyards were industrial establishments of a specialised, architecturally important kind. The accommodation for their senior officials was partly provided in terraces which were among the earliest of their type (see page 173); the buildings more peculiar to the dockyards were of varieties little known before, and not likely to occur except in places given over to the regular building, maintenance, and repair of the largest ships then afloat. Brick or stone ropewalks were built for the making and drying out of ropes stretched out to their fullest extent. These buildings were among the longest yet built in England; that surviving at Portsmouth splendidly recalls the logistic needs of the Navy under sail. Covered slipways, for the indoor building of ships of the line, ran back from the dockyard waterfronts. Their roofing, of great timber baulks ingeniously planned like that of Mansard roofs, covered spaces wider than most churches or public buildings, so that they sometimes displayed great virtuosity in timber construction. Elsewhere in the Dockyards the numerous ranges of storehouses (occasionally with pediments) anticipated the great warehouses which later distinguished England's leading ports. Office buildings were also provided; the charming clock towers and cupolas with which some were capped made them akin to such early industrial administration blocks as that of the Wedgwoods at Burslem and to the stable, laundry, and brewhouse complexes whose careful layout and soberly architectural design are often worth noting alongside the more spectacular buildings of country mansions. For these buildings' life of self-support made them industrial as well as residential concerns.

Among England's earliest industrial buildings were the mills, or barnlike sheds of masonry and dressed stone, built in Cotswold or Pennine river valleys for the cleansing operations which marked the 'finishing' of cloth made in the weavers' cottages. Many such mills dated back to the seventeenth or earlier centuries, while a few like that at Shawford near Frome have early Georgian features. As the cloth trade increased these buildings for final, centralised processes became far more numerous. The local masons who built them used window designs derived from the mullioned subdivisions of windows in houses. Such were the buildings which late in the eighteenth century became the models for the great cotton or woollen mills where spinning and weaving were done by coal-fired machinery.

Lancashire, Yorkshire, and the clothmaking districts of the western counties are the main areas for late Georgian textile mills. Their design and structure were basically the same as in the warehouses of ports and other industrial regions. Simple, squared, rectangular buildings arose gauntly in brick or stone. They might run to as many as eight storeys, their floors for the spinning and weaving machinery being reasonably lit by rows of rectangular, close-set, many-paned windows. 'Architectural' features were as few and restrained as in many terraces and villas of the time. But Venetian windows or simple classical doorways were sometimes allowed, at King's Stanley in Gloucestershire for instance, or in Smith Street, Rochdale, in a great mill only lately demolished. Slender chimneys, still simple in design and not capped by architecturally pretentious tops, stood close to these mills as they also adjoined the shafts of deep collieries and the gaunt engine houses of Cornish tin or copper mines. More interesting, in many of these mills as also in the great warehouses now built in dock areas, was the popularity of simple cast-iron classical pillars (often unfluted Doric)* to support overhanging storeys or uphold the beams (occasionally themselves of iron) on which rested the strained and creaking wooden floors. These iron columns were not basically unlike the iron pillars in churches. Of greater pioneering interest was the use of cast iron girders for the fashioning of structures more revolutionary in their nature. **[68]**

THE USE OF CAST IRON

The cast-iron industry was well established by the middle of the eighteenth century, though its products were not of an architectural character. But at Coalbrookdale in Shropshire, not far up a little valley running down to the Severn, the famous foundries of the Abraham Darbys, father and son, were active from the time of Queen Anne. Then in the 1770s there came the project for bridging the Severn near Coalbrookdale. The project's sponsors were persuaded to experiment with a bridge composed of thin, gracefully curved

* The Doric capitals of such columns were sometimes flanked by projecting brackets to make them stronger supporters of the beams above.

girders of cast iron. Their architect was Thomas Farnell Pritchard of Shrewsbury, some twenty-five years earlier the designer of the pleasing, ordinary classical church of St Julian in his home town, but now immortalised by a greater innovation. As Pritchard died in 1777 the alteration of his designs, and the supervision of the bridge's building till it was finished in 1781, seems likely to have lain with the younger Darby whose nearby foundry cast the ironwork. Between supporting piers of stone, and with a span of 100 feet, the Iron Bridge is a delicate masterpiece of curves arched above the river, with circles of iron and a faintly Gothic design to fill the spandrels between the piers, the curved supporting girders, and the gently rising roadway. [65]

The first Iron Bridge was followed, in 1796, by one a few miles upstream at Buildwas, designed by the great civil engineer Thomas Telford. The same year also saw the building of a much larger one at Sunderland. The technique of such girder bridges, of great future importance, was now well established. So in addition to ambitious structures by leading engineers like Telford or Rennie, much smaller bridges of the same type were built in the Regency period over such narrow spans as a canal lock at Bath and a pathway to Southernhay at Exeter.

More innovating still were the suspension bridges of various sizes which became common in England after the 1820s. The structural principle behind them was the reverse of that previously prevalent. For instead of the roadway being supported from below by arches or girders the horizontal element was hung from vertical bars which themselves descended from great chains. These chains, dropping down in an infinitely graceful curve, were in their turn slung from masonry or metal towers at either end of the bridge. As engineering feats the suspension bridges were bolder than those of arched girders; far more than brick or masonry structures they were a specific product of the Industrial Revolution.

Britain's first great suspension bridge was that designed by Telford to span the Menai Strait, and so to improve the road link with Holyhead and the Dublin packets. It was built between 1819 and 1826. The breadth of the channel and the slope of its banks were such that a single span was impossible; the bridge's central structure was slung from two tall tower-piers built close by the shores. More dramatic in its single sweep was Brunel's famous bridge across the deep Clifton Gorge; it was designed in 1829 and started in 1836. In so scenic a position it was mainly an awesome, romantic challenge to picturesque Nature, more the fulfilment of a cherished notion than the answer to a real economic need. Financial delays delayed its building; its completion in 1864 was after Brunel's death and was largely seen as the great engineer's memorial. The suspension bridge (or the chain pier, as at Brighton in 1822–3) was now accepted. Many of those eventually built were much smaller than the masterpieces of Telford and Brunel, or those which in London spanned the Thames. **[66]**

The first half of last century was also notable for great strides in the architecture of warehouses and docks. Many ports expanded greatly beyond their older limits, while at Gloucester a new dock area was created when the ship canal was finished in 1827; one of its new warehouses was given a row of unfluted Greek Doric columns to support upper storeys which projected till they were flush with the water's edge. The same utilitarian style was likewise used by Jesse Hartley in the splendid warehouses which he built soon after 1840 to serve the Albert and Wapping Docks at Liverpool. Behind their thin brick walls these buildings have iron columns and iron beams to make a framework for their floors; as a precaution against fire those floors were themselves made up of shallow brick vaults. Some years earlier, the engineer-architects Daniel Alexander and Thomas Telford had built some imposing warehouses to line the London and St Katherine's Docks which opened off from the Thames; Telford's Doric pillars, however, were of ponderous stone.

Two naval establishments also stood out among these monuments of blended architecture and civil engineering. From 1813 onwards the ramshackle little dockyard at Sheerness was replaced by a new establishment. The docks and buildings of the older dockyards had accumulated piecemeal. But here was a wholly new one, built in a single operation and scientifically laid out to service the largest men o' war. The designer was the elder John Rennie; after he died in 1821 the work was completed by his son and various Admiralty architects and engineers. The dockyard's layout, and the fine granite masonry of its docks and basins, belong primarily to the field of civil engineering, but 'stylistic' points occur in its church and houses and in the great quadrangle of storehouses, with its arched entrance, cast iron pillars, and horizontal girders dated 1825. More imposing still is the younger Rennie's Royal William Victualling Yard at Plymouth. Started in 1826

when the future William IV was still Lord High Admiral, it has a small
central camber. On each side, blocks of buildings are symmetrically
displayed, with a central clock tower and at the landward entrance a
monumental gateway capped by one of the few statues of the Sailor
King. But the yard's grandest aspect, like that of Greenwich Hospital,
is that gained from over an expanse of water, the view one gets crossing
the Cremyll ferry or coming down from the open expanse of the
Hamoaze.

Other buildings of this period whose interest was mainly economic
were the enclosed market halls which improved the trading facilities of
many towns. A long, rectangular space would be wholly covered over,
or else given sheltered accommodation on either side of a narrow courtyard; in a more refined manner the same principle applied in arcades
of small shops like those in London and the surviving half of James
Foster's splendid double arcade in Bristol. The street entrances of these
buildings were given some monumental treatment. So a dignified propylaeum, with bold rustication and two Doric columns, was built in
1804 at Worcester's new Market, while less imposing façades later
indicated the entrances to those of Devizes and Hereford. At Cheltenham, the now vanished Market façade of 1823 echoed the Indianisms of
Sezincote. Then in the next decade Charles Fowler of Exeter, already
the designer of the free-standing, externally colonnaded Market House
at Covent Garden, most notably adorned his home city with his Upper
and Lower Markets; a pedimented Greek Doric main entrance adorns
the former which survived the Baedeker bombs of 1942. Some covered
markets were of extra interest for the iron framing of their glass roofs.
With their unadorned, rectangular spaces for buying and selling, and
with their more monumental, somewhat unrelated forebuildings, they
set a precedent for the coming architecture of railway termini.

Much architectural design, applied to innovating structures or to
established categories of buildings, was called into being by the canals
and railways which in about ninety years from 1760 steadily permeated
England. The ancillary buildings of canals—offices, storehouses,
bridges, and cottages for toll collectors or lock-keepers—were
straightforward, and often charming in their vernacular simplicity.
Hundreds of plain, one-arched bridges were built, in brick or stone,
to carry roads and paths. Lock-keepers' houses as a rule resembled
Regency agricultural cottages or turnpike tollhouses. But some, like

the delightful Greek Doric set along the Gloucester canal, copied the lodges set at the gates of noblemen's parks, while not far away, along the Thames and Severn canal which was opened in 1789, a novel touch came in with a series of circular Gothic cottages. More daring innovations appeared in canal aqueducts and tunnels. The actual structure of the aqueducts, being adapted from that of road bridges, was fairly conventional, though Telford's early nineteenth-century masterpieces at Chirk and Pontcysyllte in North Wales were far higher above their rivers than the builders of earlier bridges and aqueducts had thought normal. Where these aqueducts were a novelty was in their basic nature, for they caused wonder whether their water was in puddled channels or else, as in Telford's pair, in cast-iron troughs. Though in the 1760s Brindley's pioneering aqueduct on the Bridgewater canal had been architecturally unassuming, more stateliness was later thought worthy of ambitious new waterways; hence in 1797, the elder Rennie's five-arched structure at Lancaster, like the bridge at Blenheim on an imposing scale unusual in English buildings. Rennie was probably inspired by Thomas Harrison's recently completed road bridge a short distance away, and he used that bridge's motif of paired pilasters or half-columns on his two single-arch aqueducts at Dundas and Avoncliff, near Bath on the Kennet and Avon canal. [67]

Architectural opportunities were also presented by the entrances to the tunnels found necessary on some canals. The earliest waterways, as at Worsley, made little of these features. But as the canal mania gathered momentum the chances proved irresistible. So some tunnel openings were architecturally embellished. The most entertaining of such treatments occurred at the Sapperton tunnel on the Thames and Severn. For while one entrance was rendered in simple Gothic, the other, in Rennie's manner though not by Rennie, is monumentally classic and was admired, on his visit from Cheltenham in 1788, by George III. Pride of achievement made the railways even keener to treat their tunnel entrances as if they were castle gateways or triumphal arches. So early tunnel mouths, whether semi-circular or paraboloid in shape, are well worth studying. Twerton at Bath and the fasces-flanked arches of Brunel's shorter tunnel at Box, Clayton near Brighton, Shugborough, and various tunnels in North London all show, among others, their varied examples of burgeoning display.

The earliest railway stations, like Crown Street at Liverpool, had unpretending ancillary buildings, of no special size or style. Nor did the first 'train sheds' use constructional methods ahead of those already seen in the iron or timber-framed roofs of covered markets. But entrances and office buildings soon assumed more monumental guises. Ceremonial screens or porticos, and urban or country mansions, were the models for the more imposing stations. The long façade of the first Lime Street at Liverpool was one of this kind. More compact were the free-standing Greek Doric propylaeum at Euston, Philip Hardwick's fine Ionic block at Curzon Street, Birmingham, unrelated to its train sheds but still standing to recall the old London and Birmingham Railway, the Grecian entrances to Cheltenham (Lansdown) and the Midland Station at Lincoln, and J. P. Pritchett's splendid blocks at Huddersfield, like a mansion in the grandest manner with flanking wings, connecting colonnades, and a great Corinthian portico looking out over the town's main square. The Gothic idiom, correctly early Tudor, was best used about 1840 when Brunel's Bristol terminus was finished. Here too, as also at Bath, the single-span train shed was of great splendour. For Brunel designed his Temple Meads roof as a magnificent timber construction, with a hammerbeam effect and supported by long Perpendicular arcades. Roofing and façade alike survive, and seem likely to endure, as the original Great Western's most imposing relic.

The spread of conscious design to new fields of building activity continued far into the nineteenth century; it was the architectural expression of a more complex, more industrialised society. Factories and mills became more 'stylistic', with Gothic among the idioms now carefully applied to make an industrial building seem like an Italian palazzo or a Gothic hôtel de ville. The summits of tall chimneys were tricked out with a growing wealth of historic detail. Even machinery shared in the prevalent trend, so that vertical boilers were sometimes flanked by iron Doric columns and canopied by pediments. Cast iron, moreover, was now exploited still more as the basic framework of vast roofs or complete buildings. Apart from Market Halls, and such buildings as London's Coal Exchange whose elaborate iron roof and inner framing of 1847–9 lay behind an ornate Renaissance forebuilding of ordinary stonework, glasshouses or conservatories with timber or iron frames, and with supporting ironwork inside, were also important. Among these was the 'Great Stove' at Chatsworth, put up between 1836 and 1841. Joseph Paxton its designer used a timber framework,

TRANSPORT AND INDUSTRY
67 Pontcysyllte, Denbighshire: the Canal Aqueduct, by Telford, completed 1805
68 King's Stanley, Gloucestershire: cloth mill, 1813
69 London: Paddington Station, by Brunel and Matthew Digby Wyatt, 1852–54

along with iron pillars and girders, to support the doubly curved silhouette of its lofty central space and lower aisles. In a few more years the even loftier Palm House at Kew had an iron frame, while Paxton's glass house at Chatsworth for the Duke of Devonshire's giant water lilies was a small-scale pattern for his iron-framed Crystal Palace.

In its original form, Paxton's great iron and glass building for the Great Exhibition of 1851 was nearly 1,850 feet long, while its round-arched transept was high enough inside to overtop the elms left standing on the site. Though it fully exploited the new technique of prefabricated iron and sheet-glass construction its design recalled great cruciform cathedrals with their naves, aisles, triforium galleries, and clerestories. It was thus a less innovating building than some of its successors. Yet its scale, and its use of materials directly foreshadowing modern steel or concrete framing, made it of more pioneering note than its sponsors foresaw. Exhibition buildings elsewhere duly followed that of 1851, while Winter Gardens like the atrocity which long defaced the Regency centre of Cheltenham exploited the same technique. But Exhibition Halls of the Crystal Palace type were essentially evanescent. More durable, and eventually more daring in their use of curved iron girders over vast single spaces, were the greater train sheds. Those planned in the 1840s, as at Euston and John Dobson's Newcastle Central, were of modest width so that a large station needed more than one. Then when Brunel and Matthew Digby Wyatt designed the present Paddington the station's ample width needed three parallel sheds, with transeptal crosspieces in the Crystal Palace manner. The high peak of such buildings was reached late in the 1860s when Peter Barlow, the Midland Railway's structural engineer,* spanned St Pancras Station with the single sweep and slightly pointed silhouette of his superb iron-framed train shed, while at Manchester the very similar Central Station takes us down to the 1880s. All these stations were of mainly structural interest; when they came to stylistic embellishment the designers were in something of a dilemma. Their earliest iron columns were classical. But though at Paddington Wyatt used flamboyant Gothic to panel the bases of his girders, he also expressed his theories on a 'vocabulary of its own' for industrial architecture when he gave the pillars capitals which were in no previously known style. Yet at York and Leeds (City) one sees mid-Victorian columns with aggressively

* He had assisted Paxton over the design for the Crystal Palace.

70 Cliveden, Buckinghamshire, by Sir Charles Barry, 1850–51
71 Babbacombe, Devon: All Saints' Church, by William Butterfield, 1868–74
72 Manchester Town Hall, by Alfred Waterhouse, 1869: a staircase

Corinthian capitals, and foliate spandrels tricked out with the heraldry of the old North Eastern Railway. [69]

By about 1850 other new types of buildings had made their appearance. Large hotels, far grander than glorified coaching inns with Assembly Rooms, arose in some spas and resorts to supersede rented lodging houses. The earliest examples, like the Regent at Leamington in 1824 and Cheltenham's Queen's of 1837–8, were well within the classic traditions; the Cheltenham building is clearly akin to an overgrown, porticoed Palladian mansion. But grand hotels, like the first office buildings and department stores, were soon caught up on the turgid currents of chaotic, unseemly Victorian taste.

CHAPTER ELEVEN

Victorian Floodtide

1840–1880

The Victorian age, from 1840 to about 1880, was important for the sheer volume and widening range of its architecture. It was repulsive in most of its aesthetic taste. Varied architectural styles and details were freely applied to buildings new in character or else seldom considered as having been worthy of 'architectural' treatment. Large towns grew from small beginnings, particularly in the industrial Midlands and North, and in seaside resorts whose piers, promenades, hotels, and residential terraces spread ponderously along strips of lonely coastline. These newly grown towns, almost more than London and other established urban centres, are fruitful for the study of uncloyed Victorianism. Bolton and Bournemouth, Southport and Bradford or Huddersfield are all repositories of Victorian taste, while the humble, standardised 'company' housing of such railway towns as Crewe or Swindon is of no mean interest. Nor can one omit the profusely decorated mansions of the newly enriched or freshly ennobled. The Duke of Omnium might still reside in the dignity of mediaeval fortresses or Palladian mansions; Sir Gorgius Midas was as likely to flaunt his riches or display his benevolence* in some version of a French Gothic or Renaissance château.

The interest of high Victorian architecture lies largely in its wide, psychologically revealing variety of imitated and adapted styles. The Greek Revival, despite its superb demonstration in the colonnaded, rounded, and porticoed exterior of St George's Hall at Liverpool, did

---

* e.g. Royal Holloway College at Egham, a Chambordesque monstrosity by W. H. Crossland, financed by the profits of Holloway's pills.

not long outlast Victoria's accession. The Gothic of early nineteenth-century churches, pre-ecclesiological in its planning and largely Perpen-dicular in style, soon yielded to a Gothic supposed by its prophets to be truly mediaeval, and a stylistic echo of England between about 1250 and 1340. But the rich repository of English mediaevalism was not the mid-Victorians' sole source of style. Thanks to Browning, Ruskin, and others for whom Florence, other cities in central Italy, and Venice were much loved haunts, the Gothic of those districts, less pure and more polychrome than that of France and England, was greatly in demand. French Gothic, moreover, was not disregarded. The Renais-sance taste of various European countries was also favoured; one may fairly say that most of the Continent was ransacked for examples. The style chosen for a Victorian building was usually a decorative veneer on a well-built load-bearing structure; the essential nature of such a build-ing, whether it was a terrace of houses, a hotel, or a row of urban shops, differed little from earlier architectural achievements. In chur-ches, moreover, pillars, walls, and buttresses did much the same work as in the Middle Ages. Metal-framed buildings, like the early ventures of the Arts and Crafts movement, were unusual and not the Victorian norm; the Crystal Palace and the vast train-sheds had long to wait before their constructional methods were widely accepted.

The Victorian age produced many important, hard-working archi-tects. Some, like Sir George Gilbert Scott, received their training in the last years of the Georgian tradition, but few showed signs that they had learnt their architecture when classical balance and symmetry were important. On a more portentous scale their kinship was closer to the designers of asymmetrical *cottages ornées*, or with the least disciplined castellations of Nash. The one quality most lacking in them (as also in the designers of furniture of the Great Exhibition period) was the ele-gance which can give the best effect with the minimum of material. English architects were now enabled, by industry and transport, to use a wider range of materials than any designers in the past. But they showed little taste or discrimination in their profusely blended crea-tions of many-coloured brick, granite, marble, alabaster, and loud encaustic tiles.

Victorian architecture, and particularly Victorian Gothic, shares one thing, if one alone, with the Georgian which went before it. It has been violently abused by hostile critics, and has passed through its hated period to a time of no less undiscriminating appreciation. Just as the Victorian designers and furnishers of churches thought Georgian classicism both pagan and debased, so the buildings of the Victorians have been rabidly loathed, and then discovered to be something that sophisticates must admire. Many of them, by now, are old enough to be respectably antique, and the immense changes of our century have hastened the process whereby Victoriana have become coveted period pieces. If only because the pendulum of taste has swung back past the mean, and because the polychrome and pitch pine of some mid-Victorian buildings are admired in a way unthinkable 30 years ago, the aesthetic content of high Victorian architecture both needs and demands some balanced assessment.

Most Victorian architecture was a rendering of Gothic or Renaissance. The second of these, in clubs, commercial, and public buildings, in Nonconformist chapels and elsewhere, is far commoner than many people imagine. Only in Anglican and Catholic churches and halls, and in schools, colleges, and other educational buildings put up before the Flemish Renaissance beloved of late Victorian School Boards, did Gothic hold a near monopoly; for educational premises, if not for churches, the Perpendicular of Oxford, Eton, and Cambridge was much in favour. In Anglican or Catholic religious buildings, and in new or much expanded public schools and 'Oxbridge' Colleges Gothic essays, of varied quality, were almost universal. Italian Romanesque oddities like Hoarwithy church in Herefordshire, John Shaw's Louis Quatorze grouping of the 1850s at Wellington College, and Brompton Oratory of the 1880s by Bernard Gribble, were all exotics in a dominantly Gothic arboretum. Victoria's reign had indeed started with an intense though brief outburst of reasonably correct neo-Norman, well seen in Fowler's church at Honiton, in work by Manners and Gill at Bath, in Christ Church, Crewe of the early 1840s, and fairly convincingly in St Peter's, Cheltenham by S. W. Daukes who later flourished as the architect of Gothic colleges and lunatic asylums. But Norman Romanesque reproduced least well of England's mediaeval styles, and the spasm was happily over by 1850. More appalling still, as in Alfred Waterhouse's Natural History Museum in South Kensington, stupendously cathedral-esque so that its central section could house such objects as model brontosauri, were the varied mid-Victorian essays in Italian or German Romanesque, chromatic riot being added to confusion of design; the same style was less unpleasant when applied to the brightening up of brick warehouses.

Just as the successive periods of the Renaissance style had based their idiom on a revived use of the Roman arch and the Vitruvian classical orders of columns, so the Victorian Gothic of Pugin and the studious ecclesiologists was supposed to revive the arch designs, tracery, and other details of English or French Gothic as pioneered in the thirteenth and fourteenth centuries. Occasionally, as in much of Pearson's Truro Cathedral, it successfully did so, while the ground-plans of some churches by Pugin and his followers resembled those of the more ambitious churches of Lincolnshire and the East Midlands. Yet most Victorian architects designed churches and other pseudo-Gothic buildings to be constructed not by slow, haphazard accumulation but in a single operation. They achieved churches not as such mediaeval buildings really were, but as these designers thought they ought to have been; the same fallacy was as rampant in their 'restorations' (with genuinely Perpendicular windows replaced wholesale by 'Decorated' fakes) as in their numerous new works. Yet their use of many-coloured, unvernacular building materials, and of such decorations as blaring brass, loud-tinted glass, and fearsome, stone-encrusted metal screens, largely destroyed their illusions of mediaevalism. They might, indeed, have built more convincingly had they chosen to ape Perpendicular, for England's late mediaeval parish churches were often almost wholly built at one time. But 'Perpendicular' was debased taboo to most Victorians. So the earlier mediaeval centuries, along with French and central Italian examples, were their principal sources. Yet mid-Victorian churches, and still more the same architects' station forebuildings, office façades, and factories, have none of the spirit and little of the detail of what arose between 1250 and 1350. Just as the high Renaissance masters, and the more daring Continental and Latin American Baroque architects, used Roman Doric, Ionic, or Corinthian columns and yet produced buildings quite unlike the temples and colonnades of Imperial Rome, so Victorian buildings and furnishings have to stand criticism on their own. It is in this very respect that most Victorian Gothic, unlike the masterpieces of a Bramante or a Bernini, sadly fails its test. Whereas the best Renaissance and Baroque designers used the ancient vocabulary, yet were able, by their wider range and by the freer handling of their classical components, to transcend the origins of their chosen style, the most opulent and dignified Victorian churches and public buildings tend to convey little but a hollow artificiality which somehow fails to strike a right note. The best Victorian churches, like some by Pugin, a few by other famous nineteenth-century practitioners, R. C. Carpenter's great chapel at Lancing, several by Pearson, and Brandon's nobly cruciform Irvingite church so oddly set in late Georgian Bloomsbury, have a real sense of spaciousness, devotion, and magnificence. But unlike the creations of a Borromini or a Balthasar Neumann they seem artificially self-conscious and seldom convince.

VICTORIAN RENAISSANCE

The sources of Victorian Renaissance architecture were more straightforward, and often handled with more dignity, than those of the Gothicists. At first, as in Elmes's St George's Hall in Liverpool, and in the small, delightfully domed and pilastered octagonal Pump Room of 1842 at Harrogate, they continued trends established by the Grecian revivalists. But with Venice and Florence in firm favour among cultured British visitors the Italian Renaissance superseded antique Greece and Rome. The Florentine or Roman *palazzo*, rectangular in elevation, with its ponderously rusticated lowermost storey, horizontal rows of pilastered and pedimented windows, and boldly bracketed cornice, became a widely accepted pattern. Charles Barry, by training a Grecian and responsible for the Houses of Parliament and other Gothicisms, was its first great exponent. Gentlemen's clubs were thought specially suitable for the *palazzo* guise. Barry himself designed such buildings for the Travellers' and Reform in London, and for the Manchester Athenaeum; other provincial clubs followed suit on a smaller scale. Banks affected palazzo-type head offices, with such opulent façades as Sansovino's Venetian Library included among their exemplars. Edward Walters built splendidly in this manner for the Manchester and Salford (now Williams Deacon's) Bank in Manchester, while few such buildings were more startling than the Bristol headquarters of the West of England and South Wales (now Lloyd's) Bank, completed in 1856 with a riot of sculpture allusive to commerce and this Bank's particular territory. Banks in other cities sometimes recall the massive *palazzi* which dominate narrow streets in Genoa. Office blocks of more general nature soon joined the Banks. More surprisingly, the same idiom appeared in colossal warehouses—in Manchester by Walters and Gregan and in Bradford by various local architects. In the latter city the Renaissance embellishment occurs not along main façades but most effectively, tier upon tier, on the narrow ends of large commercial blocks which fill triangular sites between converging roads. A few country mansions, most notably Barry's famous pilastered pile at Cliveden in Buckinghamshire, and one façade which he designed at Harewood, also borrowed the *palazzo* from the Italy of Michaelangelo and Titian. Some hotels, among them the Grand at Bristol by Foster and Wood in the 1860s, and the tastelessly ornate White Swan at Halifax of about the same time, also allowed themselves to be caught up in the fashion. [70]

Once Renaissance was firmly established, along with Gothic, in the secular and Nonconformist architectural fields its practitioners widened their choice of patterns. The Venetian or Veronese buildings of Sansovino and Sanmichele, Palladio's rich basilican façade at Vicenza, and northern and central Italy's later *palazzi* all helped to inspire mid-Victorian designers. The Renaissance or Baroque school of France was less favoured. But French motivation, with high-rising Mansard roofs and extremely ornate interiors, appeared in some ostentatious suburban or country mansions built by the newly enriched. Other Victorian Renaissance buildings blended Italian inspiration with monumental size and a distinctly Roman quality. This Roman sweep and dignity are unmistakeable in Dobson and Grainger's magnificently planned central area of Newcastle, above all in the grandly curved upward sweep of Grey Street, slowly revealing itself with its porticoed Theatre on one side and the Grey memorial column at the top. The Roman *gravitas* inherent in the Renaissance style was often thought specially apt for official buildings. It was dominant in the mind of the classically educated Whig aristocrat Lord Palmerston when he made Scott use Renaissance Italianate, not the Gothic he preferred, for the Foreign Office building overlooking St James's Park. A still stronger Roman flavour appears, at the local government level, in the Renaissance town halls and other public buildings put up in and after the 1850s. The giant Corinthian order seemed specially impressive. From 1853 onwards Cuthbert Brodrick used it to surround his imposing Town Hall at Leeds. Monumental classicism took widespread root as the chosen style for such displays of civic pride. Birmingham had led the way with Charles Hansom's famous reproduction of a peripteral

73   *Birmingham: St Chad's Roman Catholic Cathedral,*
     by A. W. N. Pugin, 1839–41

Corinthian temple. But Brodrick's masterpiece at Leeds was more influential, so that porticoed buildings, approached by ceremonial stairways, and with clock-towers of a somewhat Gibbsian type rising high above their office space, became a civic status symbol. Bolton and Portsmouth have similar Town Halls of this type, while at Birkenhead the Corinthian portico, main block, and campanile of the one completed in 1887 fit reasonably into the space left for such a hall on one side of Gillespie Graham's noble Hamilton Square. Across the Mersey in Liverpool the varied sequence of public buildings which includes the porticoed Walker Art Gallery and the strikingly circular Picton Library showed Roman classicism extending its range. [74]

THE GOTHIC DESIGNERS

Victorian Gothic presents some interesting, important subdivisions, both among church and secular architects. Church designers were not usually the same men as those who planned buildings for non-religious uses. The prolific, busy Scott was responsible for mansions and public buildings as well as for his great output of new and restored churches, while Street's vast, diversified pile of the Law Courts is more important than any one of his many churches. But in general the distinction was clear. Men like Butterfield, Benjamin Ferrey, and the Bradford firm of Healey did virtually nothing but churches, and when Jowett ruined Balliol as an architecturally appealing Oxford college he employed Butterfield for his polychrome Gothic chapel and Waterhouse for the accommodation block which impairs the charms of the Broad.

Within the religious field there was also the distinction between the Anglican architects and the Catholics who almost confined themselves to the churches of their own faith. Pugin, it is true, carried out some Anglican commissions. But religious divisions in the main remained rigid. The Catholics preferred to employ such architects as the Pugin family, W. W. Wardell in the London area, J. J. Scoles, and J. A. Hansom and his successors. Some leading Anglican architects were devout communicants, and even churchwardens, who scrupled to design places of worship for those outside their fold; their Anglican commissions were anyhow enough to fill their working time. Butterfield is said to have done penance for having designed a Bristol Congregational chapel as his first religious building. He soon made atonement, not far away in 1844–5, in his restrained, pre-polychrome church at Coalpit Heath; thereafter, like Street, he worked only for the Established Church.

The Nonconformists are, however, of much interest in this religious picture. In many chapels they continued their classical preference and adhered to some version or other of the classical tradition. All over the country one finds their pedimented, pilastered, and occasionally porticoed Victorian façades. They occur in Cornish mining towns like Redruth and in the notably Methodist Kingswood district on the outskirts of Bristol. Midland industrial towns have their quota, and they arise, in red brick with stone for their urns, capitals, and cupolas, amid the side streets of Crewe. Burnley has a particularly rich and varied collection, with one adopting a Victorian rendering of Transitional Norman, another with a curious pilastered feature in the triangle of its pediment, dates (in the helpful Nonconformist manner) on several of the buildings, and a specially ponderous and imposing Corinthian façade lending opulent dignity to the Todmorden Road Methodist church of 1861. Rochdale and Bolton, among many other northern towns, have pseudo-Renaissance Nonconformist façades, while few buildings of this character can equal the tetrastyle Corinthian portico of a great Methodist temple in the Lindley suburb of Huddersfield.

Gothic was not, however, despised by all Nonconformist congregations. So lancets and Decorated windows appeared, along with pinnacles, gargoyles, and vaulted vestibules, in many mid-Victorian chapels, while at Halifax the great tower and spire of Joseph James's Square Congregational church of 1855–7 comprise the tallest steeple in the town. The Gothic style, and with it a propensity for towers and spires aping those of many Anglican churches, was specially favoured (particularly by prosperous, educated Congregationalists) in residential districts where Nonconformists now vied with the builders of Street or Pearson churches for acknowledged position and social acceptance. So in Clifton or Cheltenham, or in such zones as the Prince's Drive area of Liverpool with its rich assortment of Victorian religious architecture, towers and spires rose above Gothic tabernacles to give them a 'church-like' mien. But the ground plans of such buildings were attuned to Nonconformist worshipping needs, and they lacked the long chancels and side chapels now *de rigeur* with Anglicans and some of England's adherents of Rome.

The obsessive idea of Pugin, of his friend and patron Lord Shrewsbury, and of the 'ecclesiologists' who succeeded the Cambridge Cam-
den Society, was that Gothic was the only Christian style. This notion,
held by some late Georgian antiquaries, was now spread with passionate
intensity. The apostles of revived Gothic considered that as Renaissance
art forms had been evolved in a pre-Christian society they had an essentially pagan nature unredeemed by the use of pediments and classical
orders on countless Renaissance and Baroque churches. From their
hatred of what they called the 'vitiated and unhappy' Italian taste, and
from their sanctification of Gothic, these early Victorian enthusiasts
went on to insist that the plans and elevations of churches should con-
form to those common in 'The Age of Faith'. They also believed that
mediaeval churches had enshrined a rich symbolism unlikely to have
occurred to the hard-headed sacrists, treasurers, and master masons
who actually built the churches so keenly followed by these Victorian
churchmen. The churches of Pugin and the early ecclesiologists thus
seldom resembled the buildings they professed to imitate; Butterfield's
applauded All Saints', Margaret Street, with its short nave, no east
window, and much polychrome brickwork, is utterly unmediaeval.
Yet many 'ecclesiological' ground-plans, with long chancels for sur-
pliced choirs, deep porches, vestries, and side chapels which could
hold the organ if not allowed to contain shrines or altars, were like
those of the Middle Ages, and much tracery was carefully copied from
the Geometrical and Decorated work in the East Midlands and elsewhere. Towers and slender spires were very popular, and in some
Catholic churches, as at Rugby, Bath, St Marie's at Sheffield, and the
Hansom churches at Cheltenham and Preston, this feature is much
better than the somewhat puny, unattractively furnished naves and
chancels. Pugin's own churches, with many thin columns and the
metal screens to which their designer was devoted, were less convincing as mediaeval essays than his ornate Gothic interiors at Scaris-
brick Hall and in Barry's new Houses of Parliament. Yet the main
pattern of the mediaevalising Victorian parish church was now
established; what impaired their antiquarian feeling was their
mechanised craftsmanship and their architects' choice of materials.
This was specially true of Butterfield's stone or brick polychromy
(well seen at Keble College, Oxford) and in the multicoloured
Gothic façades which completed the artistic ruin of several public

buildings, and of offices in such towns as London, Bristol, Leeds, and Huddersfield.

The Victorian architects, in whatever taste they worked, were a numerous, prolific band. Charles Barry belonged in essence to an earlier age, and the gorgeously late mediaeval decoration of his Houses of Parliament was mainly Pugin's achievement. Pugin himself worked on some of the new cathedrals and in many parish churches of the Catholic church he had joined as a fervent convert. Many of his churches fell short (for lack of money) of his full ambitions, but St Marie's at Derby is one that inspires, and at Ramsgate he worked typically of himself on a Benedictine abbey and on his own house. From the 1850s there came the full onrush of Victorian Gothic. Architects were 'national' or provincial. Among the former were Butterfield, Street, Anthony Salvin, Benjamin Ferrey who had been Pugin's pupil, and the lavish, overwhelming William Burges who did much domestic work as well as churches. Alfred Waterhouse started in Manchester but later ran a great national practice, Joseph Hansom designed many Catholic churches, Sir George Gilbert Scott was ubiquitous, and J. L. Pearson designed monumentally (as at Truro Cathedral, St Michael's, Croydon, and St Agnes, Liverpool) in the Early English manner, while his cathedralesque parish churches were apt to have imposing ribbed vaults. These architects were employed all over the country, in resorts and industrial cities as well as the metropolis. So High Church ladies who frequented their London churches could worship, on holiday, in a hideous Butterfield building at Babbacombe, in Street churches at Bournemouth and Torquay, or in Pearson's St Stephen's at Bournemouth. Butterfield's mature works fell sadly short of the grey stone modesty of his Coalpit Heath or Canterbury days. Scott, however, was in general more consistent, whether at Kensington in St Mary Abbots or up North, overlooking Halifax, in All Souls, Akroydon of the late 1850s. He himself thought this his best church. Geometrical in style, with a nave, transepts, chancel, south chapel, and a tall tower and spire, it has buttresses and other details which are richly ornamented as befits the gift of a moneyed donor, and is very much the ecclesiologists' pattern place of worship. [73, 76, 71]

Provincial architects, moreover, must not be forgotten. F. W. Ordish's Italian Renaissance Market Hall at Leicester shows that not all of them worked wholly in a mediaeval vein, but their varied Gothic is

*76   Truro Cathedral, by J. L. Pearson, 1880–1910;
in the foreground the mediaeval aisle of St Mary's Church*

what we have here to consider.* John Norton was such a designer in the Bristol neighbourhood, while elsewhere in the West one had Manners and Gill of Bath, and Crickmay of Weymouth who employed Thomas Hardy before he turned writer. E. W. Godwin, though Bristol-trained, was of wider importance, and a mainly secular architect as he proved in his arcaded town-hall frontages for Northampton and Congleton. In Lancashire a tremendous ecclesiastical output came from Paley and Austin of Lancaster; it was E. J. Paley who between 1867 and 1871 replaced Bolton's mediaeval parish church with a huge building very typical of the large Victorian town church in the Scott manner. It has a vaulted chancel and a tower owing much to the central one at Lincoln Cathedral. The Catholics, in the same county and elsewhere, relied much on Messrs Weightman and Hadfield whose Salford cathedral of the late 1840s was a potpourri of fourteenth-century borrowings. The towns of the West Riding gave an ample market to local designers. The Bradford architects T. H. and F. Healey (or Healey and Mallinson) cornered much of the Anglican business; All Saints', Little Horton at Bradford, is a worthwhile essay in the style of 1290, with convex triangular clerestory windows like those in the nave at Lichfield. Mainly secular, in the same Bradford area, were Lockwood and Mawson. For Sir Titus Salt they were Italianate when designing his model factory and 'company town' at Saltaire. But despite the sumptuous Renaissance décor of their Kirkgate Market in central Bradford their normal style was lavishly Gothic. Their Bradford Exchange combines Venetian Gothic with a finely sited corner feature which is much more French; the blend is a fairly convincing reminiscence of a mediaeval Cloth Hall. Their ambitious Bradford Town Hall has a campanile which seems Italian mediaeval; the whole building is very imposing and restless, with canopied statues, a vaulted outer vestibule, dormer windows, pinnacles, and other tricks from the Victorian Gothic repertoire.

Plymouth and Winchester, and above all Manchester with Waterhouse's almost Beckfordian riot of gables, oriels, grand stairs, and vaulted passageways, were other places where huge tonnages of load-bearing Gothic materials were imposed on the soil of status-proud

---

* The polychrome idiom which has been called 'Bristol Byzantine', best seen in buildings by Foster and Wood or Ponton and Gough, is really of Italian Gothic derivation.

77 Pendlebury, Lancashire: St Augustine's church, by G. F. Bodley, 1870–74

municipalities. Far finer than most was W. H. Crossland's Town Hall
of the late 1860s which adorns the middle of Rochdale. Here if anywhere is the justification of such buildings. The style is mainly that of
the Decorated to Perpendicular transition. A great central hall has a
hammerbeam roof and is reached by a grand staircase, while two dis-
similar wings are overlooked by a slender lanterned belfry of the
Flemish type. Public buildings of other kinds were also chosen for the
display of revived Gothic. Most famous of all is Scott's great St Pancras
façade, but some museums and art galleries also received Gothic
treatment. Woodward's Oxford Museum was much praised by Ruskin,
and so set a questionable precedent. Bristol's Museum of 1870 by
A. C. Ponton closely imitated the Doge's Palace at Venice, while in
the Albert Memorial Museum at Exeter mid-Victorian polychromy
was made more than typically nauseating by Hayward the local architect. [72, 75]

A mere recital of some remaining categories of High Victorian
building shows how vast was the volume of architecture, and how
numerous were the chances of aesthetic disaster. Many dwellings of all
kinds and sizes were put up. Saltaire was not the first planned area of
'company' housing, for Akroydon at Halifax was earlier, laid out as a
grid with simply styled houses, back gardens, and back alleys to put it
ahead of the 'back-to-back' slums. In the 1850s the Duke of Bedford
built neatly planned housing areas on the rural outskirts of Tavistock,
while 'model' cottages for country labourers and town artisans were a
great interest of the Prince Consort. Later still, the massive blocks of
urban flats put up by Housing Trusts were grim, yet an improvement
on jerry-built slums. Flats for the middle classes came late enough for
many of these mainly London blocks to adopt the style of the Flemish
Renaissance. More typically Victorian were the thousands of fancifully
Gothic or Renaissance villas in genteel suburbs, spas and seaside resorts,
and in the famous North Oxford paradise of married dons.* Terraces,
formal squares, and the massively classical residential expanses of Bays-
water or Kensington long lingered as a Georgian legacy. They were
often of much character, as in the weirdly Italianate Lypiatt Terrace
at Cheltenham, or in Halifax in the truly charming Balmoral Place with
its Roman Doric doorways, pedimented middle section and pavilion

* The Priory Road—Avenue Road area of Malvern is a veritable Château Yquem of
this particular vintage.

ends. Industrial and commercial buildings arose in fantastic profusion. The forebuildings of stations had a kinship of use with the varied frontages of factories, while the Gothic and Renaissance thesauri of design were plundered for large hotels, uniform rows of shops (disciplined Renaissance in Clifton or arcaded Gothic in Bradford's Manningham Lane), and office blocks. Waterhouse had his hand deep in office design, the Prudential being his client for Gothic horrors in Holborn and widely in the provinces; their harsh terra cotta and brickwork blare out, as it were, with a signature tune of ruddy cacophony. Free-standing markets, as a rule Renaissance and with much supporting ironwork, were of increased importance; those at Bolton and Burnley have outer walls whose classical entrances are of much merit, in the same vein as the more ambitious Nonconformist façades.

Educational buildings of all kinds gave Victorian architects huge volumes of work. Waterhouse did terrible things in both ancient Universities. The Public Schools were a great source of almost wholly Gothic patronage, notably in the faithful employment of Carpenter and Ingelow by the High Church Woodard Corporation. Old charitable traditions still flourished in new or reconstructed almshouses. Though Foster's at Bristol are a surprising echo (by Foster and Wood) of the flamboyant, pinnacled Hospice de Beaune, Elizabethan Tudor was more popular; one sees it in some monumentally large groupings of the 1850s at Halifax. Hospitals and, at a humbler level, stylistically rendered baths and wash-houses comprised another class of 'social service' buildings. More entertaining, often ludicrous but sometimes affectionately regarded, were the monuments, fountains, and clock towers dear to Victorian pride. The most famous are the Italian Gothic *baldachini* which enshrine Prince Albert's statues in Manchester and Kensington. Among many Gothic towers one may cite the iron erection (cast in Glasgow) on Weymouth's Esplanade, the ornate confection which lends character to the hub of Leicester, and Derry's Clock of the 1860s without which Plymouth would not be Plymouth.

The Victorian age, like that of the Elizabethans, was one of confused uncertainty in architectural taste. Good buildings occurred in its central period, but they were pitifully few. By about 1880 the utmost indiscipline prevailed. A survey of the buildings of that time, or a glance at the illustrations of papers like *The Builder* suggests that high Victorian designers had come to the intellectual and artistic dead end of what was anyhow a dubious tradition. Some churches apart, the only tolerable buildings were apt to be those simple enough to appear insipid. A reaction was needed, not only against mechanism but still more against grossly over-lavish taste. New stirrings had, indeed, been apparent for some time before 1880. Though dire horrors continued, better possibilities were clearly seen when the 1880s opened with the completion, in what *The Builder* called 'a free treatment of late Gothic', but also with 'forms somewhat of a classic character' of Norman Shaw's conveniently visited West London suburb of Bedford Park.

CHAPTER TWELVE

The Aesthetic Reaction

1880–1914

The villas of Bedford Park, demurely tasteful with their sober brick, their coves or tile-hung gables, and the white-painted woodwork of their balconies and small window-panes, were not the first architectural reaction against the High Victorians. In the year in which Butterfield's polychromy burst forth in the nave of All Saints', Margaret Street, the Red House at Bexley was built for William Morris by the fastidious young architect Philip Webb. From this beginning a new trend in architecture gathered way till it became the most influential, though not the most prolific, facet of England's building achievement.

The Arts and Crafts movement was initially more important for the decorative arts than for architecture. Philip Webb was not a copious designer, and it was not till late in the nineteenth century that the craftsmanlike simplicity of the Red House's brickwork and structural wood had many followers. Yet it soon became clear how great, and in some ways how salutary, was the break with the profuse and tasteless architecture which prevailed at least till 1880. [79]

The pioneers of the Arts and Crafts movement made heroic endeavours to regain simplicity and honesty of design, and in the execution of their chosen designs to reject the mass-production methods of mechanical industry and recapture the devoted, hand-made work of the individual artist-craftsman. Machinery, foundry moulds, and the smoky surroundings of industrial towns, were exchanged for the quiet cottage studios of dedicated, individualist artists who lived and worked in leafy suburbs or in unspoilt (i.e. unindustrial) villages in the Home Counties or the Cotswolds. The materials of houses again included the honest, traditionally English materials of hand-worked oak, oolitic limestone, and mellow red brick. Though the Red House was fairly large, awkwardly laid out, and without a bathroom (like many greater mansions of 1859) its materials, its craftsmanship, and its general spirit were deliberately far from the iron framing and technological vainglory of the Great Exhibition.

The style ushered in by Webb and Morris led to a pleasing rediscovery of the better side of England's late mediaeval and Tudor housebuilding. In their passion for unrepeated production by hand these enthusiasts failed to realise that much late mediaeval decoration—small brasses for instance, some Devonshire screen work, or alabaster panels —was apt to be standardised and mass-produced, and that the unsentimental craftsmen of the Middle Ages would have welcomed more mechanical aids had these been available. Yet their decorative work included some exquisite masterpieces of the fine arts. Printing, fabrics, and wallpaper by Morris and his colleagues, De Morgan tiles, silverware and other craftwork by Ashbee, and stained glass by Morris and Burne Jones all brilliantly countered the more frightful perpetrations of mid-Victorian glaziers and furnishers. But in the architecture and the applied arts of this movement there lay a serious flaw.

Despite the real beauty and tasteful seemliness of the craftsmanship and building work of the Arts and Crafts movement that movement was, in the context of an irrevocably industrial society, like a Quixotic crusade or Gandhian escapism from a world which could not be shunned. Designers and craftsmen refused to admit that good design could be married to industrial production. Architects and builders were all too unready to welcome such new materials as cast iron or steel, or to employ production and building methods made possible by the industry of their own time. Because iron frames and machined ornament had been unknown in the thirteenth century, now in the nineteenth they were taboo. Yet these apostles of purer taste were not alone in their anti-industrial delusion. Ruskin and the Butterfield group felt much the same; in the meantime the architecture of late Victorian protest was better and more sensitive than that which held sway between 1850 and 1880.

The secular buildings most typical of the Arts and Crafts designers were houses—vernacular in style and on a modest scale. The compact estate of Bedford Park inspired the larger garden suburbs of Bourneville at Birmingham and Port Sunlight in the Wirral peninsula of

78 *Liverpool: White Star (now P.S.N.) offices, by Norman Shaw, 1896*

Cheshire. With the spacious planning, tree-lined roads, and period taste of these new style dwelling areas the way lay open for the widely influential 'garden city' of Letchworth. Yet housing in the modest vein of Bedford Park was only a fraction of Norman Shaw's work. His quest for new styles to revive led him on to the designing of larger, more decorated buildings in various idioms much aided in their popularity by his example.

A main work of Norman Shaw, and of Eden Nesfield his early colleague, was the revival of styles disregarded by the Georgians and the earlier Victorian revivalists. Specially notable, in Nesfield's work before that of Shaw, was the renewed use of the high-pitched roofs, and of some other idioms, once popular with Wren's contemporaries and with house designers under William and Mary and Anne. The early sponsorship of this revival was mainly left to Shaw. It appears in some details in Bedford Park, in some of his South Kensington houses, and most notably in the Dorset mansion of Bryanston, built early in the 1890s with flanking wings and a great central block, all rendered in a Hampton Court mixture of red brick and silvery Portland stone. Yet 'Queen Anne' was but one of Shaw's range of favoured styles. The Gothicism of some of his large, rambling, tall-chimneyed country houses was that of the Arts and Crafts movement and of his own tile-hung, late Gothic-cum-Jacobean Renaissance work in Bedford Park; some gables in these houses had non-structural half-timbering as fussy and repulsive as anything in the more recent speculative builders' catalogues. But stone houses like Craigside in Northumberland, Adcote in Shropshire, and Dawpool in the Wirral showed his surer Gothic touch. More remarkable, and seen more in office blocks and public buildings than in private homes, were his numerous essays in the Flemish or Jacobean Renaissance, astonishing to his business patrons for their blend, in the urban setting of London and Liverpool, of stone and brightish red brick. Shaw's buildings in this much-copied style included New Zealand Chambers in the City, the kindred, baronially turreted masterpieces of New Scotland Yard and the White Star offices in Liverpool, and the towering, imposingly gabled Alliance Assurance Building (of 1903) near St James's Palace in London. From Shaw there originated a copious flow of Netherlandish allusions unknown in England since about 1600. Sir Ernest George gave Kensington its flavour of Bruges or Ghent in his astonishing sequences of brick-built, gabled,

ARTS AND CRAFTS
79 *Bexley, Kent: the Red House, by Philip Webb, 1859*
80 *Shackleford, Surrey: 'Norney', by C. F. A. Voysey, 1897*

and panelled houses. Flemish Renaissance was even more in vogue for shop or office blocks, for the great output of Board Schools, and for a riot of Technical Colleges like the genuinely impressive one of 1909 at Burnley and others, of less artistic quality, at Rochdale, Stockport, and all over England. [78]

From Shaw's more yeomanlike houses it was an easy transition to simpler, less affected homes. C. F. A. Voysey was the most notable among a group of English designers whose work made a deep impression abroad; after many Continental borrowings there now came a short time when inspiration ran sharply the other way. The typical Voysey house was long and low, with a high roof and white-plastered walls. Square-headed and mullioned windows recalled the dwellings of Tudor clothiers. Shutters and doors were often pierced with tiny, heart-shaped openings. Voysey's interior joinery and brickwork, as in his own house at Chorley Wood and in those at Windermere, was of an honest simplicity (all details being of his own design) that recalled the Red House, and linked up with the achievements of such craftsmen as Ernest Gimson, the Barnsley brothers, and others of the Cotswold school. Voysey houses, for the living of what was, by middle-class Edwardian standards, a simple life, were less varied than those by Shaw. But they were delicate masterpieces in a minor key. Their theme was sympathetically followed by men like Baillie Scott, while the vernacular revivalism of the Shaw–Voysey school was splendidly practised by Lutyens in his earlier houses. His compositions included admirable late Gothic elements transmitted by the Tudor building craftsmen. His irregularly planned, mullioned, tall-chimneyed, splendidly masoned houses are widely spread, appearing at their best in those which Lutyens, like others of the school, designed for moneyed intellectuals who chose to live in south-west Surrey, that hilly, wooded Arcady of still car-less roads and unelectrified railways, rural yet close enough to London for those householders to enjoy the herbaceous delights of their Gertrude Jekyll gardens yet keep in the swim. [80]

LATE VICTORIAN CHURCHES

In the churches of the later nineteenth century we can distinguish two main trends. Pearson's uncoloured stonework had shown that it was time to desert the heaviness and polychromy of such nightmares as those of the Butterfield-Teulon-Ewan Christian school. The refining process was perfected by the sensitive Gothic of G. F. Bodley. He had shown, in such churches of the 1860s as All Saints' at Cambridge, how a studious, more genuine mediaeval revivalism could combine with stencilled patterning and decorative effects by Morris and the Preraphaelites. But his heyday came after 1870; his notably famous and beautiful Staffordshire church at Hoar Cross was of 1871.* His style was largely late Decorated, his masonry and brickwork reverted to comparatively subdued effects, and his detail and furnishings came closer to the spirit of Pugin than to the robust insensitivity of most Victorians. Though less original than the high-Victorian creations Bodley churches nearly always convey delicacy and devotional effect, and in Bodley and others like him one finds the best justification for a reasonably close revival of mediaeval Gothicism. Bodley's works of his peak period included the vaulted church at Eccleston and the timber-roofed Holy Trinity just behind the Albert Hall. He planned conventual churches for the Cowley fathers at Oxford and at Bristol for the sisters of the House of Charity. Still in the manner of a chapel is his great work of the 1870s, the towerless St Augustine's at Pendlebury near Manchester, anticipating the chapel he designed in 1890 for Queens' at Cambridge. [77]

'Bodleyan' ecclesiastical architecture, recalling the period between 1350 and 1420, was not confined to Bodley himself. J. D. Sedding did some excellent work. His Holy Trinity, Sloane Street is impressive, though somewhat cavernous for a church of this kind, but his earlier St Clement's, Boscombe is more sensitive, is finely furnished, and has a nobly turreted Perpendicular west tower. James Brooks was another late Victorian who put some unusual, dramatic touches into his churches. The later churches of Paley and Austin improved on their earlier buildings. The great cruciform St George's, Stockport, by Austin alone and built in the 1890s by a single donor, is as splendid a building of this type as any in England. Its red sandstone is unmarred by polychromy, and its Perpendicular character is diversified by flamboyant clerestory tracery of almost Art Nouveau wilfulness. Dark sandstone is also well deployed in Manchester's impressive Rylands Library, with a vestibule and a grand stairway in the manner of

---

* He was long in partnership with Thomas Garner, the designer, after his conversion to Catholicism, of Downside Abbey's splendid choir in the manner of the 'Dec.-Perp.' transition.

Rochdale Town Hall. The dim, impressively vaulted reading room has flamboyant tracery and much metalwork prefiguring Art Nouveau; so churchlike an interior well fitted a library devoted to Biblical studies. It is the best work of Basil Champneys its architect, who also designed churches and in Newnham College, Cambridge also proved himself a Renaissance adept. J. F. Bentley was another architect skilled and sensitive in the revived late Gothic of his Catholic churches, and of alterpieces in those designed by others. But at Westminster Cathedral it was Cardinal Vaughan who was mainly responsible for Bentley's great excursion into mosaic-clad Byzantinism not without its influence on some Anglican and Catholic basilican designs. [82]

More original than the 'Bodleyan' school were the Arts and Crafts Gothic designers working soon before 1914. Though some of their designs seem a trifle precious they also contained genuine, charming originality. Like Baroque within the classical tradition their work explored new ground while remaining within Gothic confines. Segmental arches and doorways sported mediaevalising rosettes, while the heads of some smaller openings were composed of two concave curves which met in a point. W. D. Caroë (especially in his strongly designed St David's at Exeter) was one of this school, so too was the architect of the fanciful, attractive Edwardian Middlesex Guildhall in Westminster. More notable, skilled also in pseudo-Renaissance work and the designer of Manchester's functionally Jacobean Telephone Exchange, was Leonard Stokes, while the designs of Sir Giles Gilbert Scott's great Anglican Cathedral at Liverpool date back to this phase, and include pioneering detail unknown to Bodley and the earlier Victorians. Another interesting figure, very much an Arts and Crafts devotee, was the Manchester architect Edgar Wood. His houses are scattered up and down the North, while his Christian Science church in his own city pioneered its own style. More Gothic, yet also original with its symbolic sculpture, rare decoration, and green copper cap, is his beautiful Lindley Clock Tower at Huddersfield; it is astonishing for its date of 1902. [81]

Yet very few British architects between 1890 and 1914 broke away from the bonds of the traditional styles; the prophetic achievements of Mackintosh in the Glasgow area are unhappily outside this book's geographical scope. But adventurous designing did come from Harrison Townsend in his London buildings of about 1900. Best known are the frontage of the Whitechapel Art Gallery, and the Horniman Museum,

81   *Liverpool Cathedral, by Giles Gilbert Scott: the Lady Chapel, 1904–10*

self-consciously innovating with the shock effect of their asymmetrical, cavernous doorways and the chunky, brutal treatment of their turrets. Such works, with their Art Nouveau decoration, were England's nearest approach to the contemporary fantasies of the Catalan Gaudí.

But these innovations were a mere fraction of what was built in the last 20 years before 1914. Period reproductions mostly held the field. Churches like Temple Moore's impressive St Wilfred's, Harrogate, and Sir Walter Tapper's stately, vaulted Annunciation, Bryanston Street were a throwback to a more literal Gothicism; so too were such sumptuous interiors by Ninian Comper as his church at Wellingborough, the non-Georgian southern half of St Mary's, Rochdale, and his re-creation of a fifteenth-century Norfolk interior at St Cyprian's, Marylebone.

EDWARDIAN BAROQUE

More typical of this time was Edwardian Baroque. Some buildings, like H. T. Hare's Town Hall at Crewe with its cupola and pedimented gables, retained a flavour of Shaw's Queen Anne; others were more completely in the taste of Wren or even of the great Roman pioneers. Such were the War Office, the domed Central Hall at Westminster and the same architects' splendid group of public buildings at Cardiff. Sir Brumwell Thomas's fine brick and stone Stockport Town Hall has a three-tiered tower and other Wren allusions, while Norman Shaw* and Lutyens now turned over to rich Renaissance idioms. No less opulent was the architecture of pomp and circumstance, as in the canopied Victoria Memorial at Liverpool. In the same class were Sir Aston Webb's great Naval College at Dartmouth and the massive block of the Admiralty Arch which looks along the Mall to the ponderous façade which he applied to Buckingham Palace. [83]

More interesting still, for their making a genuine effort to interpret Roman Baroque of the *seicento*, were some smaller buildings. Two of these are at Cambridge. G. J. Skipper of Norwich designed surprisingly lush offices for the Norwich Union, which round the corner in Downing Street Professor Prior's Medical (now Zoology) School is more Borrominian than anything by Archer. A delightful little Bank in Clare

* Much to Voysey's annoyance. For Pugin the classical styles were un-Christian; Voysey thought them unpatriotic.

82 London: *Westminster Cathedral*, by J. F. Bentley, begun 1895
83 Stockport: *the Town Hall*, by Sir Brumwell Thomas, 1908

Street, Bristol, domed and richly pillared, should really be some octagonal chapel in Cortona or Rainaldi's Rome.

Nor did this period's factories and textile mills turn wholly from Renaissance embellishment. The main fabric of many a multi-storeyed cotton mill was bald and simple. But such embellishments as Jacobean ball finials appeared on some of their corners. Towers and turrets rose above their rooflines, being decked out with Renaissance or Baroque features, and sometimes with copper domes whose green contrasts with harsh red brickwork. Royton near Oldham has a rewarding concentration of these mills, put up when cotton really was Lancashire's King.

Yet despite these wider imitations of a once-scorned style the English architectural scene of about 1910 showed a sluggish torpor, with few moves towards the revealing construction and functionalism of what is now known as the Modern Movement.* Architectural training had long been geared to the system of articled pupillage. But academic instruction now slowly revived, though it took an École des Beaux Arts man from Paris to introduce London to steel framing, in the Ritz Hotel whose skeleton had still to be clothed in lavish Louis Quinze. Similar coverings were perforce given to other steel or concrete-framed Edwardian buildings. A gaunt factory near Chester, and a Stafford house by Edgar Wood are among England's few buildings that really heralded the eventually accepted fashion. English architecture lay deep in one of its isolationist phases, with nothing to suggest that its newest buildings were contemporary with the prophetic German works of Behrens or Gropius. As the Great War started English architects seemed unaware of what was happening beyond the no-man's-land of the North Sea once crossed by the Saxons with whose rude timber buildings we started our story.

* For a good summation of what there was, see Nikolaus Pevsner, 'Nine Swallows—No Summer', *Architectural Review*, May 1942.

A SHORT BOOKLIST

The literature of English architecture is so vast that I can do no more than mention some books which set out, individually or as part of a series, to deal with the subject not sectionally but as a whole. I have also mentioned the valuable biographical dictionaries compiled by Mr John Harvey and Mr Howard Colvin. Apart from the works here mentioned there are many others which deal with English architecture by types of buildings (churches, country houses, etc.), in particular periods (e.g. Saxon or Georgian), in separate geographical areas or towns (e.g. Cheshire, Suffolk, Cambridge, or Brighton), or which cover the work of individual architects such as Wren or Soane. For later figures like Voysey or Leonard Stokes one still has to consult articles or obituaries in various architectural periodicals. I am also aware of, but have no room to include, the many books available on the arts immediately attendant on architecture, e.g. woodwork, sculpture, church monuments, and stained or painted glass.

W. H. Godfrey, *The Story of English Architecture*, 2 vols., 1928, 1931.
A. H. Gardner, *Outline of English Architecture*, 3rd edn., 1949.

A high proportion of the total field is covered, for the general reader, by the following books originally published in the Batsford 'British Heritage' series (it is always best to consult the most recent editions):

Harry Batsford and Charles Fry, *The Cathedrals of England*, 10th edn., revised by Bryan Little, 1960.
Harry Batsford and Charles Fry, *The Greater English Church*, 2nd edn., 1944.
J. C. Cox and C. B. Ford, *Parish Churches*, paperback edn., revised by Bryan Little, 1961.
F. H. Crossley, *The English Abbey*, paperback edn., revised by Bryan Little, 1962.
Hugh Braun, *The English Castle*, 3rd edn., 1948.
Ralph Dutton, *The English Country House*, revised paperback edn., 1962.
Clive Rouse, *The Old Towns of England*, 3rd edn., 1948.

See also Ralph Dutton, *The English Interior*, 1500 to 1900, 1948; R. Allen

Brown, *English Castles*, paperback edn., 1962; B. H. St. J. O'Neil, *Castles* (H.M.S.O.), 1953; and R. Gilyard-Beer, *Abbeys* (H.M.S.O.), 1958.

Among works by other authors the following books by Mr Hugh Braun cover a good section of the total subject: *An Introduction to English Mediaeval Architecture*, 1951; *The Story of English Architecture*, 1960; *Old English Houses*, 1962.

Scholarly modern works of great importance are the volumes so far available in the Oxford History of English Art, and the relevant books, partly or wholly on English architecture, in the Pelican History of Art, edited by Professor Nikolaus Pevsner. These are as follows: In the Oxford History of Art, D. Talbot Rice, *871–1100*, 1952; T. S. R. Boase, *1100–1216*, 1953; P. H. Brieger, *1216–1307*, 1957; Joan Evans, *1307–1461*, 1949; E. B. Mercer, *1553–1625*, 1962; Margaret Whinney and Oliver Millar, *1625–1714*, 1957; T. S. R. Boase, *1800–1870*, 1959. In the Pelican History of Art: K. J. Conant, *Carolingian and Romanesque Architecture* (including English), 1959; Geoffrey Webb, *Architecture in England, the Middle Ages*, 1956; John Summerson, *Architecture in Britain, 1530–1830*, 1953; Henry-Russell Hitchcock, *Architecture, Nineteenth and Twentieth Centuries* (including English), 1958.

Other works of importance include: The county volumes in the Penguin Buildings of England series, for the most part compiled by Nikolaus Pevsner; Frank Jenkins, *Architect and Patron*, 1961; Peter Kidson and Peter Murray, *A History of English Architecture*, 1962; John Gloag, *The English Tradition in Architecture*, 1963; the relevant portions of Banister Fletcher, *A History of Architecture on the Comparative Method*, 17th edn., revised by R. A. Cordingley, 1961; Howard Colvin, R. Allen Brown and A. J. Taylor, *History of the King's Works* [till 1485, 2 vols., 1963.

Finally, the two biographical dictionaries are: John Harvey, *English Mediaeval Architects, A Biographical Dictionary to 1550*, 1954 and Howard Colvin, *A Biographical Dictionary of English Architects, 1660–1840*, 1954.

GLOSSARY

Aedicula—(i.e. a miniature temple)—A small-scale Renaissance composition, often above ground-floor level, where a niche or window is framed by pilasters and half-columns supporting an architrave, a frieze, and a pediment.

Apse—A curved or polygonal east end to a church.

Arcade—A range of arches supported by columns or piers, either open or blind, i.e. closed with masonry. Arcading was often used as wall decoration.

Art Nouveau—Mainly a decorative technique rather than an architectural style, this was an aesthetic movement of great importance for a few years each side of 1900. Its distinctive appeal is based on the fanciful exploitation of thin, sinuous curves like those seen in the leaves and stalks of some flowers, tagliatelle, etc.

Bailey—A large fortified enclosure forming the main area of a Norman castle, and containing such buildings as the keep, the hall, storehouses, etc. within its space or up against the surrounding walls.

Baroque—The latest version of Renaissance architecture, prevalent in many countries during the seventeenth century and much of the eighteenth. The classical orders, and other features deriving from Antiquity, were handled with an increasing boldness of composition, and with a curvature and sense of 'movement' which made architectural features akin to the plasticity of sculpture.

Barrel Vault—A covering of either brick or stone, generally of semi-circular section. See also **Wagon Roof**.

Battlement—A parapet cut with indentations at regular intervals, of defensive origin, but used in churches for its decorative effect.

Bay—A compartment or section of a building, e.g. a hall or the nave of a church, marked off from the next bay by the cross arches of vaulting or the principal beams of a timber roof. In some clerestories, especially in East Anglian parish churches, two windows, instead of the normal one, are found in each structural bay.

Broach—The pyramidal masonry filling the four angles where an octagonal spire rises, without parapet, from a square tower.

243

Buttress—Masonry built out to strengthen a wall and to resist the outward thrust of a roof.

Capital—The crowning member of a column or pier, giving support to superimposed arches or vaulting ribs.

Chancel—The eastern limb of a parish church, containing the high altar. So called because it was separated from the rest of the church by *cancelli*, or screens.

Chapter-House—The council-chamber of a monastic or collegiate establishment, whether or not it was a cathedral.

Clerestory—The side wall of a church above the aisle roof and arcade, pierced with windows and often, in the Perpendicular period, consisting mainly of an expanse of glass and thin dividing mullions.

Corbel—A block, usually moulded or carved, projecting from a wall and supporting a superincumbent weight.

Corbel-Table—A connected range of corbels immediately beneath the roof of a building; it can also support a parapet.

Cresting—Continuous ornament, carved or pierced, surmounting a screen, canopy, or cornice.

Crockets—Decorative features occurring principally at the angles of canopies, pinnacles and spires; usually carved and placed equidistantly.

Curvilinear Style or Tracery—The first phase in the style of the fourteenth century, in which Geometrical forms in tracery were superseded by flowing lines. (Also called Flowing Tracery.)

Cusps—In tracery, the small inner members that constitute the foliations in the form of trefoils, quatrefoils, etc.

Diapering—The more or less complete covering of a stone or brick surface with decorative patterns. In the case of stone surfaces these designs are often in low relief, are arranged in squares or diamonds, and cover the whole area.

Dog-Tooth Ornament—An ornament in the shape of small pyramids often set in a hollow moulding, and repeated either continuously or at short intervals in thirteenth-century work.

Dormer Window—A window built to light a room in an attic storey contained within a sloping roof, and projecting horizontally through the roof itself.

Fan Vault—The final development in England of Gothic vaulting, in which the curve of all the ribs is similar. The actual ribs are generally decorative rather than structural, and the fan-like shapes, or conoids, are always apparent. Sometimes pendants are introduced.

Finial—A decorative termination to pinnacles, canopies, etc.

Flying-Buttress—A buttress in the form of an open arch directing the thrust of a high vault across the roof of an aisle to the main buttress, and so to the ground.

Gable—The upper part of the narrow end of a building whose roof slopes down on each side of its central ridge. Mostly triangular in shape, gables were often, under Dutch influence in the seventeenth century, rendered in stepped form, or in more fanciful shapes involving curved profiles.

Geometrical Style or Tracery—The phase after Early English or Lancet, at the close of the thirteenth century, characterised by an early type of bar tracery designed strictly in geometric forms, in which circles and triangles predominate.

Groined Vault—A vault resulting from the intersection of two or more surfaces at an angle, the ribs, or lines of intersection, being the groins.

Hammer-Beam Roof—A wooden roof in which the tie-beam is dispensed with, and its place taken by projecting beams. The ends of these are generally treated decoratively.

Jambs—The upright sides of doorways and window openings.

Label Stop—The moulded or sculptured termination of a hood-mould (interior) or drip-mould (exterior) which runs over the top of an arch or window. Label stops are often rendered as foliage, human heads, or grotesques.

Lancet Window—A name applied to the narrow pointed window of Early English Gothic from its resemblance to a lance blade.

Lierne Ribs—Small connecting ribs used in vaulting, particularly during the fourteenth century, for decorative effect only.

Machicolation—The treatment of the gallery or parapet running along a castle wall, with the pathway projecting beyond the wall's face and supported by a continuous series of closely spaced brackets.

Modillions—Small brackets, often carved with some elaboration, which support the boldly projecting cornices of late seventeenth and early eighteenth century houses.

Mouldings—The varieties of contour given to angles, arches, and other projecting members of various parts of buildings to produce contrasts of light and shade and richness of effect.

Mullions—The vertical divisions between lights in a Gothic window, from which the tracery springs.

Narthex—A single-storey western vestibule to an early church.

Nave—The western limb of a church, used by the congregation.

Norman Architecture—The English variant of Romanesque in the eleventh and twelfth centuries, immediately preceding Gothic.

Ogee—A curve of double flexure, produced by a convex and concave curve flowing the one into the other.

Palladian Style—The classical idiom based on the work of the North Italian architect Andrea Palladio (d. 1580) and in its turn based on Palladio's study of actual Roman buildings. Found in England under Inigo Jones, and again from *c.* 1715–60.

Parapet—That part of the external wall of a building, solid, pierced or battlemented, that arises above the level and eaves of a roof.

Pediment—The treatment of the gable end of a classical building or composition whereby this is rendered with a triangular head whose projecting edges enclose a flat space which can be filled with sculpture, heraldry, etc. In the Baroque period the upper edge of a pediment was often broken, or interrupted, in the middle, thus producing a more dramatic and sculptural effect.

Perpendicular—The last of the great periods of English Gothic architecture. It flourished during the later-fourteenth, fifteenth, and sixteenth centuries.

Pier—A supporting member from which arches or vaulting spring, in form usually cylindrical, octagonal, rectangular, or clustered, i.e. composed of a collection of shafts.

Pinnacle—A tapering terminating member, vertical, and usually crowned by a finial, and smaller than a turret.

Quadripartite—A simple form of ribbed vaulting, consisting of transverse, diagonal, and wall ribs, dividing a rectangular vault space, or compartment, into four segments.

Quoin—The wrought stones at the angles or corners of buildings.

Renaissance—The great art movement by which the classical styles of architecture, as transmitted from Greece by the designers of the Roman Empire, were reintroduced into England from the sixteenth century onwards; the process was accentuated in the following century by Inigo Jones and Wren. The style appears in numerous monuments.

Respond—A half-pillar or corbelled termination to an arcade.

Rib—A structural member dividing up the compartment of a vault, generally moulded.

Rococo—A mainly decorative movement (e.g. in stucco, mirrors, silverware, and engraving) whereby the extreme elaboration of Baroque was intensified and often combined with unsymmetrical planning and design.

Romanesque—The style of architecture prevalent in Western Europe from about the ninth to the twelfth century, perpetuating the round arch of the Romans.

Rood-Loft—A gallery surmounting the rood-screen, originally supporting the great crucifix or rood, generally with flanking statues of St John and the Virgin.

Rustication—The treatment of masonry whereby the blocks are parted from each other by deep incisions, V-shaped or rectangular in profile, thus giving an impression of greater strength or boldness to the area of stonework so treated. This impression is sometimes reinforced by leaving the rusticated surfaces rough or pierced with tortuous 'vermiculation'.

Sanctuary—The easternmost, and most sacred, part of the chancel, containing the high altar, which was raised a few steps above the rest of the floor.

Sexpartite—A form of ribbed vaulting, similar to the quadripartite but having an extra transverse rib which divides the rectangular compartment into six segments.

Shaft—A smaller column, either independent or a member of a pier.

Soffit—The flat or chamfered underside of an arch; in the former case a soffit of the Renaissance period is often decorated with rosettes or other carved detail.

Spandrel—The triangular space formed between two arches, or between one arch and the rectangular lines of a door-frame.

Squinch-Arches—Arches thrown across the interior angles of a tower to support an octagonal spire.

String-Course—A projecting horizontal band or moulding on a wall, often continued around a building.

Tabernacle-Work—The carved and ornamental canopy-work over stalls, fonts, niches, etc.

Tracery—The ornamental stonework in the heads of Gothic windows, springing from and supported by the mullions. Circular windows were also filled with tracery. The earliest form is Plate Tracery, consisting of circles and other geometrical figures cut in solid stonework. After the middle of the thirteenth century, the tracery was built of stone bars (Bar Tracery).

Transepts—The cross-arms of a church, projecting transversely to the nave, chancel and aisles.

Transoms—The horizontal bars across windows.

Tympanum—The space enclosed between the lintel and the arch of a doorway in Norman and Gothic buildings, often filled with sculpture.

Venetian Window—A type of Renaissance window, particularly common in the Palladian style, whereby a central arched section rises above two narrower flanking openings of a rectangular shape.

Vault—Any form of arched roofing over a building with the exception of the domical. Vaults are either groined, as in Romanesque architecture, or ribbed, as in all Gothic architecture.

Wagon Roof—A roof of the same semicircular section as a barrel vault, but rendered in timber and particularly common in Devon and Cornwall.

Index

The numerals in heavy type denote the figure-numbers of the illustrations